T0301398

Rethinking Wealth and Taxes

RETHINKING ECONOMICS

This series is a forum for innovative scholarly writing from across all substantive fields of economics. The series aims to enrich the study of the discipline by promoting a cutting-edge approach to economic thought and analysis. Academic scrutiny and challenge is an essential component in the development of economics as a field of study, and the act of rethinking and re-examining principles and precepts that may have been long-held is imperative.

Rethinking Economics showcases authored books that address the field from a new angle, expose the weaknesses of existing concepts and arguments, or 'reframe' the topic in some way. This might be through the introduction of radical ideas, through the integration of perspectives from other fields or even disciplines, through challenging existing paradigms, or simply through a level of analysis that elevates or sharpens our understanding of a subject.

Rethinking Wealth and Taxes

Inequality, Globalization and Capital Income

Geoffrey Poitras

Professor of Finance, Simon Fraser University, Canada

RETHINKING ECONOMICS

Edward Elgar
PUBLISHING

Cheltenham, UK • Northampton, MA, USA

© Geoffrey Poitras 2020

All rights reserved. No part of this publication may be reproduced, stored in a retrieval system or transmitted in any form or by any means, electronic, mechanical or photocopying, recording, or otherwise without the prior permission of the publisher.

Published by
Edward Elgar Publishing Limited
The Lypiatts
15 Lansdown Road
Cheltenham
Glos GL50 2JA
UK

Edward Elgar Publishing, Inc.
William Pratt House
9 Dewey Court
Northampton
Massachusetts 01060
USA

A catalogue record for this book
is available from the British Library

Library of Congress Control Number: 2020940533

This book is available electronically in the **Elgar**online
Economics subject collection
http://dx.doi.org/10.4337/9781839106156

ISBN 978 1 83910 614 9 (cased)
ISBN 978 1 83910 615 6 (eBook)

Typeset by Servis Filmsetting Ltd, Stockport, Cheshire
Printed and bound by CPI Group (UK) Ltd, Croydon, CR0 4YY

Contents

Figures, tables and boxes

FIGURES

TABLES

BOXES

To those who,
seeing the vice and misery that spring from
the unequal distribution
of wealth and privilege,
feel the possibility of a higher social state,
and would strive for its attainment.

Introduction: wealth and taxes

Taxes on 'the wealthy' are a topic sure to incite venomous rants from both right-wing and left-wing ideologues. The topic attracts conflicting interpretations and policy recommendations from respected and not-so-respected scholars, detailed in a vast literature of books, journal articles and conference papers examining topics such as international tax competition, tax havens and tax evasion.[1] Proposals for tax reform consume political debate during elections and legislative sessions throughout the tax-burdened world. Much of this debate has been centred on reducing or eliminating specific taxes that, ultimately, have been and are being paid disproportionately by the wealthy in society. All this activity takes place against an opaque landscape of empirical evidence concerning the distributions of wealth and income; tax competition between countries; and tax avoidance and tax evasion by corporations and wealthy individuals. Despite claims of convincing empirical evidence for increasing inequality of wealth and income, public discourse surrounding reform of taxes paid by the wealthy is based largely on subjective opinion. Similarly, inadequate ideological interpretation of the objective information that is available reinforces the influence of subjective opinion. By stifling the availability of evidence and providing enhanced avenues for creative tax management by the wealthy, globalization has made a complicated problem almost intractable.[2]

Seeking to shed some light on this almost intractable problem of wealth and taxes, this book rethinks essential facets of the problem to account for a globalized financial system. Initially, this involves dispelling conventional myths about the wealthy derived from substantial empirical evidence for the distributions of income and, especially, wealth. In contrast to evidence from these distributions for the whole population, income and wealth holdings for the top 1 per cent and 0.1 per cent are a difficult-to-estimate extreme value tail of the income and wealth distributions. Accurate evidence on aggregate taxes paid by the wealthy, both within and across jurisdictions, is even more scarce. The skinny empirical evidence that is available is confronted with entrenched ideological biases concerning the rights and economic role of the wealthy. In this milieu, it is difficult to advance propositions without supporting one ideological position or another. In addition, the ground to cover is so vast that it is not possible to effectively introduce complications arising from the connection between tax policy and the other essential aspects of fiscal policy: expenditures and debt management. However, despite the obvious and not-so-obvious limitations, the advance of widespread poverty at a time of unprecedented economic progress calls for an empathetic and informed analysis.

Due to substantive variation across political jurisdictions and over time, there is no 'one-size-fits-all' description of tax policy. Yet, despite compelling evidence of an historic increase in aggregate personal wealth over the last few decades, in many countries the relative contribution to national government revenue of taxes imposed directly on wealth, such as inheritance and estate tax, has been declining over time. There is an implicit assumption in national revenue policy, increasingly undermined by globalization, that broad-based personal and corporate income taxes provide an effective direct method of progressively and equitably capturing gains in wealth and income. Against a backdrop of financial globalization, there has been a reduction in the relative contribution to government revenue from taxes on capital income, and loss of revenue due to personal and corporate tax avoidance and evasion. Significantly, available empirical evidence for a perverse distribution of income and wealth that allows those at the top 1 per cent of the wealth and income distributions to capture the bulk of recent dramatic gains from economic progress and technological change fails to adequately account for income and wealth that is not captured in 'the data'.[3] At the tail end of the wealth distribution is an exclusive extreme value group of the top 0.1 per cent who compose the wealthiest. The empirical implications of this group sourcing wealth and income in distinct taxing jurisdictions and deferring tax on capital income requires specific attention.[4]

Wealth is concentrated and difficult to confront politically, socially and economically. The wealthiest are important contributors to political campaigns, have disproportionate access to mass media, and the ability to fund think tanks with sympathetic agendas. The influence on public debate and public opinion is reflected in the resurgence of 'rich people's movements' such as the Tea Party in the United States (US), with agendas that favour easing the tax burden on the wealthy, such as the reduction or elimination of capital gains taxes and estate taxes.[5] Easing of controls on the international movement of capital and the restricted ability to require financial intermediaries to facilitate tax collection for such capital flows has allowed wealth and income, both personal and corporate, to be domiciled in low-tax jurisdictions and tax havens, while the *de facto* owners reside in and enjoy the social and personal benefits available in high-tax jurisdictions. The search for an inequality-reducing road to reform of taxes paid by the wealthy raises some important questions. What are the historical, economic and social processes that have allowed modern government revenue generation schemes to reduce the relative contribution from the wealthy to the aggregate tax burden? What can be learned from the comparative history and contemporary struggles of different political jurisdictions to develop revenue schemes aimed at equitably and efficiently taxing wealth gains and undeclared income?

The old adage that 'an old tax is a good tax' suggests pragmatic rethinking of wealth and taxes work within established avenues of raising revenue.[6] More precisely, many theoretically optimal but untested idealistic schemes for generating revenue from the wealthy, such as those for addressing international tax competition using multilateral cooperation, or radically altering the 'realization principle' by progressively taxing global capital, fail to address the real legal and political difficulties of practical implementation.[7] Faced with potentially insurmountable practical difficulties of implementing untested or radical taxation reforms, is it possible to retool currently available taxes on the wealthy to achieve substantive adjustment to the increasing inequality observed in the distributions of wealth and income? As it turns out, the answer to this question involves distinguishing the wealthiest 1 per cent and 0.1 per cent from a diverse group of other wealthy individuals. Various distinctions need to be made between the types of 'wealthy' to be found within this diverse group, leading to the difficult problem of identifying and taxing wealthy 'free riders'.

Can tax reform be unbundled from other aspects of fiscal policy? Is it necessary to consider whether potential revenue increases are to be matched by a reduction in the overall tax burden, such as by raising the broad-based personal exemption from income tax, or will the increased revenue be used to provide enhanced social services for the increasingly impoverished and homeless at the bottom of the wealth and income distributions who pay little or no income tax but are burdened by consumption taxes? Alternatively, is the burden on future generations of accumulating government debt to be reduced? Before addressing such relevant questions, some basic preliminary questions need addressing, such as: what are the types of situations where wealthy individuals are paying insufficient amounts of tax; that is, who are the wealthy free riders? What is an equitable amount of tax to impose for an opulent, wealthy standard of living or for ongoing substantial capital wealth accumulation? The answer to such questions requires: a precise definition of wealth; careful consideration of tax avoidance and tax evasion schemes, both corporate and personal; and close examination of the connection between wealth, income inequality and equity capital. This is challenging enough, leaving fundamental questions about the intimate connection between government revenue, expenditure and debt management policies unexplored in this book.

Precise data on the activities of the wealthy, such as the amount of income, sales, property and other taxes paid, is typically difficult to obtain, especially where income is being generated and wealth is domiciled across various jurisdictions. Legal methods of income and death tax planning across political jurisdictions, possibly involving anonymous trusts or corporations that make wealth and income difficult to identify, provide the basis for numerous tax avoidance schemes to minimize tax payments.[8] For example, while detailed income tax records are not available in Canada due to privacy concerns, is it possible (or likely) that a significant number of wealthy residents are exploiting globalization to legally take advantage of the Canadian tax system? Family wealth is transferred into Canada at the time of immigration relatively tax-free, to buy luxury items and a high-value primary residence in the name of a low-income family member, while ongoing family income is generated primarily in a lower income tax jurisdiction by another family member, corporation or trust that is not considered to be a Canadian resident subject to income tax. Income is then transferred to Canada as a gift; income that is not taxable under Canadian tax rules. While family members reporting low taxable income who reside in Canada can access health care, education and other government services, the hard-to-avoid Canadian taxes paid by these wealthy free riders are primarily property tax, user fees and consumption taxes.[9]

Based on social conventions and ethical principles stretching back to the scholastics of the Middle Ages, the guiding principles of equity in determining taxes have been 'horizontal equity' and 'vertical equity'.[10] In general, the horizontal equity or 'net benefit' principle requires that individuals living within a given tax jurisdiction with similar income, lifestyles and use of government services pay approximately the same aggregate amount of tax over time.[11] Globalization raises fundamental questions about determining horizontal equity when domicile and lifestyle of the wealthy involves ownership of property in numerous taxing jurisdictions. Assessment of horizontal equity involves numerous practical problems associated with measurement of wealth and income required to assess comparable taxes. In contrast, vertical equity poses fundamental ethical and moral questions regarding the allocation of relative tax burden across the distribution of wealth and income. Particularly, the vertical equity or 'ability to pay' principle is the basis for progressivity of marginal tax rates. Despite this stated objective, various studies claim to have demonstrated empirically that current methods of raising government revenue, relying primarily on personal income tax and consumption tax schemes, regressively place an inequitable burden on those with little or no wealth. In turn, determining precisely what contribution from the wealthiest – the top 0.1 per cent – is required to satisfy vertical equity concerns is both morally and practically problematic, especially where globalization makes residence and income source difficult to estimate. Even if that contribution could somehow be determined, an effective method of raising the associated tax is problematic due to the key role of capital income in wealth generation for the wealthiest.

Viewed from the increasingly dire perspective of those at the bottom of the wealth and income distributions, taxation outcomes achieved by the wealthiest are vertically inequitable. This moral variant of inequity is distinct from the horizontal inequity created by wealthy free riders using funds originating from a low-tax foreign jurisdiction that have not been subjected to tax in the jurisdiction of domicile, to purchase expensive primary residences, high-end automobiles, luxury goods, impressive recreational properties, and the like, that provide non-pecuniary returns not attracting taxes commensurate with the real services or net benefit provided.[12] In turn, the ethical implications of this variant of wealthy free rider exploiting globalization are distinct from the inequity posed by wealthy capitalists benefiting from the realization principle to avoid taxes on capital income arising from: deferred equity compensation paid to corporate management; deferred tax on income from equity capital shares in corporations, companies and the like; and unrealized increases in value of real estate and other capital assets. The ability to defer payment of tax provides timing options that can allow significant reduction in income tax paid relative to the *de facto* ability to pay which is the basis for calculating Haig–Simons income, the definition of income associated with distributional equity.

The variety of inequitable outcomes achievable by wealthy free riders and the wealthiest suggests that restoring a semblance of vertical and horizontal equity will require a variety of taxes to be used. Difficult-to-avoid taxes on wealthy free riders exploiting globalization that are available to address horizontal equity concerns include: property tax and transfer tax levied on real estate and other immovable property; luxury sales taxes; graduated vehicle levies on registration and licensing; and gift taxes. In contrast, a different arsenal of taxes is available to address the vertical equity concerns for the wealthiest. In addition to taxes on realized capital gains, net interest income and dividends, as well as estate and inheritance taxes, creative solutions are needed to address the various avenues that the wealthiest can use to avoid taxes by exploiting the realization principle to defer tax on unrealized capital gains.[13] Without closer examination of tax management activities, the appropriate taxes available to address the vertical inequity of the wealthiest are difficult to ascertain. Based on the estimated wealth holdings of those individuals listed in the unscientific Forbes 400 list of the wealthiest Americans, the most relevant aspect appears to be the difficult problem of taxing income accruing to equity capital shares and managerial equity compensation.[14]

In contrast to horizontal and vertical equity concerns, economic efficiency and incidence of tax changes are often identified as essential considerations in specifying practical tax adjustments to capture revenue from wealthy free riders and the wealthiest. While possibly improving morale for the voluntary compliance of non-wealthy taxpayers, there are some who argue that increasing taxes on the wealthiest and wealthy free riders could, theoretically, result in a reduction in aggregate tax revenue. For example, an increase in taxes on realized capital gains could, arguably, reduce economic efficiency by encouraging the wealthy to consume more and save less, resulting in a reduction of investment in capital assets needed to sustain economic progress. Globalization further complicates such economic efficiency arguments against capital gains tax increases, by encouraging investment in jurisdictions with lower capital gains taxes, contributing to international tax competition that reduces capital investment in the higher capital tax jurisdiction. Sorting the ideological from the objective in such claims is difficult. Even if the prediction of a reduction in tax revenue is correct, does the end – sustaining or increasing 'economic progress' to generate tax revenue – justify the means: allowing for unconscionable social inequity? Rethinking wealth and taxes cannot avoid the inherently political and ideological element involved.

Casual inspection of observable assets held by the wealthiest reveals considerable wealth held within publicly traded limited liability corporations and privately held companies. Much of the wealth generation associated with recent technological change and economic progress has been captured within such firms. Due to the realization principle associated with deferred tax treatment of capital income, the increasing value of such ownership claims largely escapes taxation as wealth is being accumulated. If reform of 'equity capital' income tax is indicated to address the increasing inequality in wealth and income distributions, the route to such reform is illusive. Attempts to capture wealth gains in one jurisdiction creates incentives to shift those gains to another jurisdiction with more favorable taxation. For example, prior to the Trump tax reforms of 2017 in the US that significantly lowered corporate tax rates, increasing avoidance of higher US corporate tax rates led to the rise of 'tax inversions' and corporations changing national affiliation to lower-tax jurisdictions that aggressively lowered corporate income tax rates, such as Ireland, or had little or no taxes, such as the Caribbean tax havens.[15] Despite recent efforts by the US administration, multilateral trade agreements, an essential feature of globalization, continue to act as a deterrent to national jurisdictions placing barriers on capital flows or using customs taxes (tariffs) as a tool to counteract such international tax competition.

Alleviating increases in wealth and income inequality by rethinking wealth and taxes raises complicated economic, political and ethical issues that reach to the heart of how the modern, globalized capitalist economy functions. Empathetically aiming to address such issues, this book is divided into two parts. Part I lays the historical, empirical and theoretical groundwork for proposals to rethink wealth and taxes as advanced in Part II. Chapter 1 in Part I commences with basic definitions and descriptions for wealth, the wealthy, the wealthiest, and the measurement of wealth and income inequality. Exploring the connection between wealth and the wealthy owners of that wealth reveals a lack of homogeneity. Colloquial usage of 'wealthy' encompasses not only those who have accumulated substantial ownership of assets, but also those with high income levels. In effect, reference to 'the wealthy' is a fiction: the wealthy and wealthy free riders come in various shapes and sizes. Close inspection is given to claims about the distribution of income, typically estimated from income tax returns. Serious difficulties with this evidence arise from the inability to represent income from unrealized gains on all capital assets and income generated in offshore jurisdictions. By comparison, available wealth distribution estimates have even more severe methodological problems. Reliance on surveys and, from tax returns, realized capital gains and estate taxes, provide incomplete and, possibly, misdirected information about the upper tail of the wealth distribution.

Description of significant, perhaps dramatic, undercounting in estimates for the upper tail of the empirical distributions for income and, especially, wealth is followed by examination of taxes on the wealthy and comparison with the traditional hard-to-tax problem. The practical difficulties of imposing net wealth taxes are identified and other, more viable, methods of raising taxes on wealth are examined. Specific attention is given to the treatment of taxes on capital assets, especially the taxation of capital gains. However, discussion of the connection to Haig–Simons income is left to Part II. Chapter 1 finally considers whether taxation of wealthy free riders can be effectively related to the traditional hard-to-tax problem. Like wealthy free riders, the hard-to-tax are not a homogeneous group. By comparison, lumping the hard-to-tax with the impoverished who have no wealth and invariably pay little or no income tax makes the lower tail of the income distribution relatively uninformative, as some of the hard-to-tax do generate substantial, if undeclared, income. Wealthy free riders who hide almost all wealth and income offshore could also contribute to estimates of the lower and upper tail that are misleading

Rethinking wealth and taxes

or uninformative. Yet, use of globalization by the wealthy to avoid and evade tax is a point of divergence with the underground economy of the traditional hard-to-tax problem.

With the ultimate objective of determining a crude estimate of the contribution that the wealthy make to the aggregate tax burden, Chapter 2 provides information on the current composition of taxes used to raise government revenue in the US, Canada and other Organisation for Economic Co-operation and Development (OECD) countries.[16] The discussion reveals a bewildering array of taxation methods in the OECD, spread across local, state/provincial and national jurisdictions: income taxes, social security, payroll/salary taxes, consumption taxes (goods and services taxes, sales taxes, excise taxes), property taxes and a small residual category of 'other taxes'. The percentage contribution of each type of tax to total tax revenue and the size of revenue as a percentage of gross domestic product (GDP) are reported. This aggregate overview is supplemented by detailed examination of government revenue sources in Canada and the US, broken down into federal, state/provincial and local jurisdictions. Specific details for British Columbia, Nevada and the city of Vancouver are provided. With this background, available imprecise estimates of the contribution by the wealthy to the various tax burdens are reviewed. The chapter concludes with a glimpse into the world of tax havens and the use that the wealthy make of these jurisdictions.

Part I concludes with Chapter 3, containing a brief historical overview of state revenue generation from ancient times to the modern broad-based income tax system. In the past, some mix of wealth, income and *ad valorem* taxes were combined with other methods of government revenue generation, such as: the leasing or sale of public lands; granting of commercial charters; collection of tithes, property taxes and port taxes; sale of patents and licenses; and borrowing. The historical timeline covers: Roman tax-farming companies, the *societates publicanorum*; the Florentine *catasto* of 1427, an early wealth tax; the 1710–17 French *dixième*, arguably the first income tax; the early English income tax of 1799–1816; and passage of the 16th Amendment to the US Constitution in 1913. The rise of the broad-based income tax during World War II is detailed, starting with the US 'social taxation' reforms of President Franklin Delano Roosevelt (FDR) in 1935, and continuing to the neoliberal reforms of Prime Minister Thatcher in the United Kingdom (UK) and President Reagan in the US during the 1980s. These latter reforms facilitated the subsequent rise of globalization and international tax competition that has seen the rise of tax havens for tax avoidance and evasion by the wealthy.[17] The chapter concludes with a discussion of globalization and the rise of international tax competition.

Having established the historical roots of the modern approach to raising government revenues, the first chapter of Part II, Chapter 4, considers insights from modern tax policy in general, and taxation of the wealthy and the wealthiest specifically. This involves some discussion of key topics from the public economics of taxation. More precisely, the traditional neoclassical public finance approach examines the equity, efficiency and distributional aspects of broad-based taxation, especially taxes on income and consumption. For various reasons, this broad-based 'optimal taxation' approach fails to adequately focus on the equity implications of taxes, especially taxes on capital, that are most applicable to the wealthy in general, and the wealthiest even more so. The discussion considers how the Haig–Simons definition of income relates to the analytical rationale for a progressive income tax. Recognizing that studies on the merits of taxing specific components of wealth rather than wage income or consumption have a history that predates the introduction of the modern income tax, the long and ongoing debate over capital income taxes is examined in detail. The symbiotic relationship between the organization of a capitalist economy and use of the realization principle to tax capital income is identified and discussed.

Recognizing a continuing theme of distinguishing between the tax bases that different levels of government control, Chapter 5 considers imposition and coordination of the arsenal of taxes that can be assessed on the wealthy across different taxing jurisdictions. Specifically, local and state/provincial jurisdictions have the ability to impose various taxes aimed at the consumption patterns of the wealthy that typically – often compulsively – involve significant expenditures on real property such as residential estates, and luxury goods such as expensive cars, boats and planes.[18] This leads to consideration of reforming taxes on the wealthy by shifting the tax burden to 'inelastic' immovables, especially real property, while reducing taxes on wage income relative to capital income. Yet, property tax is almost always assessed only by local and state/provincial governments. Due to differences across jurisdictions in tax base size and assessment practices, without enough coordination this window to rethinking taxes aimed at different types of real estate and other immovable property is problematic, if only because the wealthy are best able to migrate to avoid tax.

After considering property tax, attention pivots to taxation of consumption and expenditures. Such taxes can be imposed at the national, local and, where applicable, the state/provincial level, and can be applied to other 'immovables' including graduated vehicle licensing and operating levies; enhanced luxury and gift taxes; and graduated user fees. However, while reforms based on increased taxes on immovables have the potential to achieve a modicum of improvement in the level of wealth and income inequality at the local level where these taxes can be assessed, such reforms at the national level run the risk of disrupting the life cycle saving process. Many wealthy older individuals have accumulated wealth out of past income that has previously been adequately taxed within the appropriate jurisdictions. This wealth has been accumulated and not consumed to fund future, and likely lower, income during retirement, and in many cases, to leave bequests. Increased consumption taxes on the spending of such wealth to, say, offset reduction in income tax, inequitably penalizes those near the end of the life cycle savings process who have saved for future consumption, in favour of those earlier in the wealth accumulation cycle.

Given the complications of addressing wealth and income inequality using property tax and consumption taxes, is it possible for death taxes to play a substantive role? The implications and possible threats for democracy associated with allowing the wealthiest to transfer substantial wealth using inter-generational bequests has long been a subject of sometimes contentious debate.[19] As with the debate over equity versus efficiency, the discussion of bequest taxation has a significant, largely intractable, philosophical content. Can the associated vertical equity difficulties be resolved by accounting for the differing size and composition of physical and financial assets for the wealthiest 0.1 per cent and 1 per cent, compared to the remainder of the top 10 per cent that have the bulk of the remaining wealth available for bequests? Does the possibility of migration by the wealthy pose a significant threat to the effectiveness of death taxes? What schemes are available for the wealthiest to avoid death taxes? Seeking to address such questions, consideration is given to rethinking the use of trusts and other legal devices by the wealthiest to avoid death taxes.

Recognizing that the wealthiest often make disproportionate use of offshore trusts and corporations to avoid payment of taxes on the level of income and increase in wealth leads to identification of a fundamental problem that globalization poses for tax authorities: by providing increased jurisdictional flexibility in tax planning by using offshore corporations, trusts and the like, globalization has fuelled a reduction in a variety of taxes paid by the wealthy, undermining the unilateral use of broad-based personal and corporate income taxes to fund government programmes and address income and wealth inequality in a higher-tax jurisdiction. This situation has been compounded by the rise of tax competition across countries, permitting a variety of aggressive tax management schemes devised by accounting and legal practitioners that are used by the wealthiest to avoid and evade taxes. Various examples uncovered in recent whistleblower and legal disclosures are provided to illustrate how globalization has permitted current taxation rules to produce inequitably perverse taxation outcomes, and has encouraged tax evasion and questionable avoidance strategies using offshore tax havens. Efforts such as the Foreign Account Tax Compliance Act to stem such activity are assessed.

Given the increasing concentration of wealth arising from capital accumulation in large limited liability multinational corporations, the final chapter of Part II, Chapter 6, deals with how equity capital organization and governance has fostered increasing wealth and income inequality. Specifically, the increasing separation of ownership from control, associated with the emergence and evolution of fiduciary capitalism, has seen a marked transition of managerial compensation from wage income to capital income, using contingent equity compensation to defer the payment of tax and lower the marginal tax rate when the capital income is finally realized. This transition has been compounded by the dramatically expanded use of share buybacks instead of dividends to return profits to corporate shareholders resulting in a shift from taxation of (current) dividend income to deferred capital gains taxation. The expected common stock price increase associated with share buybacks has been accompanied by the accumulation of onshore and offshore cash balances and investment assets that further support an increasing share price. Such changes have permitted both managers and wealthy shareholders to exploit the realization principle associated with deferred tax on capital income, to fuel increasing inequality in levels of wealth and income.

What is the potential for reforming taxes on the wealthy and, especially, the wealthiest to stifle the tax avoidance and evasion that fuels increasing inequality in wealth and income? Is it possible to reconfigure managerial equity compensation by removing the self-serving distinction between personal 'wage' income and 'capital' income? What reforms are feasible to encourage the payment of taxes on current business income in lieu of the deferment of taxes on capital income inherent in the realization principle? Does allowing dividends to be tax deductible at the corporate level, with the tax implications of that income flowing through to shareholders, provide enough inducement to encourage companies to forego the tax benefits provided when the realization principle is applied to share buybacks? While the final chapter explores such questions, in the final analysis it is difficult to escape the economic, political and social biases inherent in modern capitalism toward owners of capital assets. Instead of enhancing potential for 'the good life', economic progress provided by globalization and technological change has served to exacerbate these biases, leading to increasing levels of poverty and homelessness at a time of rapidly increasing wealth and income for the 1 per cent and the 0.1 per cent. To paraphrase John Donne, it is difficult to avoid the conclusion that reform of taxes on the wealthiest are 'a chimera on my brain, that troubles me in my prayer'.

NOTES

1. There are various useful organizations, institutes and foundations with websites dedicated to exploring tax matters. Of interest in the broader public policy sphere are sites that provide information and insights such as the International Tax Justice Network (www.taxjustice.net) centred in the United Kingdom (UK). In the United States (US) there are numerous entities, including Citizens for Tax Justice (www.ctj.org), the Tax Foundation (www.taxfoundation.org), the Tax Policy Center (www.taxpolicycenter.org) and the Institute on Taxation and Economic Policy (www.itepnet.org). The 'conservative' position on taxes in the US is captured in the websites of the Americans for Tax Reform (www.atr.org), an organization headed by Grover Norquist, originating in 1985 during the Reagan tax reform era, and the older National Taxpayers Union (www.ntu.org) founded in 1969. A 'progressive' perspective on US tax policy is available from the Center on Budget and Policy Priorities (www.cbpp.org). In Canada, in addition to the Canadian Taxpayers Federation (www.taxpayer.com), tax matters are considered by a number of entities with broader mandates such as the progressive Canadian Centre for Policy Alternatives (www.policyalternatives.ca), the conservative Fraser Institute (www.fraserinstitute.org) and the non-partisan C.D. Howe Institute (www.cdhowe.org). Other notable entities dedicated to scholarly analysis of tax policy include the National Tax Association in the US (www.ntanet.org) that publishes the *National Tax Journal* and, in Canada, the Canadian Tax Foundation (www.ctf.ca), which publishes the *Canadian Tax Journal*. In an American context, Slemrod (2000) provides a useful overview of issues associated with taxing the wealthy.
2. A variety of possible definitions of 'globalization' are available. *Foreign Policy* (2004) describes some statistical measures of globalization. For example, the A.T. Kearney/ Foreign Policy Globalization Index ranks more than 60 countries using 14 variables grouped in four baskets: economic integration, personal contact, technological connectivity and political engagement.
3. The statistical evidence on perverse distribution is largely related to income, with evidence for increasing wealth concentration being opaque due to difficulties in estimating the distribution of wealth (e.g., Kopczuk, 2015; Alvaredo et al., 2016). An essential source for studies on global economic inequality measurement is the World Inequality Lab (wid.world/wid-world) affiliated with the Paris School of Economics which has compiled the open source World Wealth and Income Database (WID.world). This database was used to compile the *World Inequality Report 2018* (Alvaredo et al., 2018). In the ideologically charged milieu surrounding the distribution and taxation of income and wealth increases, even basic evidence on the share of aggregate wealth accumulation accruing to those having the largest stock of wealth is questioned. For example, Hubbard (2015), Levmore (2015) and Kopczuk (2015) review studies disputing the claims advanced by Piketty (2014) and others of a steadily rising share of wealth held by the top 1 per cent since 1970 across various countries. Given that globalization provides multiple avenues to disguise wealth ownership in order to avoid and evade taxes, such academic to-and-fro is unlikely to provide much resolution of the basic facts. The greater ability to assess evidence on earnings and income provides less, though still contentious, debate surrounding the apparently valid claim of increasing inequality using these measures.
4. Adding to the accumulating body of evidence regarding tax evasion and avoidance by the wealthiest, Alstadsæter et al. (2019) employ a 'unique dataset of leaked customer lists from offshore financial institutions matched to administrative wealth records in Scandinavia' to show that offshore tax evasion is highly concentrated among the 0.01 per cent, resulting in a 'skewed distribution of offshore wealth'. It is estimated that the 0.01 per cent wealthiest households 'evade about 25 percent of their taxes'. In addition, 'top wealth shares increase substantially when accounting for unreported assets, highlighting the importance of factoring in tax evasion to properly measure inequality'.
5. Martin (2013) provides a general history of such rich people's movements in the US; and Martin (2010) explicitly examines the campaign to repeal the 16th Amendment. A

collection of papers related to more general issues is Martin et al. (2009), where Block (2009) examines the fundamental role of taxes in the 'right wing agenda'.

6. The principle that 'an old is a good tax' has a long history (e.g., Seligman, 1914 [1911], p. 646). In the US, the principle is consistent with legal traditionalism, a perspective that 'tends to resist broad changes in established laws or concepts of taxation and [is] inclined to adjust and amend those in existence to meet changing conditions and circumstances' (Savage, 1958, p. 1009).

7. An example from September 2016 of international coordination difficulties is the resistance by the Irish government to a directive from the European Union (EU) that Apple Corporation pay $14.5 billion in corporate taxes based on a ruling that Ireland was violating EU rules on providing inappropriate tax subsidies. A similar example from February 2017 is the defeat of a Swiss referendum that would have curbed secrecy at Swiss financial institutions, despite moves by the Swiss government in that direction. The suggestion for a global tax on capital is proposed in Piketty (2014, sec. 15).

8. For example, the *Vancouver Sun*, 14 June 2015, reports that the second-poorest neighbourhood in terms of taxable income per capita in the municipality of Richmond, BC, as identified by Statistics Canada data, is composed largely of single-family detached homes valued at C$1.2 million and up. Checks of property records reveal many titles with Chinese surnames reporting 'housewife' or 'student' as occupations. A similar *Sun* item on 26 September 2015 indicates that this situation encompasses other neighbourhoods in Vancouver with average homes valued at C$2 million and above. An item from the *Sun* on 7 March 2017 reveals that more than 21 000 holders of permanent resident cards had given up their cards in the previous two years. Quoting an internal report from the Canadian immigration office in Shanghai: 'Many people are renouncing five years after landing [in Canada] rather than renewing their permanent cards, as they are working in China and do not meet residency requirements. Their children often remain in Canada to complete school and to begin their careers.' Quoting a prominent immigration lawyer: 'many people who renounce their permanent residence status are breadwinners who cannot meet Canada's two year residency requirement because they hold down jobs elsewhere, typically earning more money in their homeland than they believe they could in Canada'. Another immigration lawyer reported: 'A lot of people with permanent residence status have wanted to get their family and wealth transferred into Canada. Some have bought multiple properties. By renouncing their permanent status, they can stay below the radar and avoid Canadian taxes.' The author of the publication that broke the immigration report observes that it has become common for breadwinners to bring their entire family to British Columbia (BC) as permanent residents, and then decide 'either it's too cold or there's no way I'm going to file an income tax return and report my global interests and property and pay taxes in Canada on that'. In a number of cases, family members remaining in Canada, often living in expensive locales within Vancouver and Toronto while the breadwinner pays taxes elsewhere (if at all), are technically living below the poverty line, despite living a wealthy lifestyle. Citizenship and Immigration Canada reports that in the two years to September 2016, renunciations were for citizens from China (5407), India (2431), South Korea (1681), Britain (1416) and Taiwan (1129). Though country of birth is not reported, apparently a significant number of those renouncing from the UK were originally from East Asia.

9. Such possible schemes are not exclusively of East Asian origin. Casual inspection of the individuals identified in the Panama Papers, the Paradise Papers, the release of previously secret Union Bank of Switzerland wealth management accounts, the investigations in various jurisdictions of tax evasion and avoidance schemes perpetrated by KPMG, and so on, provide ample evidence of systemic tax evasion and avoidance by wealthy individuals from jurisdictions around the world.

10. Though equity is usually advanced as the primary criteria for major tax reform, political debate on tax changes often finds 'efficiency', 'economic stagnation' and other arguments advanced by sympathizers with those that will be subjected to increased taxes. As Head (1972, p. 49) observed about debate over the monumental 1967 Carter

Commission report in Canada that led to the 1970 White Paper on Tax Reform: 'those who stood to pay more as a result of each particular proposal remained unshakeably opposed, and the "participatory process" was dominated by precisely those vested interests whose views had already been forcefully represented'. Instead of vertical and horizontal equity considerations, the Tax Foundation seeks 'efficiencies' in promoting the 'Principles of Sound Tax Policy': simplicity, transparency, neutrality and stability. Simplicity requires a tax code that makes it easy for taxpayers to make payments and is easy for governments to administer and enforce. Transparency requires clear and plain definitions of the amount and timing of payments, with changes to the tax code being subject to democratic scrutiny. Neutrality requires that the tax code does not punish or favour specific industries, activities and products. Personal or business decisions are not encouraged or discouraged. Finally, stability requires consistency and predictability in the tax code, avoiding retroactive changes, tax holidays and temporary tax laws. Together, these four principles are aimed at encouraging economic growth by raising government revenue in the least distorting manner possible.

11. The 'net benefit' and 'ability to pay' principles of taxation have medieval roots and have evolved over time. As such, those familiar with concepts of traditional public finance will observe that the approach to defining net benefit employed here differs from the alternative of identifying net benefit with the consumption of public goods, for example in the specification of Lindahl taxes. In turn, the alternative interpretation of ability to pay also differs due to the explicit incorporation of the impact that globalization has on the determination of ability to pay.

12. Prior to globalization, it was typical for such items to be purchased with funds that had already been adequately taxed within the jurisdiction that the real property is used. Historically, property taxes were assessed on 'personalty' involving items other than land, such as livestock and the family silver. Practical difficulties with assessing such taxes led to a transition to property taxes assessed primarily on real estate.

13. Not all such taxes are available in each jurisdiction. In addition to substantive distinction between federal and non-federal states, there is ongoing conflict between locations and jurisdictions over where taxes from the wealthy are most effectively imposed and where that government revenue is spent. For examples, the income tax deductible contributions for pension assets, such as Registered Retirement Savings Plans (RRSPs) in Canada, may not be withdrawn in the same provincial taxing jurisdiction where the deduction was taken. In other words, provincial income tax loss due to the gross income deduction of the RRSP pension asset is often later recaptured in a different province.

14. Other sources, such as filings for the French net wealth tax, provide similar evidence. In addition to the widely followed shares in publicly traded limited liability corporations, such shares appear in various legal forms, varying from the traditional partnership to the limited liability partnership and the limited liability company.

15. The Tax Cuts and Jobs Act (the Trump tax reforms) was signed into law on 22 December 2017. Arguably the most thorough reform of the US federal tax code since that of President Reagan in 1986, key features of the Trump tax reforms include: lowering individual tax rates, increasing the personal exemption and reducing itemized deductions; doubling the minimum value at which the estate tax becomes applicable; reduction in taxes for pass-through entities; and lowering of the corporate tax rate from 35 per cent to 21 per cent, with a low one-time repatriation tax of 8 per cent (15 per cent for cash) for corporations that transfer profits to the US that are being held offshore. In addition, the Trump tax reforms also reduce the number of individuals subject to the alternative minimum tax and eliminate the Alternative Minimum Tax (AMT) for corporations.

16. Unfortunately, important issues surrounding taxation, inequality and globalization in non-OECD countries will not receive much attention. It is generally accepted that tax evasion in the developing countries is on a much grander scale than in the liberal democratic OECD countries. In addition, as Goldberg and Pavcnik (2007) and others have observed, globalization has, perhaps surprisingly, exacerbated inequality in developing countries.

17. There is considerable debate over the proximate causes of the inequality. For example, examining 'the last 50 years [when] the US tax system went through a striking transformation that reduced the effective tax rates for top income groups and raised transfers to seniors', Kaymak and Poschke (2016, p. 1) find: 'Changes in taxes and transfers account for nearly half of the rise in wealth concentration. Nonetheless, their impact on the distributions of income and consumption has been minor due to changes in equilibrium prices and the offsetting effects of tax cuts and transfers on the dispersion of consumption. Results highlight the role of increasing wage dispersion during this period as the main driver of trends in inequality.'

18. Such behaviour by many of the wealthiest stretches back to ancient times. The satirical critic of capitalism, Thorsten Veblen (1857–1929), made famous the notions of 'conspicuous consumption' and 'conspicuous leisure' to describe such compulsive behaviour by the wealthiest, in classics such as *The Theory of the Leisure Class* (Veblen, 1899) and *The Vested Interests and the Common Man* (Veblen, 1919). Using this insight, an appropriate method of harvesting taxes from wealthy free riders is to increase income tax on passive income above a certain threshold, and to increase sales tax, excise tax, property tax and user fees on immovable real property.

19. Dyson (2012) and Greenhouse (1994) discuss the implications of demographic transitions, such as the movement of baby boomers through the life cycle, on democracy.

PART I

The Wealthy and State Revenue Generation

1. Defining wealth and taxes on the wealthy

> 140. It is true governments cannot be supported without great charge, and it is fit everyone who enjoys his share of the protection should pay out of his estate his proportion for the maintenance of it. But still it must be with his own consent – i.e., the consent of the majority, giving it either by themselves or their representatives chosen by them; for if any one shall claim a power to lay and levy taxes on the people by his own authority, and without such consent of the people, he thereby invades the fundamental law of property, and subverts the end of government. For what property have I in that which another may by right take when he pleases to himself?
>
> (John Locke, *Two Treatises of Government*, 1728)

WHAT IS WEALTH? WHO ARE THE WEALTHY?

Defining and Measuring Wealth

Despite being a widely used term, the precise definition of wealth is both elusive and, for present purposes, crucial. Adam Smith defined 'real wealth' as 'the annual produce of the land and labour of society'.[1] This definition closely identifies wealth with income. Smith was influenced by the Physiocrats who emphasized the importance of land and agricultural labour as the source of national wealth. Such notions of wealth are consistent with a largely agrarian economy where land ownership is concentrated in an aristocratic class. Smith went on to identify productive labour, that contributed to wealth such as manufactures and agricultural production; and unproductive labour, that did not contribute to wealth such as the menial labour of servants. Special attention was given to labour that contributed to maintaining the capital stock and the rent on agricultural lands. Though antiquated, by distinguishing different types of wealth and the role of wealth in the maintenance and advancement of society, this approach to defining wealth is insightful. More precisely, wealth is not homogeneous. Wealth can be used in alternative ways which may or may not contribute to future national income.

Modern definitions of wealth tend to obscure the difference between productive, income-producing wealth and unproductive, consumption-driven wealth.[2] Because wealth is measured in monetary terms, tangible assets are emphasized compared to intangible assets due to differences in the ability to determine a marketable value. The Wealth and Assets Survey (WAS) in the United Kingdom (UK) provides a tangibles approach to the types of items included in 'wealth':[3]

> *Net property wealth.* Primary residences, buy-to-let properties, other housing, other buildings, UK and overseas land *less* outstanding mortgage debt on the main residence and other property or land.

> *Net financial wealth.* Positive balances in current accounts, savings accounts (including tax-advantaged Individual Savings Accounts), fixed-term and investment bonds, equities, gilts and other investments *less* the value of any non-mortgage debt (including overdrafts on current accounts, credit card balances and arrears, formal and informal loans and student loans).

> *Pension wealth.* Accumulated defined contribution (DC) pension funds, and the 'value' of future defined benefit (DB) income and of pensions that are in receipt. (This value is calculated as the size of fund that would be required today to purchase the future pension income stream, given current annuity rates and the number of years that an individual is from retirement (if the pension is not already in receipt)).

The WAS tangibles approach to defining wealth can be compared to the triennial United States (US) Survey of Consumer Finances (SCF) conducted by the Federal Reserve (see Table 1.1). While the SCF uses broader categories for wealth and includes income variables, some essential elements of wealth are only 'partially measured'. Important implications of such definitions are the use of 'net wealth' (total wealth net of outstanding debt) and the use of pre-tax values. The latter is particularly important in practice due to the general reduction in capital gains taxes and other wealth-related taxes that impact upon the study of wealth distributions over time.[4] Of relevance to the whole wealth distribution, the implied value of government-sponsored retirement benefits, such as Social Security in the US, is not included, if only because of the calculation difficulties determining the value of this component of wealth.

In addition to the definition and measurement of wealth used in wealth surveys, there are also definitions and measurements used in the calculation of wealth-related taxes. Only a few countries currently impose a net wealth tax, with France being the most notable until recently. Other countries, such as the US and the UK but not Canada, impose estate and/or inheritance taxes which employ wealth definitions. For example, Internal Revenue Service (IRS) Form 706 used to calculate the gross value of an

Table 1.1   Items identified in the Survey of Consumer Finances conducted by the US Federal Reserve

Income	Measured	Debt	Measured	Assets	Measured
Wages and salaries	M	Credit card debt	M	Transaction accounts	M
Self-employment/farm	M	Lines of credit	M	Savings/money market accounts	M
Tax-exempt interest	M	Mortgages	M	Stocks	M
Taxable interest	M	Installment loans	M	Bonds	M
Dividends	M	Past-due bills	M	Mutual and hedge funds	M
Real estate/business/trust	M	Loans against pensions	M	Tax-deferred retirement accts	M
Realized capital gains	M	Loans against insurance	M	Other exchange-traded assets	M
Unemployment insurance	M	Misc. personal loans	M	Annuities and life insurance	M
Welfare	M			Trusts	M
Pension and annuities	M	Bills not yet due	U	Misc. financial assets	M
Alimony and child support	M	Contractual obligations	P	Homes	M
Misc. income	M	Future obligations	P	Other real estate	M
		"Psychic debt"	U	Businesses	M
Unrealized capital gains	P			Vehicles	M
Noncash employee benefits	P			Intellectual property	M
Service flow	P			Misc. valuables	M
Inheritances and gifts	P				
In-kind income	U			Defined-benefit pension rights	P
Unpaid work for self	U			Other contingent assets	P
"Psychic income"	U			Expected future transfers	M
				Human Capital	P
				"Psychic assets"	U

Note: *M* indicates that the variable is measured to a high degree in the SCF, *P* indicates that the variable is measured in some part, and *U* indicates that no meaningful aspect of the variable is measured.

Source: Kennickell (2009).

estate for US tax purposes requires the following source-based forms to be completed for determining the decedent's estate value:

- Schedule A – Real Estate (owner-occupied plus investment properties solely owned at time of death).
- Schedule B – Stocks and Bonds (solely owned by deceased).
- Schedule C – Mortgages, Notes, and Cash (includes time, demand and savings deposits).
- Schedule D – Insurance on the Decedent's Life.
- Schedule E – Jointly Owned Property (can include real estate, life insurance and financial assets).
- Schedule F – Other Miscellaneous Property (includes art, consumer durables, private business equity and other items not included on other schedules).
- Schedule G – Transfers During Decedent's Life (beyond amounts allowed under lifetime exemption).
- Schedule I – Annuities.

From this gross amount of estate wealth, the following deductions are used to determine the net estate wealth that will be subject to estate tax:

- Schedule J – Funeral Expenses and Expenses Incurred in Administering Property Subject to Claims.
- Schedule K – Debts of the Decedent including Mortgages and Liens.
- Schedule L – Net Losses During Administration and Expenses Incurred in Administering Property Not Subject to Claims.
- Schedule M – Bequests, etc., to Surviving Spouse.
- Schedule O – Charitable, Public, and Similar Gifts and Bequests.

Using this method for determining the value of an estate as a measure of net wealth results in a somewhat different estimate of wealth than the SCF or WAS. This has implications for the empirical estimates of the aggregate distribution of wealth and associated inequality measures. Attempting to reconcile the different definitions and sources of data on wealth and income inequality has been an active research area.[5]

In addition to detailed definitions of wealth used in government surveys and tax returns, there are also conceptual and theoretical definitions. For example, there is the commonly used dynamic definition of wealth used in economic and financial theory:

$$W_{t+1} = W_t (1 + r_t) + Y_t - C_t$$

where W_t, Y_t, C_t and r_t are wealth, wage income, consumption and the return on wealth, respectively, with subscripts denoting the time date. Because debt is not explicitly identified, W implicitly represents net wealth. In addition, there is an implicit homogeneity of goods, no distinction is made between varying types of consumption goods, the alternative sources of return on wealth, the different forms that income can take, and so on. This definition has no connection to the distribution of wealth and income. Alternatively, the life cycle savings model provides an interpretation of wealth that emphasizes the uses of wealth. This approach identifies three important aspects of wealth accumulation: precautionary savings; generation of after-retirement income, so-called life cycle or 'hump' savings; and bequests. While providing an explanation for the impact of age on wealth distribution of the whole population, the life cycle model has ambiguous implications for the 'extreme value' upper tail of the distributions for wealth and income.

Measuring the Wealth Distribution

Evidence on the distribution and composition of wealth is integral to rethinking wealth and taxes to account for the profound implications of globalization for increasing inequality. Unfortunately, compared to the considerable, if incomplete, evidence on the increasing inequality of income, similar evidence on wealth is 'much more scant and conflicting'.[6] In addition to significant differences arising from available data sources, there are serious questions about the empirical evidence regarding the top of the income distribution, due to the disguising of total income by generating income in different jurisdictions or using the veil of secrecy provided by trusts and corporations, and the difficulty of estimating unrealized capital gains. As for the available data originating from corporate and individual income tax returns, the empirical evidence is more than sufficient to support claims of increasing income inequality across the Organisation for Economic Co-operation and Development (OECD), especially in English-speaking countries, though the precise degree of such inequality is less certain.[7] In addition to income tax returns, large sample finance, consumption and income surveys, such as the SCF and March Current Population Survey (CPS) in the US, supplemented by national income accounts, also provide empirical evidence supporting increasing income inequality observed in data from income tax returns. Figure 1.1 is provided by the WID.world group headed by Thomas Piketty at the Paris School of Economics, a focal point for empirical evidence on increasing inequality in income (and wealth) covering over 70 countries.

The comparably greater amount of data on income than wealth raises the possibility of generalizing results for increasing income inequality

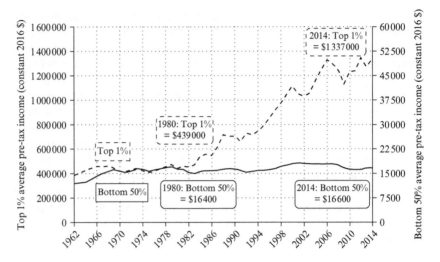

Notes: In 2014, the average pre-tax income of the top 1% was $1 337 000. Pre-tax national income is measured after the operation of pension and unemployment insurance systems (which cover the majority of cash transfers), but before direct income and wealth taxes.

Source: Alvaredo et al. (2019).

Figure 1.1   Pre-tax incomes of the top 1% and bottom 50% in the US, 1962–2014

to also represent implied evidence of increasing wealth inequality; while casual logic combined with the empirical observation that wealth and income are highly correlated would seem to imply that if the flow of income is increasingly unequal, then the accumulating stock of wealth would also become increasingly unequal. This casual logic assumes that those at the top and bottom of the income distribution are the same as those at the top and bottom of the wealth distribution.[8] Is it likely that many of those at the top 10 per cent, 1 per cent or 0.1 per cent of the wealth distribution are generating significantly less income than consumption, and that many of those at the top 10 per cent, 1 per cent or 0.1 per cent of the income distribution are below the top of the wealth distribution? If only due to the limitations of empirical estimates for the extreme value upper tails of the wealth and income distributions, the answer to this question is elusive. Focus often involves distribution quintiles, as in Figure 1.2 from the OECD, which indicates considerable variation in income by those in the 'wealthy' quintile. However, the scant evidence that is available indicates considerable overlap for members of the 0.1 per cent of the wealth and income distributions.

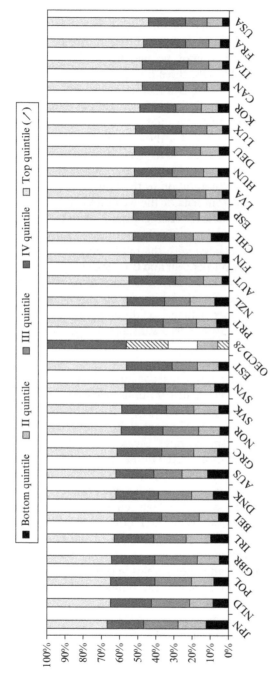

Note: The OECD average is the simple country average. For both income and wealth quintiles, data are defined at the household level and based on non-equivalised measures; this is the practice used in the **WDD** to study the joint distribution of household income and wealth.

Source: OECD Revenue Statistics 2019.

Figure 1.2 Income distribution for the top wealth quintile, 2015 or latest year available

Unlike empirical evidence on income which has been estimated directly from various sources, information on wealth is less accessible. Specifically, wealth is either not reported or is under-reported in income tax returns, used for estimating the distribution of income and earnings.[9] To estimate the wealth distribution for the US, three different methods employed in scholarly studies are: (1) a survey-based method using data from surveys such as the SCF; (2) an estate multiplier method that uses data from estate tax returns that is only applicable, if available at all, to estimating wealth at the top of the wealth distribution for those who are recently deceased; and (3) the capitalization method that uses information on capital income from individual or household income tax returns to estimate the underlying stock of wealth.[10] In addition to these three methods, there is also anecdotal information from lists of the wealthiest individuals, such as the Forbes 400 richest Americans. Being largely generated to address the issue of wealth and income inequality, attention typically focuses on the net wealth holdings associated with the upper portion of the wealth distribution, especially the top 1 per cent and 0.1 per cent. It is this portion of the wealth distribution that has the most to gain from, and is best able to access, professional resources needed to facilitate schemes aimed at exploiting globalization to 'tax manage' or disguise capital income and wealth holdings. This group also owns a substantial, but uncertain, portion of untraded, privately held capital assets which generate unrealized capital gains that are difficult to estimate.

Even though a variety of strongly stated conclusions have been extracted from empirical studies of wealth distributions, closer examination of available estimation methods reveals the opaque character of evidence on the shape and location of such distributions.[11] In general, evidence from surveys raises questions of response rates, the selection of survey participants, the formulation of questions asked in the survey, the untangling of individual versus household versus corporate wealth and, most importantly, definitions of wealth employed. For example, the response rate in the US SCF is 'only about 25 percent' and participant selection is based on 'external income tax information'. While SCF does attempt to oversample from the top of the wealth distribution, members of the Forbes 400 are explicitly censored from the sample, raising questions about the criteria used to select oversampled wealthy households in general, and the method of wealth definition used: for example, the omission of wealth held in trusts and the treatment of offshore wealth. In addition, those engaged in disguising substantial income and wealth would not want to participate in such surveys. As such, it is not possible to 'eliminate the possibility that the [SCF] sample is biased on some unobservable characteristics'.[12] Similar comments apply to survey results obtained for other countries. On balance, it seems likely that empirical evidence for holdings of many nearing the top of the wealth distribution is underestimated, perhaps severely.

One advantage of estimating the wealth distribution using survey data is the ability to determine both the full distribution and the amount of aggregate wealth within the jurisdiction of the survey participants. Unless heroic assumptions are made, it is not possible to estimate either the full distribution of wealth or the aggregate wealth using evidence from estate tax filings. In addition to the severe methodological problems of making inferences from estate tax data when available, significant differences in the calculation of estate and inheritance taxes across jurisdictions undermine the use of such estimates for cross-country comparisons. However, for present purposes, the estate tax method does provide some, albeit limited, information about the upper portion of the wealth distribution that is required to make such filings. Recognizing that the use of estate tax management strategies will impact on the value of an individual estate for income tax purposes, it follows that comparison of wealth estimates using the estate tax method with estimates using the survey or capitalization method could be used to make inferences about the gains to the wealthy over time. For example, in the US since 1980 the estate tax method has produced increasingly lower estimates of wealth shares for the top 1 per cent and 0.1 per cent than estimates using the capitalization method.[13] Limitations of the estate tax method are such that this method has been supplanted by survey estimates in most recent studies that are primarily concerned with properties of the whole distribution, not just the upper tail.

The final method used to estimate wealth involves capitalizing the reported capital income (k) from 'wealth assets' reported on income tax returns. In contrast to the estate tax method, the capitalization method can theoretically produce both a wealth distribution and an estimate for aggregate wealth. Like the estate tax method and unlike the survey method, there is a long time series for capital income available from tax returns. This methodology estimates W by assuming a rate of return on capital income (r) and solving, $k = r\,W$; that is, $W = k\,/\,r$. There are numerous limitations of this approach, ranging from complications in determining the key unobserved variable r to the absence of specific wealth income from k being reported on income tax returns.[14] For example, k would only reflect realized capital gains and not fully capture the unrealized returns from property such as real estate. Given the substantial wealth in the 21st century associated with equity capital shares in publicly traded and privately held companies, it is significant that in the last few decades firms have increasingly reduced dividends in favour of share buybacks, resulting in an ongoing increase in unrealized capital gains, which are not captured by the capitalization method. Similarly, opulent primary residences and property such as yachts and private jets generate substantial implied income that is not reflected in k. As with the estate tax method, despite substantial limitations the survey method appears to provide a more reliable approach to estimating the wealth distribution for a given population.

Despite apparent claims to the contrary, estimates of the upper tail of the wealth distribution and the aggregate amount of wealth ownership in a given jurisdiction are indicative at best, and severely misleading underestimates at worst.[15] Without sufficiently accurate estimates, it is difficult to answer important policy questions that motivate recent scholarly studies of the wealth distribution, such as:

> whether the financial crisis has led to permanent cohort differences in levels of non-pension wealth, what the relative roles of income, capital gains and inter-generational transfers are in explaining changes in household wealth over time, and how the decline of defined benefit pensions might affect the level, timing and volatility of household wealth accumulation.[16]

Seeking relevance in the contemporary policy arena, only muted effort is given to accounting for the largely unobservable impact of globalization on the sourcing of income and wealth outside the political jurisdiction of interest. Given that under-reporting at the top of the wealth and income distributions is most likely and best able to be responsible for any significant unobservable impact, even conservative adjustments must recognize that the increasing inequality observed in income and wealth is decidedly more skewed than estimated.

Who are the Wealthy?

Classifying individuals or households as wealthy is relative and subjective. 'Wealthy' could be defined by reference to a lifestyle, an income level, holdings of assets, and so on. Without adequate context, search for a homogeneous wealthy class is futile. Any search for commonalities must account for difficulties in accurately measuring the upper tails of the income and, especially, wealth distributions over time. With this in mind, Table 1.2 presents evidence for the distribution of wealth in the US generated with capitalized income tax data indicating empirical evidence that the top 0.1 per cent and 1 per cent cohorts of the wealth distributions have characteristics that differ from the 90–99 per cent cohort of those distributions. Table 1.3 presents similar results for the income distribution generated using distributional national accounts data. These results can be compared to estimates from US income tax returns, where just over 40 per cent of pre-tax income goes to the top 10 per cent of households in the US, with the 90–95 per cent cohort receiving approximately 12 per cent of that

Table 1.2　Distribution of household wealth in the US, 2012

Wealth group	Number of families	Wealth threshold ($)	Average wealth ($)	Wealth share
A. Top Wealth groups				
Full Population	160 700 000	–	384 000	100%
Top 10%	16 070 000	740 000	2 871 000	77.2%
Top 1%	1 607 000	4 442 000	15 526 000	41.8%
Top 0.1%	160 700	23 110 000	81 671 000	22.0%
Top 0.01%	16 070	124 525 000	416 205 000	11.2%

Source:　Alvaredo et al. (2019).

Table 1.3　Distribution of national income in the US, 2014

Income group	Number of adults	Pre-tax national income			Post-tax national income		
		Income threshold ($)	Average income ($)	Income share	Income threshold ($)	Average income ($)	Income share
Full Population	234 400 000	–	66 100	100%	–	66 100	100%
Bottom 50%	117 200 000	–	16 600	12.5%	–	25 500	19.3%
Bottom 20%	46 880 000	–	5 500	1.7%	–	13 400	4.1%
Next 30%	70 320 000	13 100	24 000	10.9%	23 200	33 600	15.2%
Middle 40%	93 760 000	36 900	66 900	40.4%	45 000	68 800	41.6%
Top 10%	23 440 000	122 000	311 000	47.0%	113 000	259 000	39.1%
Top 1%	2 344 000	469 000	1 341 000	20.2%	392 000	1 034 000	15.7%
Top 0.1%	234 400	2 007 000	6 144 000	9.3%	1 556 000	4 505 000	6.8%

Source:　Alvaredo et al. (2019).

income and the 95–99 per cent cohort about 15 per cent. In contrast, the top 1 per cent cohort receives about a 14 per cent income share, with about 9 per cent of that share going to the top 0.1 per cent.[17] Comparing these income cohort estimates to wealth cohort estimates reveals that the top 10 per cent cohort has almost 80 per cent of net wealth in the US, with about half of that wealth, approximately 40 per cent, concentrated in the top 1 per cent and half again, approximately 20 per cent, in the top 0.1 per cent. Though such estimates are crude and do vary over time, such results reveal significant differences in what constitutes 'wealthy' among the households in the top 10 per cent and 1 per cent cohorts of income and wealth in the US.

Being concerned with extracting insights from the aggregate distributions

of wealth and income, such estimates give limited attention to the characteristics of individuals and households within the upper cohorts of these
distributions. Consistent with the evidence in Figure 1.2, one classification
scheme that illustrates differences in the 'net benefit' and 'ability to pay'
principles of tax assessment would be to distinguish between wealthy individuals and households with: (1) high net wealth holdings, high pre-tax cash
flow; (2) low net wealth holdings, high pre-tax cash flow; and (3) high net
wealth holdings, low pre-tax cash flow. To relate this classification scheme to
net benefit and ability to pay requires assumptions about the composition of
assets that comprise gross wealth and the associated claims on pre-tax cash
flows. For example, high net wealth individuals or households in category
(3) that are retired and dedicate a large fraction of asset ownership to an
opulent primary residence would rank high on net benefit but lower on ability to pay if income from drawdown of pension assets was relatively low. It
is not difficult to generate a variety of scenarios where information about the
distributions for wealth and income is insufficient to classify the net benefit
and ability to pay if economic efficiency is also a prime consideration.

Given the voluminous evidence on the life cycle savings model, decom-
position of wealth and income distributions by age reveals characteristics of these distributions that require incorporation into any practical
definition of 'wealthy'.[18] The motivations for wealth accumulation, the
composition of wealth assets and net wealth all vary with age. Recognizing
limitations of the data, there are some estimated differences across jurisdictions and for those in the top 1 per cent cohort of the wealth distribution
compared to those in lower cohorts. Some of the more useful general
results observed are consistent with the life cycle savings model. Examining
the top 10 per cent of the wealth distribution in the US reveals lower levels
of net wealth in the below-45 age brackets, with net wealth peaking in the
55–65 age bracket just prior to retirement.[19] Below the top 1 per cent, there
is a steady decline in net wealth for post-65 age groups as retirement assets
and other financial assets are used to supplement income, with only a small
decline in real estate assets. Those in the top 1 per cent typically maintain
net wealth post-65. Gross assets for the 45–55 age bracket are slightly
less than for the 55–65 bracket, but net wealth is lower due to higher debt
levels. The top 1 per cent of the net wealth distribution also has a larger
proportion of individuals below 50 than the top 10 per cent. In addition to
the potentially severe estimation issues identified previously, such general
results are subject to variation over time and jurisdiction.

Tunnelling into the estimated change in wealth and income distributions over time and jurisdiction reveals additional reported results.
Consider the estimated difference in the reliance on capital income for
those in the top 1 per cent and 0.1 per cent of the US income distributions

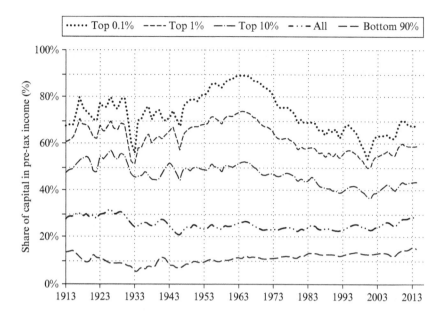

Notes: In 2014, the share of capital in the pre-tax income of the top 10 per cent was 44 per cent. Total pre-tax income is the sum of capital income and labour income. Pre-tax national income is measured after the operation of pension and unemployment insurance systems (which cover the majority of cash transfers), but before direct income and wealth taxes.

Source: Alvaredo et al. (2019).

Figure 1.3   The share of capital in pre-tax income in the US, 1913–2014

in Figure 1.3. These results from distributional national accounts differ from results from estate tax filings where there is less reliance on passive capital income and inherited wealth, and more reliance on income related to labour, than several decades ago. For the top 0.1 per cent and bottom 1 per cent, there is a consistent pattern of very high wealth and income, and very low wealth and income, going together, but with a fairly diffuse relationship for the cohorts in between. In other words, the very rich and the very poor tend to retain this status over time, but a significant fraction of those in the top 10 per cent (and below the top 10 per cent) do migrate into lower (upper) cohorts over time.[20] Extending and comparing such results for the US with other countries in the OECD is complicated by a number of factors. As the US is anomalous in assessing federal income tax on the basis of citizenship, not residence, US income tax and other data for the wealthy may be biased upward compared to other countries where the wealthy could avoid, either partially or fully, being counted in the national statistics by secreting assets offshore in non-resident entities or claiming to be resident in a low-tax offshore jurisdiction.

Venturing into the hazardous area of cross-country wealth comparisons, Table 1.4 presents empirical evidence for the distribution of wealth in the OECD, derived from survey data. Based on such empirical evidence, the 42 per cent of wealth claimed by the upper 1 per cent tail of the US

Table 1.4   Distribution of household net wealth, OECD 2015 (percentages)

	Bottom 40% share	Bottom 60% share	Top 10% share	Top 5% share	Top 1% share
Australia	4.9	16.5	46.5	33.5	15.0
Austria	1.0	8.0	55.6	43.5	25.5
Belgium	5.7	19.0	42.5	29.7	12.1
Canada	3.4	12.4	51.1	37.0	16.7
Chile	0.0	8.5	57.7	42.7	17.4
Denmark	−8.6	−3.9	64.0	47.3	23.6
Estonia	3.8	12.8	55.7	43.2	21.2
Finland	2.2	13.6	45.2	31.4	13.3
France	2.7	12.1	50.6	37.3	18.6
Germany	0.5	6.5	59.8	46.3	23.7
Greece	5.3	17.9	42.4	28.8	9.2
Hungary	5.0	15.4	48.5	35.6	17.2
Ireland	−2.1	7.2	53.8	37.7	14.2
Italy	4.5	17.3	42.8	29.7	11.7
Japan	5.3	17.7	41.0	27.7	10.8
Korea	6.0	17.7	–	–	–
Latvia	0.0	7.1	63.4	49.1	21.4
Luxembourg	3.9	15.3	48.7	36.3	18.8
Netherlands	−6.9	−4.0	68.3	52.5	27.8
New Zealand	3.1	12.3	52.9	39.7	–
Norway	−3.0	7.3	51.5	37.8	20.1
Poland	6.2	18.3	41.8	29.0	11.7
Portugal	3.2	12.4	52.1	36.5	14.4
Slovak Republic	10.6	25.9	34.3	23.0	9.3
Slovenia	5.6	17.3	48.6	37.9	23.0
Spain	6.9	18.7	45.6	33.3	16.3
United Kingdom	3.4	12.1	52.5	38.8	20.5
United States	−0.1	2.4	79.5	68.0	42.5

Note: "–" refers to non-available data.

Source: OECD, Data Directorate, Working Paper #88, June 20, 2018.

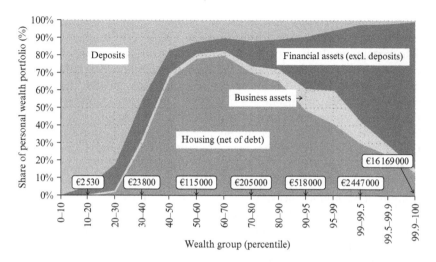

Notes: In 2012, 67 per cent of the personal wealth of the 5th decile was composed of housing assets (net of debt). All values have been converted to 2016 constant euros (accounting for inflation). For comparison, £1 = $1.1 = ¥7.3 at market exchange rates.

Source: Alvaredo et al. (2019).

Figure 1.4   Asset composition by wealth group in France, 2012

wealth distribution is anomalous, with no other country greater than 28 per cent (Netherlands, 27.8 per cent). By comparison, at 80 per cent of US wealth the upper 10 per cent tail is more comparable to the almost 70 per cent for the second-highest country (Netherlands, 68.3 per cent) with many countries at about 50 per cent of national wealth. As for the asset composition of the wealthy and wealthiest, Figure 1.4 derived from French net wealth tax data again indicates a high percentage reliance on capital income from financial assets. Globally, wealth is more concentrated than income, on both an individual and a national basis. Roughly 30 per cent of world wealth is estimated to be in each of North America, Europe, and the rich Asia-Pacific countries. These areas account for virtually all the world's top 1 per cent of wealth-holders.[21] India accounts for about one-quarter of those in the bottom 30 per cent of the estimated global net wealth distribution.[22]

Measuring Income and Wealth Inequality

The claim that wealth and income inequality is increasing over time begs numerous questions: how is inequality to be measured? How large is the increase, if any? How is the increase distributed? What data was used to support the claim? What time interval is involved? and so on.[23] The measurement of inequality in income and wealth is a topic that has consumed economists and statisticians since 1896 when Vilfredo Pareto introduced the Pareto distribution to describe the consistent pattern of wealth and income distributions over time. Subsequent contributions on the measurement of wealth and income inequality include Max Lorenz introducing the Lorenz curve in 1905, and Corrado Gini introducing the Gini coefficient in 1912 to measure the statistical dispersion of income or wealth for a given national population. Though these early contributions still play an important role as inequality measures, the increasing quantification of economics has seen the introduction of a variety of, typically, more analytically sophisticated measures, including the variance of the logarithm of income, the Kuznets curve or Kuznets ratio, and members of the generalized entropy family that include Hirschman's index, Thiel's index, Atkinson's index and Kolm's index.[24]

The presence of so many different theoretical approaches for measuring inequality is motivated by limitations in other measures, especially the widely used Gini coefficient. However, suggested solutions to address limitations almost invariably come with a substantive increase in complexity. For example, recognizing that the Gini coefficient measures inequality between individuals, with 0 representing all individuals receiving the average income and 1 representing all income going to a single individual, the Thiel index aims to measure inequality between groups of individuals. This is useful for measuring inequality based on race, ethnicity, sex, geography, and so on. To accomplish this, the Thiel index evaluates the average of the logarithms of the reciprocal of income shares weighted by income. Similarly, the Atkinson index aims to determine what part of the income distribution contributed most to observed inequality. This is determined as the complement to 1 of the ratio of the Hölder generalized mean of exponent $1 - \varepsilon$ to the arithmetic mean of the incomes. Though appealing to econometricians and statistical purists, such measures lack the intuition necessary for accurate interpretation and, consequently, raise the distinct possibility of 'the fallacy of false precision', where weak data is obscured by 'precise' statistical estimation procedures.

Focus on statistical properties of inequality measures masks a potential fundamental failing of all inequality measures: the severe distortion in estimates of the wealth and income distributions and associated changes over time if the data employed is subject to contamination. Attempts to develop inequality measures that are robust to such contamination, such as those exploiting the 'influence function', rely on assumptions about characteristics of contamination that, while relevant to coding errors and the like, do not have much applicability to the type of errors associated with the measurement of income and, especially, wealth.[25] To avoid the fallacy of false precision, attention needs to pivot to the characteristics, collection and limitations of the wealth and income data used to estimate the relevant inequality measure. In turn, such information can assist in determining the impact of contamination on specific inequality measures. Recognizing that the bulk of wealth and income is captured by 10 per cent or less of the population, the impact of data adjustment in the right-hand (wealthiest or highest income) tail of the distribution on the results of specific inequality measures is especially relevant.

Consideration of characteristics, collection and limitations of data for wealth and, to a lesser extent, income reveals an opaque landscape of conflicting evidence. Procedures used to collect wealth data differ across countries. Though surveys such as the SCF are typically used, there are subtle differences in survey methods, such that:

> Survey wealth estimates are very likely to underestimate wealth at the top, and this often by multiple percentage points. Countries that seem to have a more equal wealth distribution might not be so upon closer scrutiny . . . researchers should be warned of top wealth estimates based on surveys alone, or on simple interpolations of the survey data.[26]

Compared to countries such as the US and Spain, due to differences in wealth data collection procedures used, under-reporting of wealth is particularly dramatic in countries such as the Netherlands, Italy and Austria. One study reports under-reporting of one-quarter of the wealth held by the wealthy in Austria. To remedy downward bias in wealth estimates due to survey non-response, some studies report that adjustments using the Forbes world list of billionaires provide some improvement over survey methods alone, even though the method for constructing the Forbes lists lacks academic precision.

While useful, any attempt to address non-response bias in estimates of the wealth distribution based on household surveys must recognize that by its very nature the wealth of the non-respondents is unobserved. While it may be possible to account for some of this bias by introducing other information such as estimates from income tax data or reconciling estimates with Household Balance Sheet data, it is not possible to accurately consider wealth that is hidden in offshore tax havens and likely not counted in estimates of wealth distributions for specific countries. Despite being subject to widely differing estimates, the amount of such wealth is apparently staggering; though estimates of under-reporting vary widely. Specifically, using three different estimation methods, a 2016 Tax Justice Network report identifies $24–$36 trillion in such hidden wealth globally.

By comparison, using a narrower estimation method, Zucman identifies
$7.6 trillion hidden in tax havens, approximately 8 per cent of the wealth
that is reported globally. Given this, determining precisely what portion of
wealth hidden in tax havens and elsewhere appears in reported wealth for
individual countries is a difficult to impossible task.[27]

Recognizing that measures of inequality are likely to be biased downward, perhaps severely, due to under-reporting and other factors, it is still
instructive to consider estimates of global household wealth. One such
study that accesses survey results adjusted using household balance sheet
data, covering two-thirds of the world population and 95 per cent of the
wealth over 2000–2014, finds:[28]

> Estimated global household wealth stood at USD 251 trillion in 2014, having
> grown from USD 117 trillion in the year 2000. Wealth per adult in 2014 was
> USD 53,000. The estimated Gini coefficient of global wealth was 92.2% in 2014
> and the share of the top 10% was 88.3%. Wealth inequality fell from 2000 to
> 2007, with the share of the top 10% falling from 89.4% to 86.5%, before rising
> steadily to 2014. From 2000 to 2008 the share of financial assets in gross wealth,
> an important driver of wealth inequality, fell from 55.2% to 50.2%, before
> climbing to 55.0% in 2014.

Examining specific estimates for the US for this study, the top 10 per
cent had 75 per cent of the wealth, with the top 1 per cent holding 36 per
cent, both estimates being slightly lower than is reported in Table 1.4. For
Switzerland, the estimates were 71 per cent for the top 10 per cent and 35
per cent for the top 1 per cent. Countries reporting results for the top 10
per cent include: China, 64 per cent (OECD partner); Canada, 48 per cent;
the UK, 48 per cent; Sweden, 67 per cent; and Japan, 34 per cent. Based on
studies about the impact of survey non-response, it is likely that all these
estimates are downward biased to some extent. Accounting for wealth
hidden in tax havens, even if the sourcing of tax haven wealth to specific
countries is unknown, downward bias is likely to be substantial. By comparison, in almost every country the bottom 10 per cent is reported to have
negative net wealth, indicating a balance of liabilities greater than assets.

WEALTH TAXES AND TAXES ON THE WEALTHY

The Net Wealth Tax

While the obvious definition of a wealth tax may seem tautological – a
wealth tax is a tax on wealth – the reality is decidedly more complicated.
In particular, a wealth tax conventionally imposes tax directly on some

notional concept of net wealth, while taxes on wealth distinguish between various components of (gross) wealth in order to impose tax on specific items.[29] The most commonly used definition of a wealth tax is synonymous with a net worth tax that is assessed separately from an estate tax which is levied at the time of death. Though it is possible for such a tax to be assessed as an irregular levy to fund special situations, such as reducing the amount of public debt or to fund war expenditure, this tax is usually assessed as a supplement to the regular income tax.[30] Such wealth tax schemes have been proposed, and less often used, at various times in various countries. In the modern era of broad-based income taxes, the net wealth tax has not been a significant contributor to government revenue in any OECD country.

In practice, the form of a net wealth tax depends on whether 'natural persons' (individuals) or 'legal persons' (individuals and corporate entities) are to be taxed. Similar to items listed in IRS Form 706, the objective is to impose a levy on the total net value of the stock of personal assets, including: owner-occupied housing; cash, bank deposits and money funds; savings in insurance and pension plans; investment in real estate and unincorporated businesses; corporate stock and other company ownership claims; financial securities; and personal trusts. Liabilities such as mortgages and other loans are deducted, resulting in an estimate of net wealth that is subject to tax. Against this conceptual backdrop, wealth identification, allocation affected by globalization and valuation difficulties can pose significant practical problems. In the case of the wealthiest and the wealthy with assets spread across different taxing jurisdictions, even if wealth items could be identified and valued, the allocation of subsequent increases in net wealth tax revenue across taxing jurisdictions is unclear.

The present status of the net wealth tax raises a variety of issues. Prior to the emergence of the income tax as a critical source of government revenue, assessment of taxes based on wealth – usually in the form of a property qualification – was central to payment of certain essential government services. Though net wealth tax schemes have received considerable attention in the income tax era and were adopted in some European countries, there has been a gradual elimination of such taxes over the past two decades. As compared to income taxes and sales taxes, in the modern era the net wealth tax has not represented a significant source of tax revenue in any country. In particular, using 2011 as a reference date, 'a comprehensive and recurring tax on individual net wealth, defined as the surplus value of assets held by an individual over liabilities, existed in only three OECD countries: France, Norway and Switzerland'.[31] This situation has resulted from a recent wave of OECD countries abolishing personal net wealth taxes; for example, Spain abolished a new wealth tax in 2008, that was reintroduced as a temporary tax in 2011; Sweden abolished its wealth tax in 2007; and Finland, Iceland and Luxembourg eliminated such a tax in 2006. In 2018, France replaced the net wealth tax with a progressive property tax.

In addition to countries that adopted and then eliminated a net wealth tax, public debates about net wealth taxes have surfaced in some other counties. In Germany, for example, there was a recurrent tax on 'personal' – that is, individual and corporate – net wealth until 1997, when the constitutional court suspended the tax for being unconstitutional on grounds surrounding the lack of clarity on wealth valuation. France introduced a revised 'solidarity tax on net wealth' in 1989 to replace a previous net wealth tax that was abolished in 1986. The Netherlands introduced a de facto wealth tax as part of the income tax system by imposing an implied 4 per cent return on financial and physical capital, taxing the implied income at a flat rate of 30 per cent. In contrast, elected in 1974 with a promise to impose a net wealth tax, the UK's Labour government was ineffective in passing enabling legislation. More recently, in 2011 the independent review of the UK tax system prepared by the Mirrlees commission suggested that more effective taxation of wealth would enhance efficiency as well as equity. In Canada, the 1990 election platform of the New Democratic Party (NDP) in Ontario contained a proposal for a wealth tax. This proposal was dropped following election of a majority NDP government in September 1990. In the US, proposal for a wealth tax was part of the platform of senator and 2020 presidential candidate Elizabeth Warren.

Against this backdrop of decreasing usage of net wealth taxes to raise government revenue, there has been a revival of academic debate surrounding a policy recommendation for a global wealth tax in the recent influential contribution by Thomas Piketty, *Capital in the Twenty-First Century*, published in 2014. More precisely, Piketty recommends wealth taxes as a method of addressing the considerable compelling 'empirical evidence' of increasing wealth and income inequality. To quote Piketty:[32]

> In my book, I propose a simple rule of thumb to think about optimal wealth tax rates. Namely, one should adapt the tax rates to the observed speed at which the different wealth groups are rising over time. For instance, if top wealth holders are rising at 6–7 percent per year in real terms as compared to 1–2 percent per year for average wealth . . . if one aims to stabilize the level of wealth concentration, then one might need to apply top wealth tax rates as large as 5 percent per year, and possibly higher . . . Needless to say, the implications would be very different if top wealth holders were rising at the same speed as average wealth.

This general approach to net wealth taxation is followed by an ominous reference to the implications of globalization for disguising wealth and income: 'we need more financial transparency and better information about income and wealth dynamics, so that we can adapt our policies and institutions to a changing environment. This might require better international fiscal coordination, which is difficult but by no means impossible.'

Leaving aside the practical questions surrounding the implementation of such a wealth tax proposal, the debate about wealth taxes inspired by Piketty has prompted a number of contrary proposals from across the ideological landscape.[33] A common platitude in this debate is the need for 'a fuller understanding of the relationships among different tax bases, in particular consumption taxes, labor income taxes, and capital income taxes'.[34]

Taxes on Capital: Method and Timing

In some cases, a wealth tax is referred to as synonymous to a capital tax. This is a useful simplification for determining economic efficiency of the tax, as it relates wealth with one of the essential factors of production.[35] However, when the capital tax is assessed on the flow of capital income, the connection to taxing a 'stock' of wealth is lost. In addition, income from capital is not homogeneous: dividends and interest, realized and unrealized capital gains, imputed rents, labour income from human capital, and so on, are all avenues of income generated from capital. The ability to defer the income tax on an accrued but unrealized capital gain is an essential difference between capital and labour income. A capital tax on the stock of wealth can be imposed at death of the capital stock owner as either an estate tax on the decedent, or an inheritance tax on recipients of the estate settlement. In some jurisdictions, such as Canada, death or distribution through gift can trigger the realization of capital gains tax. Capital taxes, especially capital gains taxes, are an important touchstone in ideological debates. Right-wing proponents typically argue on efficiency grounds for capital taxes – especially capital gains taxes – to be replaced by sales taxes and labour income taxes. Left-wing prognosticators typically argue on equity grounds for higher taxes on capital in general, and for enhanced inheritance and estate taxes specifically.

As a capital tax, an equity and efficiency basis for optimal tax assessment based on net capital assets is complicated. One rationalization views a tax on the stock of wealth, somehow defined, as a desirable method of capturing the deferred capital gains income that is untaxed in the period the gain was earned. More precisely, a number of detailed empirical studies have identified three specific tax policies that have played a central role in the observed increase in US income and wealth inequality since the early 1990s: reducing the tax rate on dividends; providing inequitable treatment of capital gains compared with ordinary income; and permitting the 'step-up' basis for capital gains when assets are passed to heirs.[36] Across countries, there is significant variation in the method and timing of capital gains tax assessment, making it difficult to determine the practical implications of taxing the stock of net capital assets. For example, since 1972 Canada has abolished estate, gift and inheritance taxes, but does assess capital gains taxes prior to transferring a capital asset in a gift and at time of death. This differs from many other OECD countries where capital gains deferral or exemption at time of death is combined with an inheritance or estate tax. The potential for cross-country tax arbitrage by those wealthy individuals able to source wealth and income across different jurisdictions is apparent.

To illustrate significant and not-so-significant cross-country differences in capital taxes, consider the similar treatment of capital gains taxes in the US and Canada. For the US, the Internal Revenue Service (IRS) states:

> Almost everything you own and use for personal purposes, pleasure or investment is a capital asset. When you sell a capital asset, the difference between the amount you sell it for and your basis – which is usually what you paid for it – is a capital gain or a capital loss. You must report all capital gains. You may deduct capital losses only on investment property, not on property held for personal use.[37]

This can be contrasted with the definition of capital gain used by the Canada Revenue Agency (CRA): 'Capital gain – you have a capital gain when you sell, or are considered to have sold, a capital property for *more* than the total of its adjusted cost base and the outlays and expenses incurred to sell the property.'[38] A capital property is further defined by the CRA as:

> Capital property includes depreciable property, and any property which, if sold, would result in a capital gain or a capital loss. You usually buy it for investment purposes or to earn income. Capital property does not include the trading assets of a business, such as inventory. Some common types of capital property include cottages; securities, such as stocks, bonds, and units of a mutual fund trust; and, land, buildings, and equipment you use in a business or a rental operation.

Significantly, Canada provides an exemption from capital gains tax for a primary residence, an exemption not provided in the US where a substantial lifetime capital gains exemption limit is provided for individuals and a capital gain rollover provision for primary residences is available.

Casual examination of asset holdings for the wealthiest individuals, such as Warren Buffett, Bill Gates, Jeff Bezos and the Walton family, reveals significant deferred capital gains tax associated with equity capital shares in publicly traded corporations. Widening the wealth net slightly finds equity capital shares in privately held companies as well as publicly traded corporations. In addition to the tax-timing option associated with capital gains deferral, the income from such corporate asset holdings is taxed at corporate not individual income tax rates.[39] Despite having marginal corporate tax rates that vary from 15 per cent to 35 per cent prior to the Tax Cuts and Jobs Act of 2017, the effective US corporate income tax rate had been much lower. The Government Accountability Office (GAO) reports that in each year from 2006 to 2012, at least two-thirds of all active corporations had no federal income tax liability. Larger corporations were more likely to owe tax. Among large corporations (generally those with at least $10 million in assets), less than half – 42.3 per cent – paid no federal income tax in 2012. Of those large corporations whose financial statements reported a profit, 19.5 per cent paid no federal income tax that year. Reasons why even profitable corporations may have paid no federal tax for a given year include the use of tax deductions for losses carried forward from prior years, and tax incentives such as depreciation allowances that are more generous in the federal tax code than those allowed for financial accounting purposes. Corporations that did have a federal corporate income tax liability for tax year 2012 owed $267.5 billion.[40]

The remarkable and, for some, profoundly disturbing growth in the depth, extent and influence of equity capital during the 20th century and into the early years of the 21st century has played a central role in the increasing inequality of income and wealth.[41] This has engendered calls by Piketty and others for reform of the limited liability corporation as an avenue for mitigating this observed maldistribution. As Piketty observes: 'Without real accounting and financial transparency and sharing of information, there can be no economic democracy. Conversely, without a real right to intervene in corporate decision-making (including seats for workers on the company's board of directors), transparency is of little use.'[42] Such reform suggestions raise questions of economic efficiency. Being predicated on the notion that the limited liability corporation with autonomous shares needs, somehow, to be fixed by 'interven[ing] in corporate decision-making', such populist recommendations for reform ignore the centuries of progress that have produced a legal form adapted to capitalist commercial ventures requiring a large and permanent equity capital stock. This begs a fundamental question: is the advancement of the social justice goals of tax fairness, economic democracy and equality of opportunity, as identified by Piketty and others, obtainable using ad hoc, potentially efficiency-reducing intervention in commercial decisions?

Other Taxes on Wealth

In addition to taxes on net wealth, capital income and bequests, wealth in modern society attracts various other taxes. Included in these taxes are the most difficult for the wealthy and the less-than-wealthy to avoid: consumption taxes, user fees and property taxes. Consumption taxes can be used to recognize that capital can take various forms, resulting in problems of definition when assessing taxes. For example, if capital is viewed as a factor of production, then luxury items such as jewellery, paintings, yachts and the like would not count as capital, as such items are not involved in the production of goods and services. In application, such personal use items would fit the given definition of capital that taxation authorities use for purposes of determining a capital gain.[43] However, the income from such capital is imputed and not taxed. If such items are not sold, then no capital gains tax will be assessed. The primary tax paid on such unsold capital is the consumption tax assessed at the time of sale. While globalization allows the wealthy to avoid or evade consumption taxes on certain easy-to-transport items (such as jewellery) by sourcing such purchases through a jurisdiction with low or no consumption taxes, user fees on items that have to be registered for use in a given area (such as cars and yachts) either cannot be avoided or evaded, or it is more difficult to do so.

Subject to certain adjustments, income taxes reflect the 'ability to pay' approach to raising government revenue, while sales taxes, property taxes, transfer taxes and user fees reflect the 'net benefit' approach. Using public perception of a wealthy lifestyle as the criteria to identify net benefit to assess taxes, gross wealth held in luxury items, opulent residences and the like would attract net benefit taxes. Such easier-to-impose taxes are essential to address situations where globalization has facilitated income tax avoidance and evasion by the wealthy that undermines the horizontal and vertical equity of income taxes, and contributes to the stylized fact of increasing inequality in wealth and income. For example, consider the case of households in Canada that claim low after-tax income in Canada, yet have more than enough assets for a lifestyle that is wealthy, funded largely with funds obtained from offshore jurisdictions with low or no tax rates that is transferred to Canada as an untaxed gift from a non-resident. If ability to pay is used as a primary criterion for raising government revenue, instead of taxes on the wealthy lifestyle associated with net benefits, then by generating little taxable income in Canada such individuals or households would largely escape taxation in Canada. Because user fees and luxury vehicle levies are not substantial, the primary taxes such households pay in Canada are property taxes and consumption taxes.

To serve as a basis for offsetting the perverse impact of globalization on the horizontal and vertical equity of using income taxes as the primary method of raising government revenue, is it possible to recalibrate the importance of property taxes, transfer taxes, user fees and consumption taxes as a method of reaching wealthy free riders? To this end, other identifying characteristics such as age, occupation and geographical location would need to be recognized in establishing whether an individual or household was wealthy and warranted an increase in net benefit taxes. For example, farmers might have high net asset holdings due to ownership of farmland, equipment and animals, but many would not be considered wealthy because of low farm incomes and long, arduous working hours. An additional need for recalibrating is that, while marginal income taxes rates are designed to be progressive, property taxes, transfer taxes and consumption taxes are typically flat rate *ad valorem* taxes. While a higher-value transaction or real property value will pay a proportionately higher absolute value of tax, the marginal rate is the same as for lower-value transactions, resulting in a regressive tax outcome. Though progressivity of property tax and, where possible, consumption tax is indicated on equity grounds, the political hurdles of jurisdictional tax assessment and revenue redistribution present daunting obstacles.

WEALTH, INCOME AND THE HARD TO TAX

The Traditional Hard-to-Tax Problem

Despite claims of convincing empirical evidence for increasing inequality of wealth and income, such claims are limited by difficulties in determining estimates for the distributions of wealth and income. This opaque landscape of empirical evidence fails to account for the implications of tax competition between countries, and of tax avoidance and tax evasion by corporations and wealthy individuals. Without some knowledge about the unobservable components of wealth and income, public discourse surrounding reform of taxes paid by the wealthy is based largely on subjective opinion. Lack of knowledge permits inadequate ideological interpretation of the objective information that is available, reinforcing the influence of subjective opinion. By stifling the availability of evidence and providing enhanced avenues for creative tax management by the wealthy, globalization has made a complicated problem almost intractable. What emerges is a 21st-century evolution of the traditional hard-to-tax problem where the primary unobservable had been income, with only muted concern about wealth.

By creating a range of previously unavailable avenues for avoiding and evading taxes, globalization has altered the landscape of the traditional hard-to-tax problem, which has been concerned primarily with the avoidance and evasion of taxes within a given tax jurisdiction. While various possible aspects of the traditional hard-to-tax problem are available, the underground or shadow economy landscape – somehow defined – is typically used as a backdrop.[44] The additional complicating avenues provided by globalization include enhanced ability to transfer funds and relocate capital assets internationally; and freedom to create anonymous corporate or trust entities to source income to low-tax jurisdictions with secrecy laws that shield the identities of account and corporation owners. As such, the use of avenues provided by globalization for the wealthy to avoid and evade taxes substantively broadens the focus of the traditional hard-to-tax problem to include a combination of income and wealth. Recognizing that disguised and shielded income and assets are not and cannot be measured accurately, if at all, accounting for globalization suggests that scholarly assessments of wealth and income inequality based on available empirical evidence from national data sources are almost certainly significant underestimates. Precisely how such an unobservable underestimate overlays the available empirical evidence for wealth and income is unclear.

The traditional hard-to-tax problem arises with the failure of a given tax collection system within a specific taxation jurisdiction to identify and appropriately tax those involved in underground or shadow economy activities. There are a number of facets to this problem, but the traditional hard-to-tax problem does not typically include taxing the wealthy when income can be generated and wealth can readily be domiciled in a number of jurisdictions.[45] A central aspect of the hard-to-tax problem concerns the estimation and interpretation of the underground or shadow economy size. To this end, the underground economy can usefully be divided into three segments by transaction type: (1) barter transactions, which are 'usually assumed (perhaps incorrectly) to be minor in scale, so in estimation efforts [are] generally ignored'; (2) the informal market sector, which 'deals in legal goods and services in illegal (or extralegal) ways', where the hard-to-tax entity 'avoids reporting its activities, dodges regulations such as licensing laws, and, where possible, evades taxes'; and (3) the criminal sector, where the goods and services traded are explicitly illegal.[46] Those involved in the criminal sector are especially anxious about hiding the extent of such activities, not only from the statistician and the tax collector examining the hard-to-tax in the informal market and barter sectors, but also from identification by the criminal justice system. It is possible for individuals to operate in more than one segment; for example, a criminal enterprise that invests profits in legitimate cash businesses, bartering services with employees and suppliers and under-reporting gross income for tax purposes.

This segmentation approach to the underground economy can be similarly applied to the wealthy hard-to-tax. One segment is the wealthiest, where concerns of vertical equity are paramount and the ability to resist coercive taxation is substantial. A second segment is composed of the wealthy involved in income tax deferment using the realization principle to delay tax on capital income, including corporate executives transmuting wage income into capital income by using deferred equity compensation schemes. This segment raises issues of both efficiency and vertical equity. A third segment involves wealthy individuals exploiting globalization by sourcing income and wealth offshore, raising issues of horizontal and, in extreme cases, vertical equity. By avoiding the reporting of activities, dodging regulations and, where possible, evading taxes, this segment has similarity to the informal market sector of the traditional hard-to-tax. It is likely that the wealthiest are involved in all three segments. The final segment of the wealthy hard-to-tax, associated with income and wealth derived from criminal activities such as large scale embezzlement, drug smuggling and the like, raises issues well beyond the realm of wealth and taxes.

The intersection between the underground economy of the traditional hard-to-tax and the global and domestic activities that wealthy hard-to-tax individuals and households use to avoid and evade taxes is small, if only because tax avoidance involves legal activity and the taxation rules provide ample opportunity for the wealthy to legally avoid taxation, especially on capital income. Most wealthy tax evaders would be classified as only a small part of the informal market sector. The hard-to-tax rural agricultural producers in low-income developing countries, where the underground economy constitutes a significant proportion of gross domestic product (GDP), have little in common with the largely urbanized wealthiest 1 per cent and 0.1 per cent of the population in the high-income OECD countries. This begs an important question: can insights from the traditional hard-to-tax problem be usefully adapted to rethinking wealth and taxes? More precisely, can suggested methods aimed at raising government revenue from the hard-to-tax be adapted to the wealthy tax avoidance and evasion that is driving increasing wealth and income inequality?

Ideology, Morality and the Hard-to-Tax[47]

Though the tax avoidance and evasion activities of the wealthy are identified in some definitions of the hard-to-tax, the underlying political, ideological and moral differences to the traditional hard-to-tax problem go unrecognized. This problem was elevated into the policy arena by numerous empirical estimates that started to appear in the late 1970s, claiming the underground economy as a percentage of officially recorded GDP was significant. Though such estimates varied with the methodologies and heroic assumptions made, typical results found that the average size of the underground economy varied from 8–10 per cent for high-income OECD countries such as the US, Japan and Switzerland, to about 75 per cent for low-income countries in Africa such as Egypt and Nigeria.[48] Such estimates for the size and growth rate of the shadow economy depend on the definition used for identifying activities that fall within the underground economy. An important early researcher on the 'unobserved' and 'irregular' underground economies, Edgar Feige, finds two elements of 'conceptual linkage' between the various constituent activities of the underground economy: concealment and immorality.[49] Put in a simple policy context, participation in the concealed activities of the underground economy is perceived as a 'social bad'. In contrast to the traditional hard-to-tax, the wealthiest can dedicate considerable political, social and economic resources to promoting the perception that extreme wealth at a time of increasing poverty is a 'social good', not a 'social bad'. Altering this perception would seem to be essential to developing a democratic solution.

An illustration of concealment and implied moral condemnation is provided by a 1992 US Department of Labor publication that distinguishes among aspects of the US underground economy according to the following categories: illegal; unreported; unrecorded; and informal. The illegal sector of the underground economy is defined as 'economic activities pursued in violation of legal statutes defining the scope of legitimate forms of commerce', using examples such as prostitution or the trade in drugs. The 'unreported economy' involves 'those economic activities that circumvent or evade . . . the tax code'; 'the unrecorded economy' captures those 'that circumvent the institutional rules that define the reporting requirements of government statistical agencies'; and finally, 'the informal economy' is defined as 'those economic activities that circumvent the costs of . . . the laws and administrative rules covering property relationships, commercial licensing' and other similar government regulations. The difficulties of providing precise estimates of inherently 'unobserved' activities is reflected in this Department of Labor report where estimates of $42 billion to $1.096 trillion are reported for the size of the aggregate underground economy in the US, depending on the estimation method and the definition categories included.[50]

By identifying the immorality linkage between different sectors, Feige was an early contributor to the debate on the moral and ideological implications of the underground economy. As for the individual sectors, Feige maintains that the 'most serious consequence' of illegal activities 'is to undermine the stability and responsibility of political, legal and economic institutions'. Such a position reflects deeply held ideological and political predispositions about criminality. On similar moral grounds, Feige condemns unreported and unrecorded activities: 'Tax noncompliance shifts the burden from the dishonest to the honest, increasing the costs of adherence to any system of rules and regulations.'[51] It is a small ideological step to a policy conclusion that flight into the unreported and unrecorded sectors is due to individuals and households being increasingly overburdened by government taxes and regulations. The possibility goes unrecognized that the tax code permits the wealthy to legally avoid paying more tax than those typically lower-income tax evaders in the unreported and unrecorded activities of the traditional hard-to-tax.

Taxing the Hard-to-Tax

'Most policy advisors and government practitioners have no trouble in agreeing on the main [traditional hard-to-tax] culprits: the self-employed; the agricultural sector; small firms, moonlighters, and informal sector providers of services.'[52] Given this, there is an incongruence between these traditional lower- and middle-income hard-to-tax and the wealthiest 1 per cent and 0.1 per cent and wealthy 'free riders' who are hard-to-tax for alternative reasons. In contrast with traditional culprits, these hard-to-tax exploit increased international mobility of financial wealth, favourable tax treatment of capital-related income, and the proliferation of tax and bank secrecy havens, to effectively avoid and evade taxes. Despite this incongruence, both types of hard-to-tax have the same implication: that the overall tax incidence associated with raising a given amount of government tax revenue requires an even greater share of the personal tax burden to fall on the least informed or least mobile, effectively the 'honest' wage and salary income earners. In turn, available empirical evidence on the traditional hard-to-tax in OECD countries indicates that 'an increased burden of taxation and social security payments, combined with intensive labor market regulation, quality of state institutions and the tax morale are the driving forces for the shadow economy'.[53]

Against this backdrop, consider a simple but persistent question surrounding underground economy activities: what alternative to the status quo should we consider? One path asks whether further coercion is required to make violators comply with the law. The other path asks whether it is best to relax the norms, so that activities now underground will rise to the surface and receive the protection of the law.

Perhaps a large and growing underground economy: 'is an indication that the economy is over-taxed and over-regulated and a neo-liberal adjustment is needed to free it up? . . . Clearly such political conclusions depend on having a good theoretical as well as sound quantitative foundations and both these components are generally missing.' Others question the actual response to the hard-to-tax problem that took the 'form of empty slogans about the need to cut taxes, roll back regulations, and privatize public functions'.[54] In sharp contrast to the neoliberal perspective, the central issue with the wealthy hard-to-tax is not taxes that are too high, but taxes that are, arguably, too low on vertical equity grounds for those in the wealthiest 1 per cent and 0.1 per cent. On balance, assessing the various potential solutions to the hard-to-tax problem, 'one should also be aware of a political dimension'.

In 2004, the eminent public finance economist Richard Bird provided the following assessment of the difficulties that globalization poses for the enforcement of tax evasion by the wealthy:[55]

> while sophisticated cross-border evaders are the bane of all tax systems, this group may pose such great problems for administrations that are not well-equipped to play in this league that it sometimes has been suggested that it is important to keep some 'on-shore' channels of tax evasion sufficiently open to avoid driving not only tax revenues but also real resources and real economic activity offshore. Such measures as withholding taxes on cross-border financial flows, vigilant policing of cross-border trade, and, especially, cooperating with the neighbors both with respect to such flows and trade and keeping tax rates roughly in line, as well as facilitating information exchange relevant to taxation may help, though none of these approaches is without its own problems.

Recognizing the significant difficulties posed by the wealthy 'exit option', various possible approaches to taxing the hard-to-tax have been identified. These approaches can be loosely classified as: legitimization, enforcement, indirect taxes and presumptive taxes. Within each of these general classifications, there are a variety of possible avenues. For example, legitimization could involve exempting income (allegedly) earned offshore or having tax holidays. Of these four classifications, presumptive taxes are often recognized as being the most effective method of reaching the hard to tax. In turn, the presumptive tax classification is a broad basket of possible taxation avenues, including property taxes and the alternative minimum tax. Despite some progress on multilateral coordination in recent years, enforcement is still open to concern raised by Bird about the tax authorities being ill-equipped to deal with the wealthy hard-to-tax. For a legal traditionalist, this discussion begs the question: what combinations of revenue sources are currently being employed to raise government revenues that would be available to raise additional taxes from the wealthy?

NOTES

1. Adam Smith (1776, p.5).
2. Wolff (1990) identifies the three possible theoretical approaches to defining wealth, as household (or individual) disposable wealth, augmented wealth and capital wealth. Household disposable wealth is a market value concept that references the market value of tradeable assets less tradeable liabilities. In turn, augmented wealth calculates the present value of the discounted future stream of net income (this could include human capital). This specification raises the issue of whether the difficult-to-measure value of future public and private pension payouts are technically wealth components. Capital wealth captures the ownership of income-producing assets. Most empirical studies employ some form of household disposable wealth. Piketty (2014, p.45) defines capital 'as the sum total of nonhuman assets that can be owned and exchanged on some market'. This ignores human capital and non-traded capital. It also assumes that the market valuation of intangible and other assets at a point in time is correct.
3. This UK government survey is discussed in Crawford et al. (2016). Balestra and Tonkin (2018, Appendix A) lists available survey data collected in relevant OECD countries. In Canada, the Survey on Financial Security, conducted most recently in 2016, provides useful data on wealth and income (Uppal and LaRochelle-Côté, 2015). Jäntti and Sierminska (2007) provide an overview of sources on wealth holdings in the OECD countries. Katic and Leigh (2016) discuss the use of surveys to estimate the wealth distribution for Australia. Ward (2014) examines the use of survey data in evaluating the evolution of the wealth distribution for China.
4. On the implications of the difference between pre-tax and after-tax calculation of wealth, see Looney and Moore (2016). For detail on differences in wealth calculations between the SCF and 'capitalized' administrative tax data, see Bricker et al. (2016, p.272, Table 1).
5. Many of the numerous studies in this area reference the contributions of Piketty, Saez and Zucman, often focusing on Piketty (2014). For example, building on Galbraith (2012, Ch. 2) and Galbraith (2016), Galbraith (2019) critiques the use of 'sparse, inconsistent and unreliable' tax data used in Alvaredo et al. (2017) claiming to improve methods of estimating income and wealth inequality from surveys. In addition to contributions from the Centre for Tax Policy and Administration at the OECD, an important forum for such inequality research is the World Inequality Lab at the Paris School of Economics, with an executive team of Alvaredo, Chancel, Piketty, Saez and Zucman.
6. This claim is from Kopczuk (2015, p.47). This relatively conservative statement on the state of empirical knowledge for the wealth distribution refers primarily to studies such as Kopczuk and Saez (2004). In addition to the contributions from the World Inequality Lab and the associated database WID.world, the current status quo for research on estimation of wealth distributions and wealth inequality measures appears in recent OECD-sponsored publications (Balestra and Tonkin, 2018; Alvaredo, 2018), the evolution of the OECD wealth distribution database (OECD, 2019a), and contributions to the OECD Conference on Wealth Inequalities: Measurement and Policies (April 2018) that included contributions by a number of leading academics in the area. As reflected in UNDP (2019) and other contributions to the associated World Inequality Lab, the OECD is not the only transnational organization dedicating substantial resources to research on the measurement and implications of economic inequality. There are also numerous less recent contributions, primarily for the US, that examine issues surrounding increasing wealth inequality, including Wolff (1992, 1994, 1995, 1996, 1998), Winnick (1989), Welch (2001), Smith (2001) and Yunker (1994). Though results from earlier studies are affected by the same data limitations as more recent work, there is evidence of increasing wealth inequality dating to the 1980s.
7. The considerable literature on the increasing inequality of income and earnings includes the influential Piketty (2014), which extends earlier work on income inequality (e.g.,

Piketty and Saez, 2003; Atkinson et al., 2011), to include the more complicated issue of wealth inequality. Differences in income inequality estimates arising from the two most widely used data sources for the US – the CPS and income tax data – is discussed in Burkhauser et al. (2009). Meyer et al. (2015) identify serious limitations involved in the use of household surveys. Armour et al. (2013, 2014) examine the relationship between market-based and Haig–Simons income measurement. Evidence for the UK is provided in Atkinson (2005), and for Canada in Saez and Veall (2005). The project associated with the World Top Income Database, which initially provided income distribution data for 22 countries, aiming to expand to include another 45 countries, is discussed in Piketty and Saez (2013).

8. Bricker et al. (2016) explore the relationship between wealth and income distributions in the US and, in addition to demonstrating significant differences in the estimated distributions using SCF and income tax data sources, also assert that these distributions are highly correlated.

9. For example, Fagereng et al. (2016, p. 651) observe: 'Data on the stock of wealth of the very wealthy are rare. Yet, people at the top of the wealth distribution control a large share of the total assets in the economy . . . Unfortunately, measuring wealth at the top and its evolution over time is difficult. Survey data are problematic. The wealthy are too few to be sampled and even oversampling some leaves out too much wealth. Furthermore, underreporting is notoriously a problem, it is increasing over time and, importantly, likely to be more relevant precisely among wealthier households.'

10. According to Alvaredo (2018) and the wealth inequality survey by Davies and Shorrocks (2000), there are five possible data sources for estimating the distribution of wealth: household wealth surveys, inheritance and estate tax records, rich lists, net wealth tax data, and investment income data such as reports of realized capital gains, interest and dividends. Such data are often combined to offset limitations of relying on one source. Saez and Zucman (2016), for example, capitalize investment income information from US tax returns and compare with results using other data sources. For many OECD countries, there are less than five data sources available; for example, the US and UK do not have net wealth tax data. Various sources discuss the difficulties and different results obtained by different estimation methods; for example, Kopczuk (2015), Looney and Moore (2016) and Eckerstorfer et al. (2016). Slemrod (2016) discusses limitations of using tax return administrative data. In turn, lists of the wealthiest are observed to be particularly inaccurate due to being based largely on estimates of gross wealth, omitting the amount of debt, and not accurately accounting for individuals with large inheritances.

11. Failings of survey methods to accurately represent the wealth distribution and associated wealth inequality measures is an active research area. Kennickell (2019) reviews previous studies and details the mechanics of survey methods, to conclude: 'problems in making comparisons of wealth inequality measures when there are specific defects in the measurement of the upper tail of the distribution . . . indicate that in the absence of effective controls on the measurement of the upper tail of the wealth distribution, great caution should be the rule in the interpretation of most commonly used measures of wealth inequality from a given survey, comparison of such measures across the waves of the survey, and perhaps even more strongly, comparison across independently designed and managed surveys'.

12. Kopczuk (2015, p. 52).

13. Kopczuk (2015, p. 50, Figure 3). One appealing feature of the estate tax method is that results from the survey method are relatively recent in historical terms, while estate tax returns have a long lineage. For example, the first survey directly concerned with wealth in the UK is from 2006, while estate tax information goes back over three centuries.

14. Bricker et al. (2016, p. 272, Table 1) provides a detailed comparison of the capitalization method and survey method.

15. For example, O'Brien (1988, p. 256) observes: 'Tax evasion qualifies the usefulness of income-tax returns and this objection to using the statistics must be discussed at

the outset. Two factors are involved in assessing the accuracy of estimates of income made for taxation purposes, administrative efficiency on the one hand and social co-operation on the other. Because only the first is capable of objective assessment, it tends to bulk large in any discussion of tax evasion, but the latter is undoubtedly at least as important.'

16. Crawford et al. (2016, p. 53).
17. The income cohort estimates for all but the top 0.1 per cent are from Burkhauser et al. (2009) for 2006, obtained from the CPS, and the estimates for the top 0.1 per cent are from Jones (2015). Reconciliation of results from income tax data with national income accounts is an active research area. The wealth estimates are from Kopczuk (2015). Saez and Veall (2005) report similar pre-tax income shares for Canada for 2000. This source also identifies an acceleration in the shares of the top 1 per cent and 0.1 per cent for both Canada and the US starting in the mid-1980s.
18. The life cycle hypothesis can be interpreted to imply a strong relationship between age and wealth. Consequently, measured inequality of wealth at a given point in time could be due primarily to an age effect. In other words, given complete equality in all respects other than age, there could still be a significant amount of measured inequality due to the impact of age arising from life cycle savings behaviour. While available evidence on this hypothesis is mixed for the whole population (e.g., Almås and Mogstad, 2012), an age effect is less likely to be significant when applied to the wealthy and wealthiest.
19. There are various sources that provide information on specific features of the wealth and income distributions. Specifically examining IRS data from estate tax filings, Raub and Newcomb (2012) provide detailed information on the 2.3 million Americans in the top 1 per cent of the wealth distribution with gross assets of $2 million or more. For Canada, Macdonald (2015) examines information on the full wealth distribution from the Statistics Canada Survey of Financial Security. Morissette and Xuelin (2006) provide earlier evidence for Canada.
20. Kennickell (2017, 2006) provides detailed discussion of such estimates for the US. Saez and Veall (2005) report that this result is less robust in Canada for the high-income cohort. For example, in 2000 the probability of remaining in the top 0.1 per cent of income earners two years later is approximately 50 per cent. Examining a Norwegian sample of those born between 1953 and 1973, Hansen (2014, p. 457) observes: 'recruitment into the top wealth groups is extremely restricted, and most so in recent years. Having wealthy parents, and especially top wealth origins, is important for wealth attainment. The very top category appears to be a rentier class, with higher income from capital than from earnings.'
21. These estimates are from Davies et al. (2008).
22. Within the US, Raub and Newcomb (2012, p. 166) report for 2007 that the states with the largest number of residents in the top 1 per cent are California (329 000), New York (160 000), Florida (155 000) and Texas (100 000). As a percentage of residents, the top-ranking states are Wyoming (1.5 per cent), Connecticut (1.3 per cent), New Hampshire (1.3 per cent), Vermont (1.2 per cent), California (1.2 per cent) and South Dakota (1.2 per cent).
23. Even using the more plentiful data available for the distribution of incomes, it is not clear whether pre-tax or post-tax income is the relevant variable to estimate income inequality. For example, after recognizing that data availability concerns are inevitable, Armour et al. (2013, p. 173) demonstrate that differences between using pre-tax or post-tax income 'profoundly impact observed levels and trends in "income" and its distribution'. Comparing pre-tax and post-tax income for the US, Piketty et al. (2018) find that, 'The government has offset only a small fraction of the increase in inequality' since 2000.
24. Relevant references include Gibrat (1931) for the variance of the log of income, Kuznets (1953) for the Kuznets curve or Kuznets ratio, and for members of the generalized entropy family, Hirschman (1945) for Hirschman's index, Thiel (1967) for Thiel's index, Atkinson (1970) for Atkinson's index and Kolm (1976) for Kolm's index.

25. Discussion of the influence function and robust inequality measures is provided in Cowell and Victoria-Feser (1996). Schluter (2012) examines the impact of heavy-tailed distributions – typical of situations where considerable wealth is located with a small cohort located at the right tail of the wealth distribution – on inequality measures resulting in estimates of inequality that are substantially biased lower. Eckerstorfer et al. (2016) and Vermeulen (2018) demonstrate that estimates of the right tail of the wealth distribution obtained from household surveys significantly understate the amount of wealth. Procedures for correcting the bias are proposed.

26. Vermeulen (2018, pp. 384–5). The estimate for Austria is from Eckerstorfer et al. (2016).

27. For these estimates, see Zucman (2015) and an update of Henry (2012) at: https://www. foreignaffairs.com/articles/panama/2016-04-12/taxing-tax-havens.

28. See Davies et al. (2017). Notice that if the poorest people have negative net wealth, it is possible for the Gini coefficient to be greater than 1.

29. There is a substantial literature on wealth taxes in general, and the net wealth tax in particular. Early contributions on wealth taxes in the modern era of the broad-based income tax include Tait (1967), Sandford (1971) and Sandford et al. (1975). More recently, there are collections of useful papers from two symposia related to wealth taxes published in *Canadian Public Policy* in 1991 for Canada, and *Tax Law Review* in 2000 for the US. Proposals for implementing a net wealth tax in the US are advanced in Dugger (1990) and Sewalk and Leaman (2014). Practical difficulties of implementing wealth taxes are examined in Smith (1993) for Canada, and Glennerster (2012) for the UK. Discussion of the European experience with net wealth taxes can be found in Bird (1991), Lehner (2000) and Escobar (2007). A recent survey of the issues surrounding net wealth taxes is available in Schnellenbach (2012). In addition to academic sources, the role of wealth taxes received attention in various government studies considering broad-based tax reform, as well as commission reviews of the UK tax system associated with the Meade Report (Meade, 1978), and the two-volume Mirrlees Review (Mirrlees et al., 2010) published in *Fiscal Studies* (Mirrlees et al., 2011). Coincident with the Mirrlees Report are similar efforts in Australia – the Henry Review – and the report of the New Zealand Tax Working Group examined in Evans (2011).

30. For example, following on proposals advanced by the Green Party representative in the German federal parliament, Bach et al. (2014) propose a one-time net wealth levy to reduce the public sector debt in Germany. Glennerster (2012) details the inability of the UK Labour government to implement a wealth tax. In the Canadian province of Ontario, the election of the NDP government in 1990 stimulated Smith (1993) and the studies published in a special issue of *Canadian Public Policy* (1991).

31. The quotation is from, and the following discussion is adapted from, Schnellenbach (2012, pp. 369–70).

32. Piketty (2015a, p. 51).

33. Included in this debate are Hubbard (2015), Auerbach and Hassett (2015), Jones (2015), Piketty (2015a, 2015b) and Acemoglu and Robinson (2015).

34. Auerbach and Hassett (2015, p. 41). A similar comment appears in Hubbard (2015, p. 419). Scholarly debates on the issue of capital taxes and wealth distribution have a long history (e.g., Brown, 1924; Atkinson, 1971; Bird, 1976).

35. For example, see Atkinson (1971), Domeij and Heathcote (2004), Yunker (2014) and Hays (2003).

36. See Looney and Moore (2016, p. 81).

37. IRS, 'Topic 409: Capital Gains and Losses', https://www.irs.gov/taxtopics/tc409.

38. CRA, 'Definitions for Capital Gains', https://www.canada.ca/en/revenue-agency/ser vices/tax/individuals/topics/about-your-tax-return/tax-return/completing-a-tax-return/ personal-income/line-127-capital-gains/definitions-capital-gains.html.

39. Discussion of the tax implications of equity capital shares at this point is only general. Specifics for the taxation of capital income vary across countries. For example, in addition to the partnership and sole proprietorship, the US provides four different organizational structures that have distinct taxation implications for equity capital: the

limited liability company (LLC), limited partnership, S corporation and C corporation. Most publicly traded corporations, important sources of wealth for the wealthiest, are organized as C corporations that are subject to corporate taxes on profits and dividend taxes on shareholders. In Canada, the use of the flow-through feature available to the LLP, S corporation and, in many cases, the LLC is subject to considerable restriction.

40. See GAO (2016).
41. The relevant developments and references to equity capital are given in Poitras (2016, Pt 3).
42. Piketty (2014, p. 570).
43. Specific treatment of capital gains on personal use items depends on details of the income tax code for that country. For example, in Canada, sales of personal use items below $1000 are exempt and capital losses on such items are not allowable deductions against other capital gains.
44. Both the hard-to-tax and the underground economy are subject to varying definitions. Schneider and Enste (2000, pp. 78–9) discuss problems of defining the shadow economy where 'a precise definition seems quite difficult, if not impossible' and 'the definition often varies depending on the chosen method of measurement'. Similar issues are discussed in the June 1999 edition of the *Economic Journal* ('Controversy: On the Hidden Economy'). An overview of the differing definitions of the hard-to-tax is available in the volume by Alm et al. (2004).
45. Bahl (2004, p. 339) provide a definition of the hard-to-tax which includes: 'Those who can take advantage of loopholes for tax avoidance.' Bahl recognizes that 'such avoidance introduces a new sector of the economy to the hard to tax story and one that is neither small nor informal'. The connection with globalization is not developed.
46. See Naylor (2005).
47. The recognition of ideology in economic analysis has reached the mainstream with the appearance of Piketty (2020).
48. As Thomas (1999, p. F382) observes: 'the guestimation[s] of the size of the black economy . . . are not based on any economic theory, but . . . rely on heroic assumptions to justify the manipulation of certain numbers'. Reported estimates are from Schneider and Enste (2000, p. 80).
49. Priest (1994, p. 2294).
50. See Priest (1994, p. 2283) for a discussion of the US Department of Labor report.
51. Feige (1990).
52. Bahl (2004, pp. 338–9).
53. Schneider (2009, p. 1079).
54. Naylor (2005, p. 44).
55. Bird and Wallace (2004, p. 122).

2. Raising government revenue

> In all the governments that there are, the public person consumes without producing. Whence then does it get what it consumes? From the labour of its members. The necessities of the public are supplied out of the superfluities of individuals. It follows that the civil State can subsist only so long as mens' [*sic*] labour brings them a return greater than their needs.
> (Jean-Jacques Rousseau, *The Social Contract*, 1762, Essay 3, Sec. 8)

COMPARING GOVERNMENT REVENUES: ORGANISATION FOR ECONOMIC CO-OPERATION AND DEVELOPMENT (OECD) COUNTRIES[1]

Taxes and the Wealthy

Practical implementation of vertical and horizontal tax equity requires information about the actual tax burden of specific groups of individuals. With some provisos, the task of estimating the tax burden of a specific group increases with wealth and income. In other words, more wealth and income increase the amount and number of taxes that can be imposed, and the associated deductions and exclusions that can be claimed. For a host of reasons, modern structuring of tax systems employing an array of taxes across a range of jurisdictions obstructs the ability to accurately calculate the tax burden of a specific group of individuals. Where the wealthy and, especially, the wealthiest are a concern, the practical problem of determining a tax burden is, at least, particularly acute; and at worst, intractable. For example, the wealthy own a more than disproportionate share of businesses that, in some cases, are subject to tax, and in other cases such as flow-through entities pass the tax burden to the wealthy owner or, in other cases, to some possibly offshore entity. Where a business operates in various taxation jurisdictions, tracing the taxes paid in each jurisdiction is a daunting task. In addition, it is not clear whether and how to credit tax paid – if any – by a business to the owners, especially if the business is a 'legal person' such as a corporation.

Absent practical calculation of the aggregate tax burden for a specific group, public discourse surrounding reform of taxes paid by the wealthy is based largely on subjective opinion. Similarly, inadequate ideological interpretation of the objective information that is available reinforces the influence of subjective opinion. Consider the following April 2014 United States (US) example of subjective ideological interpretation from Andrew Lundeen published by the Tax Foundation think tank.[2] The preamble starts innocuously: 'Do the rich pay their "fair share" in taxes? It's never particularly clear what the rich currently pay, nor is it clear what share of taxes is fair for them to pay. A good place to start would be to determine exactly what high-income earners currently pay.' This is followed by a subjective claim based on reference to seemingly credible sources: 'Estimates from Congress's Joint Committee on Taxation and recently highlighted in the *Wall Street Journal* make it abundantly clear that high-income earners pay a disproportionate share of taxes in relation to their income in the US.' The evidence provided seems compelling:

> According to the *Journal*, taxpayers with income over $100 000 a year earn 60 percent of the nation's income and pay 95.2 percent of the [federal] income taxes in the United States. If we consider all federal taxes paid (income, payroll, and excise taxes), those making over $100 000 (a little over 20 percent of taxpayers) pay for 75.7 percent of total federal taxes (this excludes the burden on corporate and investment taxes).

Ignoring the issue of determining a tax burden using all taxes paid, not just federal income tax, or all federal tax, and accepting that the evidence that 20 per cent of taxpayers earn 60 per cent of the 'national income' is correct, it is apparent that Lundeen is advancing a subjective opinion about progressive taxation. The continuing discussion reinforces this point:

> If we break this down further ... the level of progressivity in the tax code becomes even clearer. Those making over $200 000 comprise just over 5 percent of the nation's taxpayers, earn 32.3 percent of the income, but pay 46.7 percent of total federal taxes and 70 percent of federal income taxes.

Precisely what level of tax is to be required from the wealthy 5 per cent of taxpayers who earn 32.3 per cent of national income? The implicit metric being used is reflected in the following:

> As we move down the income scale the ratio of taxes to income decreases. Those making between $100 000 and $200 000 a year make up 15.6 percent of all taxpayers, earn 27.7 percent of income, pay 29 percent of total federal taxes and 25.2 percent of federal income taxes.

The ideological interpretation of this evidence is captured in the conclud-ing rhetorical statement: 'So, there is the information on who pays what. Now a question for you: do the rich pay their fair share?'

If there is any doubt about the answer Lundeen is suggesting to the rhetorical question, the evidence provided about those making less than $100000 clarifies the issue:

> Those between $50000 and $100000 make up about a quarter of the country, earn 23.6 percent of all income, pay 18.6 percent of federal taxes and 11.3 percent of federal income taxes. Finally, taxpayers making less than $50000 a year represent about half of the country, earn 16.4 percent of the nation's income, pay 5.6 percent of [federal] taxes and have a negative share of [federal] income taxes because they receive more back than they pay out (largely due to refundable tax credit programs).

Half of those required to pay federal taxes earn 16.4 per cent of national income and pay 5.6 per cent of federal tax. Is it surprising that the progressiveness of the federal income tax results in those earning higher incomes also paying substantially more federal income tax? Why are non-progressive taxes – state and local consumption taxes, property taxes and the like – excluded from the calculations? What are the implications of excluding the 'burden on corporate and investment taxes'?[3]

Absent accurate and detailed information about the tax burden of specific groups it is difficult, if not impossible, to avoid subjective bias in assessing vertical and horizontal equity associated with taxes paid by the wealthy. The temptation to 'cherry pick' evidence from the buffet of available taxes to advance ideological objectives can be irresistible. This general problem of the absence of data is compounded by the bewildering array of taxes that can be imposed across political jurisdictions. Lacking information about such taxes paid specifically by the wealthy and the wealthiest, it is necessary to fall back on examining the decidedly more plentiful information about the overall tax burden in specific countries. Given the diversity of rules governing specific taxes across jurisdictions, such information is, at best, only a basis for intuitive interpretations. Such diversity extends well beyond jurisdictional rules for assessing income taxes to include, for example, the method of assessing sales taxes and property taxes. In the US at the federal level, there is excise tax but no sales tax; at the state and local level, there is a diverse combination of sales and excise taxes, with distinct rates and items covered. By comparison, Canada has both federal sales and excise taxes, as well as both sales and excise taxes in almost every province, and in some cases local excise taxes are also assessed.

Taxes in the OECD

The search for current government revenue sources reveals a host of complications and variations across political jurisdictions. Numerous types of taxes can be levied across various levels of government. Tax regimes and specific taxes are a moving target that can change significantly over time, so comparisons and overviews can quickly become dated. The so-called Trump tax cut legislation of December 2017 provides a recent example. Different taxing jurisdictions do not tax certain types of income, assets or transactions, while others do. In some jurisdictions, certain revenues (such as unemployment insurance payments or government pension plan contributions) are classified as (payroll or social security) taxes, while other jurisdictions treat these items separately from taxes. Significantly, with increasing financial globalization, the residency of the tax-paying entity can be shifted to minimize the tax burden, making it difficult for political jurisdictions to control the tax base. Taxation of individuals and corporations in a globalizing world has become so complex that a large industry of tax accountants, lawyers and consultants has emerged to assist those with enough wealth and income to make tax avoidance and, possibly, evasion feasible. The tax authorities in different political jurisdictions have reacted to those wealthy that exploit financial globalization to avoid and evade taxes with a range of initiatives: the Foreign Account Tax Compliance Act (2010) (FATCA) in the US, the OECD/G20 Base Erosion and Profit Shifting (BEPS) project and the OECD Global Forum on Transparency and Exchange of Information for Tax Purposes (GFTEITP) being important recent examples.

The OECD *Revenue Statistics* publication is an invaluable resource for obtaining detailed information about the tax practices in numerous countries reporting this data to the OECD.[4] The time series and cross-section information is substantial and detailed. It is not possible to give a full accounting here, only a cursory view. The considerable differences in general tax structures for the OECD countries are given in Figure 2.1, Figure 2.2 and Table 2.1. Such aggregated data is only indicative. For example, there are fundamental differences in the implementation and collection of the various types of taxes to be accounted. In many countries, there is a division of taxing authority between the federal/national, provincial/state and local jurisdictions; that is, county, municipal, township, council, and so on (see Figure 2.2). The details of this authority differ from country to country. Ignoring differences in the level and variety of government services ignores the associated 'net benefit'. Given such provisos, in Table 2.1 there is obviously wide variation in the use of the four identified funding categories. The US is anomalous in imposing the smallest amount of

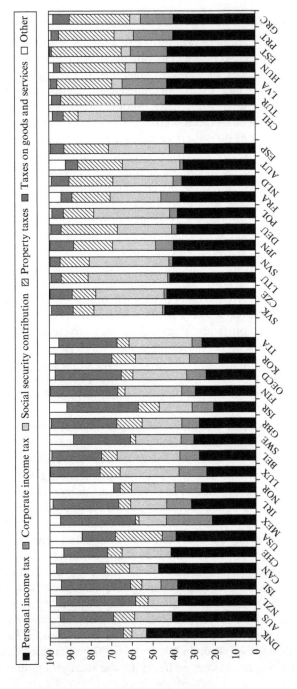

Note: Countries are grouped and ranked by those where income tax revenues (personal and corporate) form the highest share of total tax revenues, followed by those where social security contributions, or taxes on goods and services, form the highest share.

Source: OECD (2019c, p. 25, Figure 1.5).

Figure 2.1   Tax structures in the OECD, 2017

goods and services taxes, mostly due to state and local sales taxes, while Chile and Mexico are the most reliant upon goods and services taxes. These results need to take account of information about the tax shares as a percentage of gross domestic product in Table 2.1.

As for recent trends in tax regime changes, the annual OECD *Tax Policy Reforms* reports that, in 2015, 'the tax wedge on labour income stabilized after years of steady increases'.[5] In turn, the 2019 report indicates: 'In the area of personal income taxes (PIT) . . . countries are continuing to cut labour taxes, after several years of PIT increases following the crisis'. This has resulted in significant reforms: 'A stated rationale for these reforms among many countries is to support employment and those on low and middle incomes.' Consistent with a weak trend of shifting the tax burden away from labour income and towards personal capital income, the 2019 report states: 'several countries raised tax rates on dividends and other sources of personal capital income. The increase in statutory tax rates on personal capital income, both since the crisis and over the last year, could be a response to a renewed focus on inequality and the differential tax treatment between labour and capital income.' However, as for the trend of corporate income tax rate reductions driven by international tax competition:

> Corporate income tax (CIT) rate cuts have continued in 2019, but these rate reductions have been less significant than the ones introduced in 2018. Interestingly, the countries that are introducing the most significant CIT rate reductions tend to be those that exhibit higher initial CIT rates, leading to further convergence in CIT rates across countries.

Of special interest, both the 2015 and 2019 OECD reports find that various countries introduced corporate income tax base-broadening measures, 'to protect domestic tax bases against tax avoidance by multinational enterprises. In response to the recommendations agreed upon as part of the OECD/G20 BEPS project, a number of countries enacted specific anti-avoidance legislation'. In addition, the regressive increases in standard value-added tax (VAT) and sales tax rates that had been 'a clear trend since the end of the crisis until the beginning of 2015'; by 2019: 'The stabilisation of standard value-added tax (VAT) rates observed across countries in the last couple of years is continuing. High standard VAT rates in many countries have limited the room for additional rate increases without generating potentially high efficiency and equity costs.' Recent efforts on VAT have switched from altering rates to increasing enforcement. Perhaps the most relevant observation in the OECD report concerns property taxes. Both the 2015 and 2019 reports find that there were 'only a limited number of reforms in the area of property taxes', with 'unclear' trends across

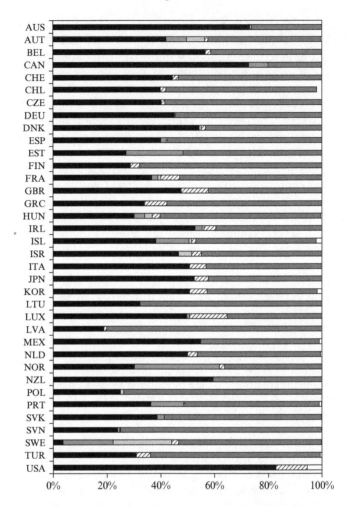

Notes: The left-hand panel refers to only those taxes which are classified as central government taxes. Social security contributions paid to social security funds are excluded. The right-hand panel refers only to those taxes which are classified as sub-central taxes (local and (where relevant) state taxes). Social security contributions paid to social security funds are excluded.

Source: OECD Revenue Statistics 2019.

Figure 2.2   Composition of tax revenues: federal or central government (left) and sub-national governments (right), 2017

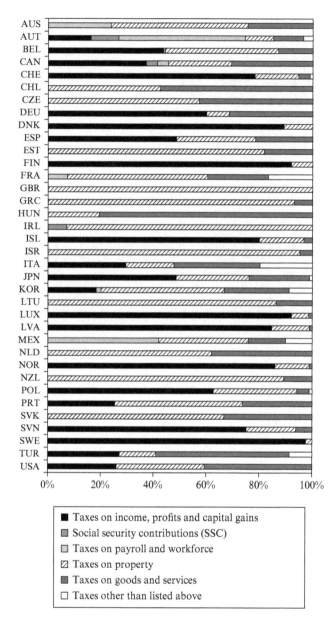

Figure 2.2 (continued)

Table 2.1 Tax revenue in OECD, selected years 2000–2018

	Tax revenue as % of GDP				Tax revenue as % of total tax revenue in 2017						
	2018p	2017	2016	2000	Taxes on income, individuals (PIT)	Taxes on income, corporates (CIT)	Social security contributions (SSC)	Taxes on property	Value added taxes	Other consumption taxes	All other taxes
OECD – Average[1]	*34.3*	*34.2*	*34.4*	*33.8*	*23.9*	*9.3*	*26.0*	*5.8*	*20.2*	*12.2*	*2.6*
Australia		28.5	27.6	30.5	40.3	18.5	0.0	10.3	12.2	13.9	4.8
Austria	42.2	41.8	41.9	42.3	21.7	5.9	34.9	1.3	18.3	9.8	8.1
Belgium	44.8	44.5	43.9	43.5	27.2	9.3	30.5	7.9	15.2	9.0	0.9
Canada	33.0	32.8	33.2	34.7	35.7	11.4	14.1	12.0	13.7	9.9	3.2
Chile	21.1	20.1	20.1	18.8	9.7	21.1	7.3	5.4	41.6	13.2	1.8
Czech Republic	35.3	34.9	34.2	32.4	11.5	10.7	43.0	1.4	22.0	10.9	0.5
Denmark[2]	44.9	45.7	45.7	46.9	52.9	7.2	0.1	3.9	20.7	11.1	4.1
Estonia	33.2	32.8	33.5	31.1	17.4	4.7	34.1	0.7	27.8	14.8	0.5
Finland	42.7	43.3	44.0	45.8	29.2	6.3	27.8	3.6	21.0	11.8	0.2
France[2]	46.1	46.1	45.4	43.4	18.6	5.1	36.4	9.5	15.3	9.2	6.0
Germany	38.2	37.6	37.4	36.2	27.1	5.4	37.9	2.7	18.4	7.9	0.6
Greece	38.7	38.9	38.7	33.4	16.0	5.0	29.6	7.9	20.9	18.5	2.1
Hungary	36.6	38.2	39.1	38.5	14.2	5.5	32.1	2.8	24.8	18.2	2.5
Iceland	36.7	37.5	50.8	36.0	38.0	8.2	9.1	5.5	23.8	9.9	5.5
Ireland	22.3	22.5	23.4	30.8	31.2	12.3	17.1	5.7	19.6	12.8	1.3
Israel[3]	31.1	32.5	31.1	34.9	20.7	10.1	16.2	10.0	22.9	11.8	8.4
Italy	42.1	42.1	42.3	40.6	25.7	5.0	30.3	6.2	14.8	13.6	4.4
Japan	–	31.4	30.7	25.8	18.8	11.8	39.9	8.2	13.0	8.0	0.2
Korea	28.4	26.9	26.2	21.5	17.9	14.2	25.7	11.7	16.0	11.8	2.8
Latvia	30.7	31.1	31.2	29.1	21.1	5.1	26.9	3.3	25.7	17.3	0.6
Lithuania[2]	30.3	29.5	29.7	30.8	13.1	5.1	41.5	1.0	26.6	12.0	0.8
Luxembourg	40.1	38.7	37.9	36.9	23.6	13.6	28.6	9.6	15.9	8.4	0.3

Mexico[4]	16.1	16.6	11.5	21.4	21.8	13.3	1.9	23.1	13.2	5.3
Netherlands	38.8	38.4	36.9	21.6	8.5	35.7	4.0	17.4	11.7	1.1
New Zealand	32.7	32.1	32.5	37.8	14.7	0.0	6.0	30.2	8.3	3.1
Norway	39.0	38.7	41.9	26.5	12.5	26.6	3.3	22.1	8.8	0.1
Poland	35.0	33.5	32.9	14.6	5.6	37.5	4.0	22.8	14.1	1.3
Portugal	35.4	34.1	31.1	18.8	9.4	26.8	3.9	25.1	14.9	1.1
Slovak Republic	33.1	32.3	33.6	10.2	10.4	43.9	1.3	21.1	12.1	1.1
Slovenia	36.4	36.5	36.6	14.2	4.9	40.0	1.8	22.3	16.3	0.5
Spain[2]	34.4	33.3	33.2	21.8	6.8	34.0	7.5	19.1	10.2	0.5
Sweden	43.9	44.2	48.9	29.9	6.3	21.8	2.2	20.9	6.9	11.9
Switzerland[2]	27.9	27.7	27.6	30.3	10.7	23.6	7.6	12.0	9.1	6.8
Turkey	24.4	25.3	23.6	14.5	6.8	29.3	4.5	20.1	23.3	1.3
United Kingdom	33.5	32.7	32.9	27.2	8.5	19.2	12.5	20.7	11.1	0.8
United States	24.3	25.9	28.3	38.7	6.5	23.0	16.0	0.0	15.7	0.0

Notes:

1. 2018 provisional average calculated by applying the unweighted average percentage change for 2018 in the 34 countries providing data for that year to the overall average tax to GDP ratio in 2017. The 2016 OECD average tax-to-GDP ratio includes the one-off revenues from stability contributions in Iceland.
2. The total tax revenue has been reduced by the amount of any capital transfer that represents uncollected taxes.
3. The data for Israel are supplied by and under the responsibility of the relevant Israeli authorities. The use of such data by the OECD is without prejudice to the status of the Golan Heights, East Jerusalem and Israeli settlements in the West Bank under the terms of international law.
4. 2018 provisional: Secretariat estimate, including expected revenues collected by state and local governments.

Source: OECD Revenue Statistics 2019.

OECD countries: 'some countries raising property tax burdens and others lowering them'. The property tax reforms introduced in 2019 'were limited in number and in scope, confirming that the revenue-raising and equity-enhancing potential of property taxes, especially through recurrent taxes on residential property, remains under-utilised', though there had been minor reforms 'focused on increasing taxes on high-value immovable property'.

SPECIFIC GOVERNMENT REVENUES: CANADA AND THE USA

Tax Revenues in Canada

General cross-country information available from sources such as the OECD disguise the subtle variations in tax codes across taxing jurisdictions. Of specific relevance to the wealthy are tax rules associated with gift taxes, estate and inheritance taxes, capital gains realization, property taxes, vehicle levies, corporate taxes, top-bracket personal tax rates, assessment of tax by residence versus citizenship, and luxury taxes. Despite an adjacent geographical location, the tax codes of Canada and the US have substantive differences in the design of such taxes, although in practice some of these differences become insignificant. For example, instead of a death tax – imposed on either inheritance or estate – combined with a gift tax, Canada requires the deceased to make a deemed disposition of capital gains and tax-deferred pension assets in the year of death. Bequests from the after-tax proceeds of the estate are then transferred as a gift. In contrast, the US has a gift tax and an estate tax with a combined exemption level that has the estate and gift taxes being applied to only a small fraction of the population, some of whom take further advantage of gift tax and trust loopholes to significantly reduce the tax paid. Combined with the US allowance of capital gains basis carryforward for bequests, the end result is that while the US has formal death and gift taxes, the impact of taxes on the estate of a wealthy decedent in many cases would be less than in Canada, which has no formal death tax.

While useful, aggregated tax revenue statistics provided by the OECD and other entities disguise many subtle differences in the tax regimes of different countries that impact upon the wealthy. As in many other countries, taxing authority in Canada is constitutionally mandated to the provincial and federal governments, both having taxing authority to fund areas of constitutional authority. As illustrated in Table 2.2, in Canada the C$263.09 billion in tax revenue at the federal level (83.9 per cent of total revenue) for 2017–18 comes primarily from personal income tax

Table 2.2 Canadian federal government revenue sources

	2016–17 ($ millions)	2017–18 ($ millions)	Net change ($ millions)	(%)
		Revenues		
Tax revenues				
Income tax				
Personal	143 680	153 619	9939	6.9
Corporate	42 216	47 805	5589	13.2
Non-resident	7071	7845	774	10.9
Total	192 967	209 269	16 302	8.4
Other taxes and duties				
Goods and Services Tax	34 368	36 751	2383	6.9
Energy taxes	5634	5739	105	1.9
Customs import duties	5478	5416	(62)	(1.1)
Other excise taxes and duties	5868	5913	45	0.8
Total	51 348	53 819	2471	4.8
Total tax revenues	244 315	263 088	18 773	7.7
Employment Insurance premiums	22 125	21 140	(985)	(4.5)
Other revenues	27 055	29 378	2323	8.6
Total revenues	293 495	313 606	20 111	6.9

Source: Canadian Department of Finance.

(58.4 per cent resident + 3 per cent non-resident), corporate income tax (18.2 per cent) and sales tax (13.97 per cent). Together with an energy tax (2.2 per cent), such taxes are also charged at the provincial level, though with different percentages. Only customs and (most) excise taxes (4.3 per cent) are solely within federal jurisdiction. This method of calculating tax revenue ignores a tax for employment insurance premiums which adds an additional 6.74 per cent on top of tax revenue. While fees for government-funded medical services plans are assessed primarily at the provincial level, there is a lump sum transfer of federal tax revenue to the provinces to offset the cost of universal medical care reflected in the provincial revenue sources for British Columbia (BC) given in Table 2.3. Though some portion of property tax revenues do accrue to the provincial government, the bulk of this revenue is the primary funding source for municipal governments, as reflected in Table 2.4 for the city of Vancouver, BC at 42.1 per

Table 2.3   British Columbia provincial government tax revenue

	In $ millions	
	2019	2018
Personal income	11364	8923
Provincial sales	7362	7118
Corporate income	5180	4165
Property	2617	2367
Property transfer	1826	2141
Carbon	1465	1255
Fuel	1015	1010
Tobacco	781	727
Employer health	464	
Harmonized sales	7	13
Other	633	602
Total	32714	28321

Notes:
Personal income tax and corporate income tax revenues are recorded after deductions for non-refundable tax credits. Deductions allowable in the calculation of personal income tax revenue were $110 million (2018: $91 million) and corporate income tax were $108 million (2018: $111 million). The types of tax credits adjusting personal income tax and corporation income tax revenues are for foreign taxes, logging taxes, venture capital, scientific and experimental development tax, and mining flow-through shares.

Personal income tax revenue was also reduced by $162 million (2018: $161 million) for the BC Tax Reduction.

Personal and corporate income tax refunds may be issued under the *International Business Activity Act.* Corporate income tax refunds were $8 million (2018: $11 million).

Property tax revenue was recorded net of home owner grants of $829 million (2018: $814 million).

Source: Government of British Columbia.

cent, with an additional 12.98 per cent from 'developer contributions', which is derived from construction activity.

In most countries, the division of taxing authority is constitutionally determined. However, such authority can be complicated. In Canada, while a major government expenditure item – medical services – is under provincial jurisdiction, the federal government exercises considerable control through general taxing authority and provincial transfers to ensure similarity of access to medical care across the country. Similar tax jurisdiction issues arise with property tax that is imposed at the municipal/ provincial level, with a division of revenues raised allowing municipalities some discretion over the total levy. Charges for various utilities, such as garbage collection and water services, are imposed at the municipal level.

Table 2.4 City of Vancouver, Consolidated Statement of Operations, year ending 31 December ($'000s)

Revenues	2018 Budget	2018	2017
Property taxes, penalties and interest	789 894	833 414	753 152
Utility fees	274 384	277 143	260 786
Program fees	111 609	123 888	116 664
License and development fees	75 117	94 828	74 458
Parking	94 556	98 063	93 010
Cost recoveries, grants and donations	80 816	152 553	123 441
Revenue sharing	19 150	22 489	21 918
Investment income	21 757	37 681	28 497
Rental, lease and other	55 403	66 813	69 567
Bylaw fines	21 918	22 352	20 490
Developer contributions	127 020	256 763	331 587
Loss on sale of tangible capital assets	–	(7094)	(6973)
Total	1 671 624	1 978 893	1 886 597

Source: City of Vancouver.

Electricity charges vary across provinces, with some provinces using a Crown corporation charging for usage and generating revenue for the provincial government, while other provinces have privatized this service. In addition, some provinces raise (lose) revenue from the provision of mandatory auto insurance. All levels of government receive other revenue from the sale of assets and, in some cases, from Crown corporations. Precisely how such revenue sources (and related expenditures) impact upon the wealthy is difficult to determine.

Tax Revenues in the US

The contrast in government revenue assessment and collection methods between Canada and the US is striking. Some of these differences originate in the mandated structure of expenditures. In Canada, 'big ticket' expenditures items, such as medical services and various social welfare programmes, are provincial responsibilities. Consequently, total government revenues in Canada are raised more at the provincial level than at the federal level; for example, in 2013, of C$584 billion in total government revenue slightly less than half (C$271 billion) was raised by the federal government. In turn, with a substantial amount of federal revenue transferred to the provinces as equalization payments and to partially fund medical services, the effective federal tax burden is even less than the amount collected indicates. By contrast, in the US, about two-thirds of tax revenue is raised at the federal level, which has responsibility for social security expenditures and key social welfare programmes. Due to a tradition of inter-provincial coordination, the characteristics of provincial taxing jurisdictions across Canada are decidedly similar. As illustrated in Figure 2.3, the variation in the usage of different revenue sources across US states is dramatic.

In Table 2.5, at the federal level in 2017, individual income tax (47.9 per cent), payroll taxes that fund social security and medicare (35 per cent) and corporate income taxes (9 per cent, down from 11 per cent in 2015) composed the bulk of federal revenue, with excise and customs providing only an additional 4 per cent of revenue. There is no US federal sales tax. As illustrated in Figure 2.3, it is at the state and local level that there are significant differences in both the composition of tax revenue and the total tax burden. For example, seven states do not currently assess income tax on individuals, with two other states only imposing small levies. Four of these seven states do not charge corporate income tax. While all states impose some form of sales tax, four states only impose selective sales taxes. Three of the four states that charge no general sales tax make up the revenue by charging the largest proportion of some other tax, property taxes in New Hampshire, state income tax in Oregon and resource extraction fees in Alaska. Given this, information on the proportion of state revenue raised with the major tax sources needs to be conditioned with information on the portion of total state revenue that goes to state and local expenditure items.

The Tax Foundation informs us that the US average of state and local tax burdens as a share of state income fell from 10.7 per cent in 1977 to 9.9 per cent in 2012. 'During the 2012 fiscal year, state-local tax burdens as a share of state incomes decreased on average across the US. Average income increased at a faster rate than tax collections, driving down state-local tax burdens on average.'[6] As for specific states, New York imposed the highest tax burden, recording 12.7 per cent of state income going to state and local taxes. New York was closely followed by Connecticut (12.6 per cent) and New Jersey (12.2 per cent). States with the lowest tax burden were Alaska (6.5 per cent), South Dakota (7.1 per cent) and Wyoming (7.1 per cent). Recognizing that tax shifting across state lines is not uniform across states, on average taxpayers pay taxes mostly to the state and local governments of residence. In 2012, 78 per cent of taxes collected were paid within the state of residence, up from 73 per cent in 2011. For the bulk of states, the state and local tax burdens are similar, with slight changes in taxes or income translating to seemingly dramatic shifts in rank. For example, Delaware (16th) and Colorado (35th) differ in tax burden by

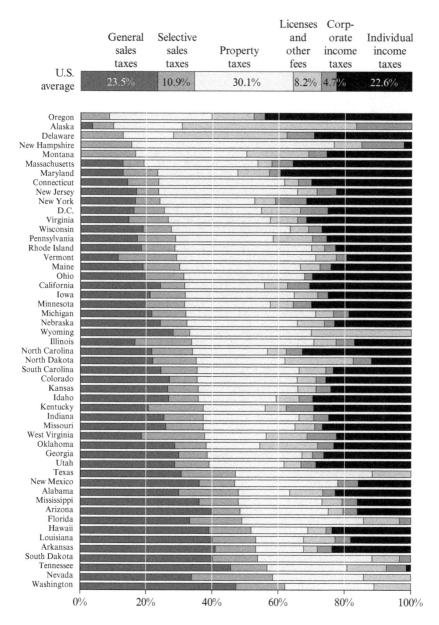

Source: Tax Foundation (taxfoundation.org).

Figure 2.3 State and local government revenues

Table 2.5 US federal government sources of revenue, 2001–17 (percentages)

Fiscal Year	Individual Income Taxes	Corporation Income Taxes	Social Insurance and Retirement Receipts			Excise Taxes	Other	Total Receipts		
			Total	(On-Budget)	(Off-Budget)			Total	(On-Budget)	(Off-Budget)
2001	49.9	7.6	34.9	9.4	25.5	3.3	4.3	100.0	74.5	25.5
2002	46.3	8.0	37.8	10.0	27.8	3.6	4.3	100.0	72.2	27.8
2003	44.5	7.4	40.0	10.6	29.4	3.8	4.3	100.0	70.6	29.4
2004	43.0	10.1	39.0	10.6	28.4	3.7	4.2	100.0	71.6	28.4
2005	43.1	12.9	36.9	10.1	26.8	3.4	3.8	100.0	73.2	26.8
2006	43.4	14.7	34.8	9.5	25.3	3.1	4.0	100.0	74.7	25.3
2007	45.3	14.4	33.9	9.1	24.7	2.5	3.9	100.0	75.3	24.7
2008	45.4	12.1	35.7	9.6	26.1	2.7	4.2	100.0	73.9	26.1
2009	43.5	6.6	42.3	11.3	31.1	3.0	4.7	100.0	68.9	31.1
2010	41.5	8.9	40.0	10.8	29.2	3.1	6.5	100.0	70.8	29.2
2011	47.4	7.9	35.5	11.0	24.6	3.1	6.1	100.0	75.4	24.6
2012	46.2	9.9	34.5	11.3	23.2	3.2	6.2	100.0	76.8	23.2
2013	47.4	9.9	34.2	9.9	24.3	3.0	5.5	100.0	75.7	24.3
2014	46.2	10.6	33.9	9.5	24.3	3.1	6.3	100.0	75.7	24.3
2015	47.4	10.6	32.8	9.1	23.7	3.0	6.2	100.0	76.3	23.7
2016	47.3	9.2	34.1	9.3	24.8	2.9	6.5	100.0	75.2	24.8
2017	47.9	9.0	35.0	9.4	25.7	2.5	5.6	100.0	74.3	25.7

Source: Office of Management and Budget, Historical Tables.

only just over one percentage point. However, while burdens are clustered in the centre of the distribution, states at the top and bottom can still have substantially different burden percentages: for example, New York (12.6 per cent) and Alaska (6.5 per cent).[7]

The substantial differences in types of taxes used to generate state revenue suggest further tunnelling into the procedures of a specific state. Nevada has a sizeable proportion of non-resident taxpayers (a characteristic of the wealthy is ownership of multiple properties used for residential purposes). Due to the popularity of Las Vegas as an entertainment destination, non-residents or residents of convenience include both vacationing visitors and owners of second homes, primarily Californians. According to Tax Foundation data for 2012, Nevada ranks 43rd in state and local tax burden, at 8.1 per cent of state income. Nevada is one of the few states with no personal or corporate state income tax. As illustrated in Figure 2.4, the bulk of state revenue is from sales taxes composed of excise taxes and a general state sales tax of 6.85 per cent with variation by county, up to 8.375 per cent in Clark County.[8] Nevada ranks 4th in

TAX REVENUES

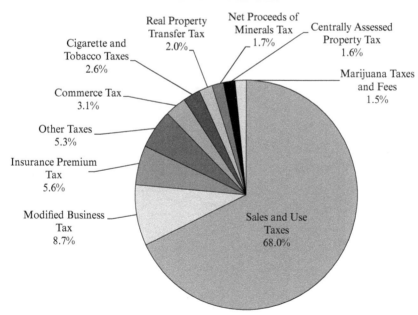

Source: Government of the State of Nevada.

Figure 2.4   Nevada state tax revenues, 2019

the relative amount of state income raised by these sales taxes. Nevada also imposed the 10th highest gasoline tax and the 17th highest cigarette tax. This apparent reliance on sales taxes is somewhat misleading as the method of determining property tax involves the Nevada Tax Commission certifying property tax rates proposed in budgets submitted by local governments and school districts. Though Nevada only ranks 35th in the per-person property tax assessment, the aggregate state and local tax burden does include a significant property tax component. Nevada also imposes a variety of substantial vehicles levies (registration fees and insurance tax) that depend on vehicle assessed value. Absent a state income tax combined with limitations on property tax rates, taxation at the state level in Nevada, though not onerous, is somewhat regressive.

From this general background on the overall federal, state and local tax structure, it is possible to discern implications of the government revenue structure that directly impact upon the wealthy. Examining the evolution of the major US revenue categories over time in Figure 2.5, it is apparent that taxes paid disproportionately by the wealthy, especially corporate income tax, are falling; while the contribution from social secu-

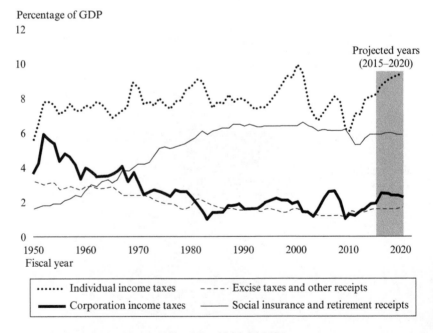

Source: Government Accountability Office (GAO-16-363).

Figure 2.5 US federal tax revenues as a percentage of GDP

rity receipts, assessed only on the first $118 500 of income (2016 amount), are rising. The Federal Insurance Contributions Act (FICA) requires a payroll tax to be paid by employees and employers, at 6.2 per cent each on the gross compensation of the employee up to the $118 500 ceiling, and a further 1.45 per cent each to pay for Medicare, an assessment that is not subject to a gross compensation limit. The total withholding of 15.3 per cent of gross compensation may be augmented by withholdings imposed in various states, such as withholding for state income taxes that further fund such programmes. For a variety of reasons, FICA contributions are viewed as a regressive tax, if only because FICA is not assessed on interest, dividends and property income. In addition, there is no standard deduction or personal exemption associated with FICA.

Finally, a fundamental empirical question confronting tax reform on the wealthy concerns the distribution of the tax burden across income groups. Table 2.6 provides information on this question, albeit from income tax records, a source that captures only reported income and taxes paid. This would not count income earned by the wealthy from deferred

Table 2.6   Incomes and federal, state and local taxes in 2015

	Average cash income	Shares of		Taxes as a % of income		
		Total income	Total taxes	Federal taxes	State & local taxes	Total taxes
Lowest 20%	$15 000	3.2%	2.0%	7.1%	12.1%	19.2%
Second 20%	30 500	6.7%	5.1%	11.8%	11.3%	23.2%
Middle 20%	48 900	11.0%	9.8%	16.4%	10.8%	27.2%
Fourth 20%	81 300	18.4%	18.4%	19.7%	10.7%	30.4%
Next 10%	125 000	14.2%	14.7%	21.1%	10.5%	31.6%
Next 5%	176 000	10.1%	10.7%	21.9%	10.2%	32.1%
Next 4%	310 000	14.4%	15.2%	22.3%	9.7%	32.0%
Top 1%	1 735 000	22.2%	23.8%	24.3%	8.3%	32.6%
ALL	$86 200	100.0%	100.0%	20.3%	10.0%	30.3%
Addendum:						
Bottom 99%	$69 500	77.8%	76.0%	19.0%	10.7%	29.8%

Notes:
1. Taxes include all federal, state and local taxes (personal and corporate income, payroll, property, sales, excise, estate etc.).
2. For calculations of income shares and taxes as a percentage of income, income includes employer-paid FICA taxes and corporate profits net of taxable dividends, neither of which is included in the average cash income figures shown.

Source: Institute on Taxation and Economic Policy (www.itep.org).

capital gains, or increase in property values, or offshore avoidance and evasion. In other words, only one group of the wealthy – those generating significant taxable income – are being examined. Given this, Table 2.6 illustrates that the mildly progressive federal income tax rate is offset by the regressive state and local tax structure, resulting in a more-or-less effective flat rate tax on the top 40 per cent of taxpayer incomes. The ideological chasm that underpins any rethinking of taxes for the wealthy is captured in the almost 24 per cent of total government taxes paid being raised from taxpayers in the top 1 per cent of reported incomes. Supporters of the entitlement perspective of Robert Nozick or Ayn Rand would see such numbers as evidence that those with the highest incomes already pay enough. Supporters of social taxation would empathetically point to the lack of progressivity in marginal rates, and the social hardships arising from increasingly unequal distribution of after-tax income and wealth.

A PRIMER ON TAX HAVENS AND THE WEALTHY

What is a Tax Haven?

The notion of a tax haven is complicated and evolving over time. The Tax Justice Network observes that the term 'tax haven':

> is troublesome, because these places offer facilities that go far beyond tax . . . [providing] facilities that enable people or entities to *escape* . . . the laws, rules and regulations of other jurisdictions *elsewhere*, using secrecy as a prime tool. Those rules include tax – but also criminal laws, disclosure rules . . . financial regulation, inheritance rules, and more.[9]

Recognizing that many countries engage in the use of preferential tax regimes aimed to attract capital from offshore jurisdictions or to provide a competitive tax advantage to onshore companies, it is conventional to restrict the term 'tax haven' to omit such activities. As such, the definition of a tax haven requires the intentional creation of enabling legislation to facilitate transactions undertaken by commercial entities without de facto operations in the jurisdiction, or by individuals who either are not resident or are residents of convenience. Until recently, tax havens typically offered substantial legally protected secrecy to allow the actual location of economic or financial transactions to be disguised as transactions in the tax haven, allowing the low or zero tax liability of the tax haven to be assessed instead of the tax rate that would be imposed in the actual location of the transaction.

Though the history of tax havens is ancient, the modern history has several strands that eventually coalesced into the global network of tax haven countries that feature specialties aimed at distinct activities.[10] One strand has origins in the emergence of the limited liability corporation during the last half of the 19th century, and the subsequent jurisdictional competition to attract corporations by writing liberal laws of incorporation. In the US, allowing incorporation without state residency and doing little or no business in the state begins with an 1875 Act in New Jersey and, following the passage of various anti-trust Acts from 1898 to 1914, in Delaware. The emergence of the income tax as an important source of government revenue led to an eventual merging of the desire to avoid tax with the ability to create non-resident corporations. This strand begins with a series of British legal decisions starting in 1929. These decisions determined that a business incorporated in the United Kingdom but not doing business there would not be subject to British tax. The merging of these two strands became the pillar on which the network of British dependency tax havens, centred on the City of London – British Virgin Islands, Cayman Islands, Bermuda, Bahamas, the Isle of Man, Jersey, Guernsey – developed into the 'Treasure Islands' exposed by Nicholas Shaxson of the Tax Justice Network,[11] and others.

Another strand along which tax havens developed is associated with the emergence of European tax havens following the passage of the 1924 Company Law in Liechtenstein that imposed no requirements or restrictions concerning the nationality of shareholders in Liechtenstein companies; the Swiss Banking Act of 1934 that placed protection of bank secrecy under the criminal law requiring 'absolute silence in respect to a professional secret', and the passage of a holding company law in Luxembourg that provided an exemption from income tax. Over time, the Swiss–Liechtenstein connection evolved into a massive tax evasion scheme involving high net worth individuals from around the world, using the major Swiss banks to secret billions of assets that have been uncovered in a series of whistleblower events and insider leaks. For example, a 2008 leak uncovered 900 German citizens estimated to have avoided €4 billion in taxes. In 2016, a crackdown by the US authorities led to $1.3 billion in penalties being assessed on 80 Swiss banks, identified as having secreted some 34 000 accounts, holding an estimated $84 billion in undeclared funds. More recently, in March 2017, Dutch authorities uncovered tens of thousands of accounts associated with Credit Suisse suspected of tax evasion. In Luxembourg, a 2014 investigation by the International Consortium of Investigative Journalists uncovered more than 340 companies using Luxembourg to perpetrate dubious tax avoidance schemes.

Based on this background, modern tax havens can be roughly organized in three groups. One group, likely the largest, is composed of the British dependency-based tax havens centred on the City of London. The central position of London in the Eurocurrency deposit market, where funds are deposited in international banks operating outside the source country, provides an essential conduit for tax havens to trade and transfer funds into legitimate channels. This network encompasses the Crown dependencies and overseas territories, certain Pacific atolls such as Samoa, as well as Singapore and Hong Kong. The second group consists of tax havens domiciled in Europe, with a Swiss-centred subgroup exploiting secrecy laws to facilitate tax evasion by individuals using large private banks to hold and manage hidden investments. Another subgroup, including Luxembourg, Ireland and the Netherlands, caters to multinationals conducting legal, if ethically dubious, tax avoidance. The third and final group consists of various countries that seek to capture gains from conducting tax haven activities by emulating certain practices of the other two groupings. This group includes countries such as Panama, Uruguay, Taiwan, Mauritius and Dubai. In addition to these three groupings are locations that provide access to low or no personal taxes once residency is obtained through a golden visa or an investor investment programme, most notably Monaco and Malta.

Multilateral Initiatives Against Tax Havens

By the early 21st century, activities of tax havens had reached incredible proportions. According to the Bank of International Settlements, the Cayman Islands was the fourth-largest financial sector in the world. The US Treasury reports that the third-largest foreign holdings of US Treasury securities, following China and Japan, were the Caribbean financial centres. The Tax Justice Network estimated that in 2017 the 410 000 companies registered in the British Virgin Islands (18 companies per inhabitant) were responsible for $37.5 billion in global tax losses. A 2016 report by the International Monetary Fund (IMF) estimated annual global tax losses due to activities in tax havens of $650 billion; about one-third of this loss occurring in developing countries. A more detailed 2017 United Nations University World Institute for Development Economics Research (UNU-WIDER) study pegs the annual global loss at $500 billion. Such figures can be compared to Institute on Taxation and Economic Policy estimates of US multinationals holding at least $2.1 trillion offshore, mostly in tax havens, and avoiding up to $767 billion in federal tax.[12] Whatever the size of the tax avoidance and evasion numbers, it is certain that the bulk of the immense value from such activities accrues to wealthy free riders and, in many cases, the wealthiest. Such unreported amounts raise serious questions about the robustness of the empirical evidence for the upper tail of the wealth distributions provided in an array of scholarly studies.

Until the beginning of the 21st century when the first serious cracks began to appear in the tax haven networks, national tax authorities were either compliant with or frustrated by the nefarious tax evasion of wealthy individuals and, to a lesser extent, the tax avoidance of multinational corporations. Bilateral and multilateral agreements requiring either 'Exchange of Information on Request' or the related 'Automatic Exchange of Financial Account Information' (AEFAI) were essential to breaking the wall of secrecy protecting wealthy free riders and corporations operating in tax havens. Inspired by FATCA and initiatives emanating from the European Union Council and G20, 2017 marked the beginning of a new era of multilateral cooperation on tax transparency with the creation of the GFTEITP to identify and put pressure on jurisdictions that are non-cooperative or non-compliant, for purposes of revealing information required by tax authorities in other jurisdictions. As a result of such efforts, there has been a decided increase in transparency and cooperation by many jurisdictions operating as tax havens that have been the source of blatant tax evasion, even though a partial veil of secrecy remains intact for tax avoidance. An important piece in the multilateral effort was the passing in April 2017 of United Kingdom (UK) legislation requiring UK overseas territories – including the important Caribbean tax havens – to reveal the ownership of companies that are incorporated in those jurisdictions if requested.

Though progress has been made reining in tax evasion abuses by the wealthy, as evidenced in the release of the Panama Papers and the Paradise Papers, ample opportunities remain to engage in tax haven activities that are ostensibly legal tax avoidance. In addition, there are still jurisdictions that are deemed to be non-compliant and partially compliant, providing multinational corporations with avenues for abusive tax avoidance, and those in the 1 per cent and 0.1 per cent willing to risk the consequences of detection with offshore avenues for tax evasion. Tax avoidance schemes associated with using 'golden visas' and residency via immigrant investor programmes still lie outside the scope of current initiatives. In addition, as an October 2018 report prepared by the Greens/EFA for the European Parliament details, there are still significant loopholes in the AEFAI rules for creative accountants and lawyers to exploit.[13] Finally, there is always the possibility that future political events may overtake these initiatives, resulting in a retrenchment by key players, such as the Swiss or the UK, that will open the door to a return of the unrestrained use of tax havens by wealthy free riders to evade and avoid taxes.

NOTES

1. There are various reasons to focus on the Organisation for Economic Co-operation and Development (OECD) countries. These include availability and comparability of data sources and the substantial fraction of global wealth and income that is concentrated in these countries. Recognizing that there are even more significant data limitations, wealth and income inequality in non-OECD countries is an active research area, with China and Russia receiving specific attention. For example, Alvaredo et al. (2018) find that inequality in Russia and China is comparable to the US, the OECD country with the highest estimated degree of inequality. Piketty et al. (2019) for China, and Novokmet et al. (2018) for Russia, provide more detailed support for this claim about inequality. See also Piketty (2020) for the connection between inequality, capital and ideological predisposition.
2. https://taxfoundation.org/do-rich-pay-their-fair-share.
3. It would also be interesting to see the evidence on: the percentage of national income and federal tax paid by the 0.1 per cent of those earning the highest incomes; what fraction of state and local tax – not just income tax – was paid by the half of federal taxpayers with the lowest reported earnings; and what is included in 'national income'; for example, does 'national income' include unrealized capital gains or income earned in other nations by domestic companies?
4. Though discussion is limited to the OECD, this is due more to the availability and comparability of information than to the acuteness of income and wealth inequality. Available evidence, though relatively scant and anecdotal, does indicate that in non-OECD countries tax evasion and avoidance by the wealthiest is more pronounced.
5. OECD (2016, p. 8). The following quotes are from this source and OECD (2019b).
6. Tax Foundation (2016).
7. Figures from Tax Foundation (2016).
8. Increases in the sales tax have been proposed for various initiatives.
9. https://www.taxjustice.net/faq/tax-havens/.
10. Palan et al. (2010) provides an overview of the modern history of tax havens.
11. Shaxson (2012).
12. Sources for these estimates are:
    https://www.taxjustice.net/2018/05/04/yes-britain-is-closing-its-tax-havens-but-lets-not-forget-it-created-them-in-the-first-place/; https://itep.org/fortune-500-companies-hold-a-record-26-trillion-offshore/; Cobham and Janský (2017); http://ticdata.treasury.gov/Publish/slt3d.txt. In the most recent data, the Caribbean total is approximately the same as the fourth-place holder of US Treasury securities, Brazil.
13. Knobel (2018).

3. State revenue from antiquity to the modern income tax

> The proprietor of stock is properly a citizen of the world and is not necessarily attached to any particular country. He would be apt to abandon the country in which he was exposed to a vexatious inquisition, in order to be assessed to a burdensome tax, and would remove his stock to some other country where he could either carry on his business, or enjoy his fortune more at his ease.
>
> (Adam Smith, *Wealth of Nations*, 1776, p. 520)

STATE REVENUE FROM ANTIQUITY TO LOUIS XIV

Historiography and Taxes on the Wealthy

An important, if often untold, lesson from history, especially ancient history, concerns the need for objectivity when confronted with limited sources. Such lessons from history can provide guidance in modern times when rethinking wealth and taxes to alleviate increasing income and wealth inequality. Specifically, if proposals for reform of taxes on the assets and income of the wealthy lack the empirical evidence required for objectivity, then is it inappropriate to claim data that is available, however plentiful, can be sufficiently massaged to support a specific proposal or conclusion? Privacy concerns surrounding taxes paid, secrecy of tax havens, the corporate veil for privately held corporations, the difficulty of determining unrealized capital gains, and the like, conspire to restrict the availability of information concerning the taxes, assets, liabilities and income of the wealthy. This situation creates a conundrum. Seemingly dire moral, political and economic implications of inequality in wealth and incomes, both within countries and across countries, call for cutting rebukes in response. In such a situation, the incentives to overstep what available data can support are considerable, and subjective opinion, supported by rhetorical flourish, enters the picture.

What reasonable grounds for objectivity can be obtained based on evidence that is available about the net assets and income of the wealthy? As numerous academic studies have detailed, tax records, surveys and the like provide only a limited amount of evidence. There is also fragmentary evidence on the offshore activities of the wealthy, from leaks such as the Panama Papers; criminal and civil legal proceedings; and reports in the media. The challenge of combining such sources into a cohesive interpretation differs only in degree from the challenges of the historian investigating ancient Egyptian tax farming or the early 18th century English slave trade. The history of state revenue collection and assessment contains substantial primary sources on state revenue through time that detail the central role of taxes on the wealthy in government revenue generation. State finances are a constant both in the political harangues of the day and, as taxes require laws to be implemented, in the legal record. What the resulting historical record reveals is an evolving diversity of approaches to state revenue generation. Each approach is fundamentally dependent on characteristics of the tax jurisdiction that is using the revenues. Historical events associated with substantive changes in tax regime, such as the introduction of the income tax in England in 1799, or passage of the 16th Amendment in the United States (US) in 1913, reveal insightful ideological and social perspectives regarding reform of taxes on the wealthy captured in the primary sources of those events.

Tax Farming during the Roman Republic and Empire

In Roman commercial history, difficulties arise from the substantive evolution of Roman commercial activities from kingdom to Empire, and the relative absence of sources about these activities. Conquests that fuelled growth of the Roman state from the early to late Republic created dramatic changes in the demand for infrastructure and the availability of resources to fund military adventures, colonial administration and other state activities. Though the sources provide only fragmentary detail, partnerships of *publicani* – the *societates publicanorum* – served an essential role in taking up the state contracts to provide the skills, manpower and capital needed to support Roman expansion. The *publicani* were members of the *equites*, the wealthy officer and merchant class. In the timocratic Roman state, *equites* possessed status just below that of senators, who were barred by law from participating in the business of state contracting. The coming to power of the Emperor Augustus marks a fundamental change in methods of state contracting from that employed during the Republic; change that substantively reduced the role of these *societates* largely to tax farming.

One fascinating aspect of Roman commercial history is the construction of intricate narratives based on scarce or absent sources detailing commercial activities. Origins of the Roman state contract system are unknown, possibly dating as early as the founding of the Republic in 509 BC, though more likely somewhat later. This inference follows because, during the Republic, state capacity for infrastructure construction, managing state assets and raising revenues was limited, and the resources needed were under private control. Little is known about the state contract system until the Second Punic War (218–201 BC) when the sources start to provide some detail. The awarding of contracts – typically with a five-year term (*lustrum*) – was largely by public auction (*censoria locatio*), conducted by the censors. Initially, as state assets were insignificant compared to later years, the contract system was largely concerned with infrastructure construction, tax farming and supplying the military. As territories were conquered and Roman rule in the provinces solidified, contracts for tax-farming and managing state assets gradually assumed a central role in the contract system.

The timocratic and militarist state of ancient Roman civilization differs dramatically from the modern welfare state. At the peak, the Roman Empire was a vast collection of conquered territories that required revenue to support both the local administration and the military garrisons. The rate of Roman expansion gradually outpaced what a state centred in Rome was able to control. Starting in 27 BC, in the early stage of Empire, the fiscal reforms of Augustus resulted in a decentralized system of revenue collection that gave increasing authority to provincial governors and cities, at the expense of the *publicani* in Rome. From the *Lex Sempronia* of C. Gracchus in 123/22 BC until the fiscal reforms of Augustus, the *societates publicanorum* were important for raising taxes, especially in recently conquered territories in Asia.[1] The revenues needed to sustain the Republic and the Empire required collection of taxes (*vectigalia*) that were, in a narrow sense, 'dues levied on *ager publicus*', and in a wider sense, 'all regular and ordinary sources of Roman revenue, as distinct from the extraordinary *tributum*'.[2]

As the Romans often adopted tax practices previously used in conquered territories, the importance of a specific tax varied by location. For example, at Ephesus customs duty (*portorium*), including revenue from public buildings and markets associated with trade at the seaport, was an important source of local revenue. In many jurisdictions, the important *vectigalia* were the *decumae* (the tithes, a fixed percentage of crops) and the *scriptura* (grazing fees). Additional Roman state revenues for collection could include rents for houses on public land (*solarium*), sale of timber on public land (*vectigal picariarum*), revenue from salt works (*salinae*), revenue from mines (*metalla*) and various taxes on goods sold. The practice of farming state revenues to private collectors likely predates the appearance of cuneiform writing; it was not unique to the Romans. The Egyptian, Sumerian, Babylonian empires and the Greek city states all farmed state revenues, though the precise methods employed varied over time and location. The practice continued into the 17th century in England, the 18th century in France, and the 20th century in South East Asia.[3] Tax farming during the late Republic was unusual in ceding control of the tax farms to a narrow class of middlemen located in Rome – the *equites* involved as *publicani* – not in the locations where taxes were collected.[4]

The ancient world presents an extreme case of the hard-to-tax problem. Following ancient practice, to confront this problem the Roman state relied on taxes and taxation methods that were relatively resistant to tax avoidance and evasion. Identifying modern equivalents of these taxes is not a transparent exercise. Consider the *decumae* (the tithe, a fixed percentage of crops). Given the agrarian character of ancient society, the tithe had an income tax element. However, as the tax falls only on the owners of agricultural land and resources, the tithe can also be viewed as a property tax. Similarly, while the *scriptura* (grazing fees) had elements of a user fee, grazing animals were also a source of wealth, making the *scriptura* also a rudimentary wealth tax. The *solarium, metalla, salinae* and *vectigal picariarum* are all instances where revenues were generated from leasing state-owned salt mines, forests, grazing land, buildings and the like that were, in many instances, acquired through conquest. As for customs, tariffs and excise taxes (*portorium*):

> The main interest of the state in the extraction of customs was fiscal. Trade was to a large extent viewed as a flow of resources which could be tapped for the sake of revenue ... Customs were not something mainly charged on exports, and especially imports ... the imperial systems taxed the internal movement of goods as well as of those crossing their boundaries almost indiscriminately.[5]

Such hard-to-avoid taxes are comparable to modern consumption taxes.

The *Catasto* of Renaissance Florence[6]

The roots of the Renaissance can be traced to the profound impact that the Crusades had on trade of the Italian city states. This lucrative trade, dominated by the Italians, connected the Levant and other areas around the Mediterranean with Northern Europe. Starting in the 12th century, growth in this trade was accompanied by military and economic competition among the Italian city states. The resulting financial conundrum resulted in creation of city government debt issues (*montes*) to cover the excess of state expenses over revenues. Evolution of this general fiscal problem differed substantively across city states, providing a rich texture of possible approaches to raising government revenue when both debt and taxes are available. While private, voluntary loans were used if available and not expensive, Italian city state debt was typically raised using forced loans on the wealthy citizens. It is among the methods of making specific assessments that the historically important 1427 *catasto* of Florence appears. The *catasto* provides extensive written inventories of household liquid assets and land used for the assessment of direct taxes and forced loans: 'The thousand-odd volumes of the Florentine *catasto* constitute the richest source for the social and economic history of any European community prior to the French revolution'.[7]

Florence during the *Quatrocento* (15th century) was, arguably, the apex of the Renaissance. In contrast to the aristocratic and socially cohesive Venetians, or the feuding factions of the Genoese commune, the ruling commune of the Republic of Florence involved a relatively democratic combination of upper-class merchants and guild leaders that controlled the Florentine Council following the Ciompi revolt of 1378. Unlike the maritime states of Venice and Genoa, Florence was an inland city that, in addition to merchant banking, relied on manufactures, especially woollen goods, that gave considerable political and economic strength to the medieval guilds. Eligibility for communal office required a contribution to the *monte* – effectively a property qualification – and a fully paid tax assessment. Allowing taxes to be in arrears (*allo chio*) restricted availability for communal office for three, five or even more years, depending on the time involved in organizing a new assessment round to determine eligibility. For families with enough wealth, access to the political process was needed to deal with 'the conspiracies, false pretenses, and clienteles of the most powerful citizens' that contaminated the direct tax and forced loan assessment process; this need to minimize individual tax assessment using the 'patronage networks of the Florentine establishment'[8] was balanced by overwhelming demands for military expenditures that were inflated by the Florentine practice of using mercenary armies to prosecute military conflicts with Milan, Pisa and Lucca; conflicts that stretched from 1390 until well after the *catasto*.

The *catasto* was the 1427 resolution reached by the 200 or so members of the Florentine Council to address the quandary of balancing individual tax burden with state survival, 'because assessments would be determined on sure evidence rather than uncertainty clouded with favouritism; thus, it would contribute to domestic peace'.[9] More importantly, the *catasto* aimed to address failings of the previous direct tax and forced loan assessment method – the *estimo* – that was based on landed wealth and did not accurately account for the increasing wealth accumulation by manufacturers and merchant bankers. At the time of the *catasto* about three-quarters of state revenue was from the *gabelles*, a collection of sales, salt, customs, excise and document taxes paid by all residents within the Republic.

As the *gabelles* were regressive taxes, there was significant concern that attempts to obtain an even greater share of state revenue from the *gabelles* could lead to revolt or economic collapse. Paying for increasing military expenses required increased contribution from direct taxes and forced loans. The *catasto* was a surprisingly democratic attempt to bring equitable balance to tax assessment and the ongoing struggle for state survival.

Prior to the *catasto*, about one-quarter of government tax revenue for the Republic of Florence was from direct taxes on the countryside immediately surrounding the city (the *contado*) and on subjugated cities, especially Pisa and San Gimignano, and the countryside surrounding those cities (the district). These direct taxes were determined based on need, and provided a conceptual basis for the *catasto*. However, few wealthy Florentines lived in the *contado* and the district, so when funds from the regressive *gabelles* and direct taxes on landed wealth were insufficient, primarily when military expenditures dictated, the deficit was covered by forced loans on the wealthy in the city of Florence and, when possible, from private loans. As the *estimo* system of assessing wealth for the imposition of forced loans involved secret judgments of tax commissions (assessment *per arbitrio*), the resulting perception that the forced loan assessment method was unfair contributed to the peculiar democratic extension of direct taxation to the city of Florence with the *catasto*. The recognition of household liquid assets accumulating in the hands of manufacturers and merchants as a legitimate source for raising government revenue has reflections in the need to recognize and tax unrealized capital gains in modern times.

Like the Roman experience, substantive difference in historical context limits direct insights from the *catasto* of Florence to broad-brush observations. Florence during the *Quatrocento* underwent an economic Renaissance, becoming a centre of manufacturing and merchant banking activities that were not directly taxed under the traditional *estimo* method of measuring wealth using landed property. This connection between a shift in wealth-producing activity and the subsequent need for substantive tax reform is a theme found in the early adoption of the income tax in England and passage of the 16th Amendment in the US. This strongly suggests that rethinking taxes and wealth in the 21st century needs to address the dramatic shift in wealth-producing activity associated with globalization and the revolution in information technology and communications.

The *catasto* was the outcome of a partially successful struggle for democracy against aristocratic government. Unusual at a time of aristocratic city states, the *catasto* appeared as the result of a democratic process, seeking equity in direct tax and forced loan assessment on the wealthy. In addition to a high exemption limit from direct tax applicable to most guild members and other less wealthy Florentines, the only excluded property in the *catasto* wealth calculation was residential real property and contents, including furnishings; works of art; and household animals. Physical evidence of tax avoidance by the wealthiest in Renaissance Florence survives today in the palaces, churches and art galleries that attract millions of tourists to modern Florence. The sharp reduction in revenues from the 1431 and 1433 *catasto* census is further indication that direct tax avoidance and evasion by the wealthy became common. The modern implication is that whatever method of tax assessment on the wealthy is imposed, recognition and exploitation of avenues to avoid and evade taxation are a predicable systemic response.

The Enlightenment and the *Dixième* of Louis XIV

Arguably, the *dixième* of Louis XIV – a 10 per cent tax on propertied income introduced in 1710 – was the first attempt at a modern-style income tax. Though this tax did not impact upon labour income, the tax did reach propertied income and, most importantly, tax assessment ignored exemptions based on social status. This identification of the income generated as a basis of tax assessment was a dramatic break with the traditional taxation principles of French society that gave preference to the social status of the property owner. Given that unevenly distributed wealth in the France of Louis XIV was concentrated in about 10 per cent of the population, with the remaining 90 per cent either starving or simply surviving, the *dixième* was an assault on privilege brought on by the financial disarray that years of war inflicted on the French monarchy.[10] The *dixième* was not a permanent tax, lasting only two years after the death of Louis XIV in 1715. After two brief periods where the *dixième* was revived to deal with demands for revenue associated with military expenses during times of war, a 5 per cent direct tax on propertied income, the *vingtième*, was made permanent in 1749. However, the implementation of both the *dixième* and the *vingtième* was fraught with difficulty and the *vingtième* was swept away in the French Revolution.

In comparison with city state revenue assessment and collection problems in the 15th century Republic of Florence, the finances for France under Louis XIV are several degrees more complicated. The *dixième* was not an ordinary source of revenue. Introduced by the controller general of finances, Nicolas Desmaretz, nephew and long-time assistant of the important 17th century finance minister Jean-Baptiste Colbert, the *dixième* was an extraordinary assessment to deal with the extreme financial distress brought on by years of prolonged military engagement. The ordinary revenues of the French state under Louis XIV can be divided into direct taxes (*impositions*) and indirect taxes, including sovereign revenues (*perceptions*).

One of the administrative successes of Colbert was to complete the long process of combining four types of *perceptions* into the General Farms that were leased to a syndicate of 40 financiers operationally responsible for running the administrative apparatus of the General Farms and being a source of short-term credit for the government.[11] There were four types of 137 separate taxes included in the first lease of the General Farms in 1681. These types were: the *aides*, a sales or excise tax on certain types of goods, especially alcohol; the *traites*, tariffs collected on the movement of goods across provincial and national boundaries and for entering certain towns; the (French) *gabelles*, a salt tax that was combined with required salt purchases for some locales; and the revenues of the royal domain, consisting of rents, dues and income from the king's personal holdings.

In contrast to the collection of *perceptions* by tax farmers, the *impositions* – primarily the *taille* – were connected to venal office holders who owned the right to receive moneys paid for taxes and were responsible for receiving *taille* collections. The *taille* was a complicated direct tax from which the nobility, clergy, public servants working in the tax farms, venal office holders and various others were exempt. It was also possible to purchase exemption letters by making a substantial payment to the monarch. The *taille* taxed rural areas disproportionately compared to urban areas. Important cities such as Paris, Lyon and Marseilles were also exempt. Except in provinces with legislatures (*estates*), the *taille* was assessed by the royal government. The tax was assessed on the head of a *taillable* household according to a complicated process that resulted in gross assessments by the royal government eventually being passed to individual parishes. 'Residents of the parish subject to the *taille* took turns acting as collectors. Each parish had two to seven collectors, depending on its size. The collectors apportioned the parish's taxes among its *taillables* by estimating their ability to pay.'[12] The complicated process of taxation collection and payment can be described as: 'Parishioners owed the collectors, who owed the *receiver particular*, who owed the receiver general, who owed the government'.[13] Each stage in this process was governed by contracts that required fixed payments on specific dates to be made.

This backdrop of ordinary taxes was insufficient to support the monarch in the War of the League of Augsburg (1688–97), when France combated all the major powers of Europe alone. With ordinary taxes approaching a maximum, and desperately seeking new sources of revenue, a graduated form of poll tax, the *capitation*, was introduced in 1695. The design of this new tax was strongly influenced by views of Enlightenment thinkers 'calling into question the propriety of wealth . . . The critique of luxury spans the age and is inseparable from the spirit of the Enlightenment'.[14] The upshot was a progressive tax that would be assessed on all citizens according to ability to pay. In debate and practice, there was divergence over whether the *capitation* would be assessed based on wealth or social status. A scale with payments varying from 2000 *livres* to 1 *livre* based on social status was proposed in the 1695 *capitation*. This form of the tax did not produce the expected revenue, at least partly due to the reluctance and ability of *non-taillables* to make payments, and in 1701 the *capitation* was reformulated as a proportional gross-up to the *taille* for *taillable* households and *non-taillables* 'were to pay amounts based on estimates of wealth made by the provincial intendant in conjunction with other members of the group to be taxed'.[15]

Passage of the *dixième* in 1710 took place against a backdrop of debate among inspired idealistic Enlightenment reformers calling into question the propriety of wealth. A common theme of the reformers was a call for the suppression of 'inequitable' taxes, to be replaced by a tax based on ability to pay. In the end, the *dixième* did not achieve all that the reformers desired. Though the *taille* and salt tax were reduced, the basic structure of older French taxes did not change. 'Even so the *dixième* was a radical departure from traditional Old Regime tax policies because, by taxing all property equally, it did not recognize the difference between noble and common property'.[16] By taxing income from property but not labour, the *dixième* was not a formal income tax. However, by taxing the income from land, mills and woodlands, rent from houses, seigneurial and feudal dues, and the income from rights and privileges of government officials, the *dixième* was like a modern capital income tax. In addition, the *dixième* required 'that all people file a declaration of their income under penalty of fines for filing late or making false declarations'.[17] This was an important step in allowing the government to track property ownership.

Included in the broad-brush insights surrounding the *capitation* and *dixième*, such as the difficulty of getting the previously untaxed wealthy to pay assessments, there is the insightful debate among Enlightenment reformers. In recommending that 'removing barriers to trade and releasing the taxpayers from their strait-jacket could directly contribute to the nation's prosperity and make tax flow', reformers such as Pierre Boisguilbert were making suggestions with similarities to modern neoliberals; yet, the reformers also had decidedly progressive sentiments: 'would-be reformers such as Boisguilbert, the *maréchal* de Vauban and the *abbé* de Saint-Pierre pointed to the glaring inequalities of wealth in their society and denounced the arbitrary and irrational distribution of the burden of taxation which perpetuated or exacerbated these inequalities'.[18] In 1702, Boisguilbert coined the term '*laisser-faire*', arguing for free roads and just taxes. Whether based on a land-register or an assessment of personal means, taxes had to be paid out of revenue, out of what was sold and consumed.

'In order not to impoverish his subjects, the king should see to it that his taxes were certain and not arbitrary . . . that they were proportionate to the ability to pay, convenient in their manner of collection, and that they passed cheaply and directly.'[19]

Recognizing the need for revenue to support the state, Boisguilbert and other reformers argued that fundamental reform of the *taille* required certainty and predictability of assessments such that the rural taxpayer would know the tax burden in advance, instead of having the *taille* being increased suddenly and disproportionately when there was a prosperous harvest. For the *taille* to be distributed equitably, the 'rich must pay as rich, the poor as poor'; and further: 'Taxes are excessive or moderate not in relation to the absolute amount of the sums demanded, but in their relation to the value of the property from which they are exacted'.[20] Boisguilbert was a forward-looking reformer in predicating that a certain complexity in tax design is essential to achieving flexibility and fairness. Such debates did not end with the *dixième*. Important Enlightenment thinkers such as Rousseau made later contributions:

> For Rousseau, taxation was the social instrument to achieve balanced growth and to arrest luxury . . . Rousseau advocated a poll tax on a progressive scale, to tax individuals according to their wealth. All other taxes had to be sales taxes levied on discretionary consumption or on the consumption of luxury goods. Here Rousseau literally followed Montesquieu, who argued that luxury grew along an exponential scale.[21]

FROM PROPERTY TAX TO THE MODERN INCOME TAX

Evolution of the English Property Tax

The modern relevance of the medieval English property tax may seem obscure, but there is much to be learned about tax policy from a feudal society with dramatic differences in wealth and a gradual emergence of an unlanded commercial class that was not encumbered by aristocratic obligations. Looking back to the Middle Ages in England, 'property was simple but obligation complex'; in the medieval period, 'property' was:

> almost exclusively land and the fruits thereof, but obligation came in many forms, reflecting two general principles. One principle was feudal: obligation was seen to be a consequence of rank. The other principle was corporate: obligation was seen to be a consequence of membership, as in a guild, town, or parish.[22]

The tenor of the medieval property tax is reflected in an eleventh-century statute of King Canut: 'Let the heriots be as it is fitting to the degree'.[23] As such, the rank of a subject determined the extent of individual obligation to the sovereign. 'Originally the tenant made his lord a gift, a *donum*, the amount of which should be commensurate with his importance'.[24] Initially, feudal tenant gifts consisted of real goods, such as crops and livestock, combined with an obligation for military service. Gradually, this system of real goods in exchange for the protection of the lord and the right to farm a plot of land transformed into cash payments in the form of so-called quit rents or rack rents.[25]

Unlike the obligation of rank, the obligation of membership was associated with the 'corporate levy' used by the sovereign to raise revenue primarily from urban freemen not directly connected to the feudal system of nobles and serfs.[26] What ensued was a process of incorporating by royal charter a municipality or town that involved an agreement about initial and ongoing payments by the 'body corporate', together with the provision of military duties. This corporate obligation would be distributed among the citizens of the town. A variety of scholarly sources recognize that the resulting allocation was an early instance of basing taxation on 'ability to pay'. However, in an era of emerging and competing nation states, English monarchs required increasing sources of revenue to pay for 'more ambitious domestic policies'.[27] Increasing needs of national defense outstripped the traditional revenue sources that were relatively fixed due to tradition or charter agreement. To increase revenues, 'a new justification would have to be found for the taking of subjects' wealth. It was the search for such a new "principle" of obligation that led to the evolution of the property tax'.[28] The basis for this evolution was an acknowledged principle of medieval law allowing the monarch to levy taxes: '(1) if the tax were a feudal obligation; or (2) if the king could make a case for the necessity of a specific levy'.[29]

Because tax on much of the land and its produce was already covered by the feudal obligations, it is significant that 'property' had a meaning distinct from modern usage. The property tax introduced in 1194 was an extension of the *danegeld*, 'the first assessed payment in England' that was a fixed charge per hide of land – where a hide was enough land able to support one family for one year.[30] The objective of this tax was to move past feudal status to tax landholding directly. Given that the increasing wealthy urban populations largely escaped this tax and were only subject to the corporate levy, a property tax was introduced – the 'aid on movables' – based on 'personalty', that is, livestock, crops, tools, household goods, especially household luxuries such as silver plate, and so on.[31] Implementation of the tax was aided by the process for collecting the corporate levy. However, while the amount of tax required for the corporate levy could be assessed in an agreeable fashion and *danegeld* only involved determined units of land in use, the aid on movables introduced a tax that required a crude estimate of market value to be determined. This was an innovation allowing 'the chief magistrate [to] know men's estates'.[32] An unfortunate consequence of taxation based on personalty is the need to identify taxable items. Because this could involve searches of homes by tax assessors, the aid on movables could be time-consuming, expensive and difficult to verify.

In areas where the corporate levy applied, potentially high information costs associated with the aid on movables were controlled using the decentralized administration by local subjects, acting in the King's name, that was already in place. Initially, members of the gentry were selected to form a jury to make assessments. However, as even the poorest could own some ratable property, such as pigs or goats, some assessors not associated with the gentry were also selected to be jurors.[33] The accomplishment of this major tax reform, aimed to get at an increasing amount of untaxed wealth accumulation, was largely achieved by transforming the fixed sums due under a charter or feudal obligation to a combination of traditional fixed payments and a variable sum based on property assessments. The aid allowed the Crown the added flexibility of determining a total amount of revenue required and then apportioning that according to the estimated movables wealth of the different towns, villages and manors. Each local jurisdiction would then determine the rate as the fraction of the estimated value of movables that each resident would be assessed on. In the common event that the rate was set too low to meet required revenue, local officials could ask for a reduction in the traditional fixed component. 'For this reason the corporate levy created a bargaining opportunity. Towns in particular seem to have availed themselves of this opportunity repeatedly, extracting concessions on municipal privileges in return for higher tax yields, or deliberately under-assessing so as to return lower yields.'[34]

In practice, the aid gave local officials considerable discretion in determining the taxation of specific residents. Total tax assessments were not typically based on property alone. Tenants often had aid assessments based on the productivity of the fields under cultivation. The expenses of position and size of family were also typically taken into the accounting.[35] Foreshadowing a problem that would plague the property tax for centuries, there is also evidence that corrupt influences on assessments were present from the very beginning of the aid on movables. Over time, this method of taxation had unintended consequences for the special feudal status of land. In the feudal economy:

land was possessed by right immemorial or by royal favor. Inheritance was controlled by family law, and the greatest portion of land not in the hands of the king or the Church was held by a very small number of subjects. Land was rarely sold in an open market, and therefore it could not be reached by *ad valorem* assessments because it could not have a market value.[36]

While land could be taxed indirectly through the aid, this was not expedient or sufficient. The upshot was the emergence of a political battlefield between the great landlords and the monarchy.

Local administration of government revenue gave an important role to local juries that were not typically dominated by the gentry. Faced with a need for additional revenue, the local jury often turned to the great landlords for tax revenue. In this fashion, the local jury often acted in the interests of the Crown seeking to extract tax revenue from a reluctant nobility. This gave rise to a 'contest between the landed and the moneyed interest, between rent and profit'.[37] This contest pitted the rising urban merchant class against the feudal rights of the landed aristocracy:

> By the sixteenth century, this contest had largely been won by the middle class. By then, income had been incorporated into the list of ratables, including income from land rents, and along with income from office, profession, and wage labor. In the absence of an accounting and reporting system, however, the most visible form of income was rent.[38]

With the decline of feudal rights came increasing poverty as the most vulnerable became displaced. Starting in the 14th century, the resulting problem of vagrancy was dealt with by statute. However, these statutes were largely ineffective, leading to the beginnings of the Poor Law, starting in 1536, and continuing with a codified Poor Law in 1587–98.

The decline of the feudal economy and the subsequent need for the Poor Law put increasing demands on local administrations for funds. Given that land rent proved to be the most lucrative – eventually almost the sole source of local tax revenue – by the 17th century the aids was referred to as the 'Land Tax'.[39] Seligman observes that such 'slippage' is invariably a feature of a property tax. Items that can be concealed – especially household valuables – are dropped from the assessment lists due to the high cost and possibility of inequitable assessment. Similarly, other difficult-to-assess items such as professional income and forms of intangible wealth were also dropped. In the end, only the most visible and immovable form of property – real estate and the income derived from it – is left in the tax base.[40] This was applied both to the national tax and to the local direct taxes; the so-called scot, lot, town tax and parish rate. On the eve of the English Civil War, English taxation had come full circle to once again be primarily a tax on landed classes, as was the case with the early feudal tax payments. Consequently, the landed gentry became the governing class, the most heavily taxed, with representatives filling Parliament. The attitude of the middle class, by contrast, is suggested by Bacon's remark that 'the Englishman is the least bitten in purse and most the master of his own valuation' of any nation in Christendom.[41]

The Early English Income Tax[42]

While the *dixième* had some features of the modern income tax, the early English income tax initially introduced in 1799 was some steps closer to the modern design. Like the *dixième*, the 1799 English tax was not permanent, being revised in the Income Tax Act of 1803, eliminated after Waterloo in 1816, and reintroduced and made permanent in 1842. The English landscape following the Glorious Revolution of 1688 differed substantively from the privileged aristocratic absolute monarchy of Louis XIV. In conjunction with parliamentary control of taxation, the adoption of Dutch techniques of government finance established the basis of the Financial Revolution that provided for a dramatically expanded use of borrowing in the private capital market as an essential source of government revenue. Through the 18th century, the need for a steady and significant revenue source to support an expansionist foreign policy fuelled a steady march toward a tax on income, although this did not become a reality until 1799:

> A long series of 'mercantilist wars', occupying nearly half of all the fiscal years from the reign of Charles II through to that of George IV, imposed ever increasing tax burdens on the incomes of British citizens and upon their economy. In real terms the burden rose nearly eighteen times over this long period.[43]

The war-related burden was met primarily with borrowing and varying the tax rate on land from 5 per cent at times of peace to as high as 20 per cent in wartime.

An advantage of financing extraordinary and significant military expenditures with government borrowing was the ability to avoid sharp and sudden tax increases in the excise, stamp and customs duties that were paid by the whole population. As illustrated in the peacetime results for 1788–92, such indirect taxes represented about 80 per cent of government tax receipts, with direct taxes levied on manifestations of wealth and income contributing the remaining 20 per cent. Higher indirect tax rates encouraged evasion, especially smuggling, resulting in increased costs of enforcement at a time when severe revenue constraints would be driving such rate increases.[44] Though the use of borrowing made expansionist foreign policy more palatable with Parliament and the landed voting constituency, the hidden cost of taxation to finance present and future interest payments mounted decade by decade. Prior to being adopted, the merits of an income tax to provide a significant and stable new government revenue source were recognized. It was, however, the impetus given to 'a tax of this nature by the development of the democratic ideal and the increased importance of exchange and the earning of money incomes in an expanding commercial society, that resulted in its eventual adoption in the very late eighteenth century'.[45]

In contrast to the taxation system of France that was riddled with exemptions for the privileged, the English approach captured 'the sentiment that more of the tax burden should be carried by those of greater means'.[46] In particular, the 17 years that William Pitt the Younger served as British prime minister (1784–1801) witnessed a variety of luxury taxes imposed directly on items such as saddles, carriages, racehorses, hats, perfumery and manservants. Though the revenue from such taxes paled in comparison to such widely consumed items as beer and malt, or to the property tax based on rack-rent estimates, there was the perception of distributional equity which encouraged overall tax compliance. One subtle additional benefit from the use of property and luxury taxes was that Pitt created an administrative framework to collect such taxes which facilitated the initial introduction of the income tax. Introduced primarily to fund the hostilities with France that stretched from 1793 to 1815, the income tax was a new tax. This posed a substantive problem: how to design such a tax to prevent evasion and encourage compliance? The abortive initial attempt at design appeared in 1798 with the passage of 'An Act for granting to His Majesty an Aid and Contribution for the Prosecution of the War'.

Consistent with having an administrative apparatus to collect property and luxury taxes, the 1798 Act imposed additional duties on those with incomes of £60 or upwards. This was not an income tax per se but, rather, additional duties assessed based on an income qualification. This tax was not a successful revenue producer, if only due to what Pitt characterized as 'shameful evasion, or rather, scandalous frauds'.[47] This led to the passage of Pitt's Act of 1799 that repealed the 1798 duties and imposed a regular tax on incomes at the rate of 10 per cent. This Act required each taxpayer to provide a general statement of income from all sources. The tax assessment on total income was subject to certain deductions, for example for children and for property repairs. Consistent with the 1798 Act, incomes under £60 were not subject to the tax, with a graduated assessment between £60 and £200, with the full 10 per cent levy only on incomes of £200 and above. The success of the tax was evident in the first year's revenue of more than £6 million. Such large revenue demands on the propertied class were not popular, and in the brief period of peace following the Treaty of Amiens in 1802, Prime Minister Addington repealed the 1799 Act, arguing that such a tax was to be assessed only during periods of war.

The respite for the propertied from the income tax was brief. The resumption of hostilities with France led to a revival and 'improvement' in the Tax Act of 1803. 'In this Act is embodied for the first time a principle which has been of incalculable benefit to the revenue this country, and which in spite of some modern encroachments remains the great buttress of Income Tax stability and efficiency – the principle of taxation at the source.'[48] The 1803 income tax calculation was based on assessing income from five schedules, a method of calculating income that survives in modern income tax systems. In adopting schedules, the requirement of the 1799 Act for statements of total income was dropped, replaced by statements of income from specific sources. In addition to the taxpayer not having to disclose total income, the use of schedules for specific income sources aimed to alleviate tax evasion. Schedule A covered income accruing to the owners of land, houses, tithes and other minor categories of real property. Schedule B covered income from 'occupation of the land', effectively farming. Schedule C captured 'Profits from annuities, dividends or shares of annuities payable to any person, persons or corporate bodies out of public revenue'. Schedule D, 'in every way the most unsatisfactory income category', involved 'All profits from professions, trades, vocations and employments exercised in Britain'.[49] Finally, Schedule E was assessed 'Upon every public office or employment, upon pensions annuities or stipends payable by H.M. Government' resulting in duties being charged 'Upon all public salaries, fees, profits or pensions whatsoever'. The success of the 1803 Act in achieving enhanced compliance is reflected in the similar revenue generated from the 1803 tax at 5 per cent compared to the 1799 Act at 10 per cent.

One useful artefact of the early English income tax is the survival of records from the Board of Taxes. These records have been trolled through to provide evidence of the wealth and income distributions in England at the beginning of the 19th century.[50] Circa 1800, less than 15 per cent of British families admitted to receiving an annual income £50 and above. Similarly, in 1812 less than 14 per cent of English families claimed spending more than £5 a year on shelter. This suggests the number of families with annual incomes above £50 a year was small at the beginning of the 19th century, implying that only a minority of the population was liable to pay income tax. The income tax schedules indicated that most income of those subject to the income tax came from the ownership of property. Investment income from the traditional sources of land, houses and the national debt seems to have exceeded income from the ownership of industrial assets. In 1800, there were only about 80 000 returns – 25 per cent of about 320 000 total income tax returns – that claimed an annual income above £200. Available estimates indicate that this same group received 67 per cent of taxable income assessed for that year. The upshot is that, circa 1800, wealth and income in England was concentrated in a very small part of the population. 'Only the armies of Revolutionary France and the probable collapse of public credit prompted the political classes to accept a policy which translated into law their oft-proclaimed principle that Englishmen should contribute to the needs of the state in accordance with their abilities to pay.'[51]

Passage of the 16th Amendment[52]

The slow process of introducing a federal income tax in the US republic can be attributed to the unique attributes of the federal Constitution and to the ideological struggle that still consumes American politics. In particular, Article I, §8, para. 1 provides that, 'the Congress shall have power to lay and collect taxes, duties, imposts and excises . . . but all duties, imposts and excises shall be uniform throughout the United States', and §9, para. 4 provides that, 'no direct tax shall be laid unless in proportion to the census or enumeration hereinbefore directed to be taken'. From this point, the path to the 16th Amendment is a sequence of conflicting legal decisions by the Supreme Court that led, ultimately, to the federal Income Tax Act of 1894 being deemed unconstitutional by the Supreme Court in a ruling that found the 1894 income tax to be a 'direct' tax and, therefore, not a tax that could be assessed by the federal government. This led ultimately to passage of the 16th Amendment to the US Constitution by Congress in 1909, with final ratification by the states in 1913. This amendment states: 'The Congress shall have power to lay and collect taxes on incomes, from whatever source derived, without apportionment among the several states, and without regard to any census or enumeration.'

Commenting on the amendment during the approval process, the *Harvard Law Review* observed in 1909: 'The proposed amendment presents the anomaly of a Federal power of taxation absolutely unrestricted, and entirely opposed to the principle of the Constitution requiring either the rule of apportionment or the rule of uniformity govern in every instance.'

As initially conceived in the 19th century, the US federal income tax was not a broad-based tax; that development was introduced to satisfy funding needs during and after World War II. The first appearance of a proposal for federal income tax was during the War of 1812 against the British. At this point in time, federal government revenue came primarily from the tariff system passed by Congress in 1789. 'In a special report on the state of finances, Secretary of the Treasury A.J. Dallas proposed an income tax to generate revenue for the war effort, the first instance of a government official publicly recommending a federal income tax.'[53] The end of the war, a few months after the income tax proposal was advanced, ended Congressional consideration of the proposal. The relatively successful use of the income tax by the English to pay for various and considerable war expenditures at that time likely contributed to the income tax getting serious consideration in the US Congress as a method of dealing with the sharp increase in government expenditures due to war finance. Recalling that the British made the income tax permanent in 1842, the maximum effort required by the Civil War marks the first time that the US federal government implemented an income tax. This tax was part of a larger reorganization of the federal fiscal structure captured in the Act of 1862, designed to comprehensively capture as much revenue for the war effort as possible (Box 3.1).

Framers of the 1862 Act were acutely aware of the constitutional complications of assessing an income tax. There was general agreement

---

BOX 3.1   EDWIN SELIGMAN DESCRIBING THE US INCOME
TAX OF 1862

The law of 1862 imposed a comprehensive code of internal revenue taxes, of which the income duty formed only a part. In addition to a series of taxes on the gross receipts of certain specified corporations, all railroads were required to withhold and to pay over to the government as a tax three per cent on the interest of their bonds and the dividends of their stock; and all banks, trust companies, savings institutions, and insurance companies were to pay a duty of three per cent on dividends, and on assessments added to their surplus or contingent funds. A tax on salaries of government officials was imposed at the rate of three per cent on incomes over six hundred dollars, and the paymasters and disbursing officers of the government were required to withhold the duty at the time of the payment of the salary or pay. The 'income duty' proper consisted of a tax of three per cent upon 'the annual gains, profits or incomes of any person residing in the United States, whether derived from any kind of property, rents, interest, dividends, salaries or from any profession, trade, employment or vocation carried on in the United States or elsewhere, or from any source whatever', to the extent that the income exceeded six hundred dollars. If the income exceeded ten thousand dollars, the rate was to be five per cent. In the case of citizens residing abroad, the rate was also five per cent, while in the case of income from government bonds the rate was one and one-half per cent. In estimating the annual gains, profits, or income subject to duty, deductions were allowed for all other national, state, and local taxes assessed upon the property or the source of income, as well as for all incomes taxable under the other sections of the law.[54]

during the Congressional debate over the Act that 'a direct tax in the constitutional sense denoted only a tax on real estate and slaves and a poll tax', referring to the income tax as an 'income duty'.[55] The tax had similar features to the British income tax, including an exemption level of $600 that allowed most to escape the levy, progressive increases in marginal rates, and allowance for certain deductions in calculating taxable income. The tax was to be imposed for three years starting in 1863, but the demands of Civil War finance resulted in a new Act being passed in 1864 that increased the marginal rates to 5 per cent on incomes from $600 to $5000, 7.5 per cent between $5000 and $10000, and 10 per cent beyond $10000, these progressive rates were amended the following year to assess a flat rate of 10 per cent on income above $5000. As the revenue demands of the Civil War subsided, the last Act empowering collection of the tax in 1867 imposed a flat rate on incomes above the exemption level. Finally, in 1870 and 1871, the last two years of the Civil War income tax before it expired in 1872, the tax was assessed at a flat rate of 2.5 per cent on incomes above $2000.

Ideological aspects of the political to-and-fro over whether the marginal rates in the Civil War income tax needed to be progressive or flat rate survive to the present. Referencing constitutionally protected rights, there were the 'flat taxers' who argued against the graduated schedules of increasing marginal rates at higher income levels. In some cases, even the exemption level was seen to be a violation of constitutionally guaranteed 'equality'. In contrast, one of the Founding Fathers of the American republic, Thomas Paine, argued forcefully in *The Rights of Man*[56] that democracy requires 'a progressive tax on estates in order to protect democracy against the corrupting influence of large fortunes'. Themes in Congressional debates surrounding the lapsing of the income tax in 1872 reappeared surrounding the passage of the 16th Amendment. Ultimately, it was difficult for legislators to ignore a potentially lucrative tax that earned nearly 30 per cent of all internal revenue collected in 1866; a tax that was paid by a small fraction of the richest individuals in the US population.

Despite the considerable ability to generate revenue, the 'income duty' was permitted to lapse in 1872 in favour of raising revenue using more traditional and regressive excise and customs taxes. As proponents of retaining the income tax stressed, these were 'taxes upon consumption that oppress the poor and take coppers out of the dollars of the people who earn them by their daily work'.[57] Those aligned against the income tax were not a homogeneous group. Some were against the tax based on obvious evidence of evasion and under-reporting of income, such that the tax was only paid by the honest for the benefit of the dishonest. Others argued the tax was only implemented as a temporary war measure and, given the substantial reduction in expenditures, such taxes needed to be reserved for use in future instances of excessive fiscal demands. Representatives from states that paid the bulk of the income tax felt the tax was an inequitable burden: New York paid about one-third of the tax alone, rising to 60 per cent if Pennsylvania and Massachusetts were included. These three states were particularly averse to the tax.[58]

Lapsing of the income tax in 1872 coincided with the beginning of a period of profound growth in the industrial and commercial sectors of the US economy. Facilitated by the emergence of the trusts to organize equity capital and monopolize certain industries, large personal fortunes were amassed in these monopolized sectors that attracted a significant democratic backlash, including the Sherman Anti-Trust Act and the Income Tax Act of 1894. Though political support for graduated income taxes persisted following the lapse of the tax in 1872, representatives from the industrial Northeast US states that would be most burdened by such levies were able to prevent consideration of various bills introduced in the House by representatives from the traditionally Democratic low-income states in the South Atlantic and Midwest farming regions. It was the emergence of the Populist Party as a political force, and passage of the McKinley tariff by the Republican-controlled Congress in 1890, that laid the political basis for the Democrats to win the 1890 congressional elections and the presidential election of 1892, setting the stage for passage of the 1894 income tax amendment that was subsequently declared unconstitutional by a unanimous Supreme Court ruling in 1895. As the 1894 law was modelled almost word for word after the Civil War income tax law, this ruling reflects the complicated legal and political interplay that can be involved in tax reform.

In the intervening years between 1895 and 1909, support for the income tax became a key difference between the pro-tariff Republican Party under President McKinley and the opposing Democrats and Populists. A Democratic proposal in 1898 for a federal income tax made in defiance of the Supreme Court ruling was defeated in the House. In contrast to McKinley, the more 'progressive' Republican President Teddy Roosevelt was in favour of a 'graduated income tax of the proper type [that] would be a desirable feature of federal taxation, and it is to be hoped that one may be devised which the Supreme Court will declare constitutional'.[59] By 1908, support for the progressive income tax was such that the Democrats included a proposal for a constitutional amendment permitting the federal government to assess income taxes 'to the end that wealth may bear its proportionate share of the burdens of the federal government'. Though the newly elected Taft administration was more in favour of raising revenue using a progressive inheritance tax which had received approval for federal use by the Supreme Court in 1898, such a tax was not supported by some states. Public and legislative support for the income tax led in June 1909 to Taft altering his position on the income tax, coming out in favour of a constitutional amendment. Votes on the income tax amendment were passed by both houses of Congress almost unanimously, with most states passing the amendment with substantial margins in the period from 1909 to 1913.

From the 16th Amendment to the Tax Reform Act[60]

The election of Franklin D. Roosevelt (FDR) as President of the United States in 1932 marks the beginning of a dramatic transition in the approach to raising federal and state government revenues. At the start of 1933 when Roosevelt assumed office, more than half of federal government revenue ($1.5 billion of $2.6 billion total federal revenue, with a $1.6 billion federal deficit) came from *ad valorem* taxes, mostly customs and excise taxes assessed on consumer goods, with income taxes contributing about $1 billion. At the same time, state governments relied primarily on *ad valorem* taxes ($1.7 billion of $2.3 billion) – a combination of sales taxes and property taxes – with $4.3 billion of $5.4 billion in local government revenue coming largely from property taxes. By 1950, after the gradual reduction in rates following World War II and before the increase in taxes to pay for the Korean War, income taxes generated $26.2 billion of $39.4 billion in federal government revenue, with *ad valorem* taxes generating about one-third of the revenue produced by income taxes ($8.7 billion), with a $5.4 billion federal deficit. At the state and local level, *ad valorem* taxes were still the most important revenue source ($6.6 billion of $11.5 billion state revenue, and $7.9 billion of $11.7 billion local revenue), though a variety of alternative revenue sources – income taxes, social insurance contributions, user fees and business charges – were increasing in usage.

The Revenue Act of 1935 is an important step on the path from initial passage of the 16th Amendment, to a narrow federal income tax base of 4 million wealthy Americans in 1939, to a broad-based income tax base of 45 million in 1945. Though New Deal reforms implemented under FDR extend well beyond the Revenue Act, the introduction of 'social taxation' – the creative use of tax policy to achieve social and economic reform – embodied in the Act 'was a pivotal victory for the New Deal – and a landmark in the history of American taxation'.[61] The words of FDR in proposing the Act are eerily similar to the modern situation:

> Our revenue laws have operated in many ways to the unfair advantage of the few ... They have done little to prevent an unjust concentration of wealth

and economic power . . . Social unrest and a deepening sense of unfairness are dangers to our national life which we must minimize by rigorous methods.[62]

The 'soak the rich' Revenue Act proposal advanced by FDR differed only somewhat from the final Act passed by Congress. Instead of a new inheritance tax, Congress elected to change this to increasing the top estate tax rate from 50 per cent to 70 per cent, combined with a lowering of the exemption level. The top marginal income tax rate was increased, from 59 per cent on incomes above $1 million, to 75 per cent on incomes above $500000. Perhaps most significantly, the Act introduced a graduated rate structure for the corporate income tax.

The Revenue Act of 1935 was significant in advancing the cause of social taxation, not in broadening the income tax base or in raising substantial amounts of additional tax revenue. It was the revenue demands brought on by World War II that produced fundamental change in the American income tax system. The US war mobilization that peaked in early 1943, during some of the heaviest fighting of World War II, was anticipated by the Revenue Act of 1942 that mandated the largest expansion of the income tax in American history in support of war finance. Prior revenue Acts in 1940 and 1941 had expanded the tax base by lowering exemptions, raising corporate taxes and implementing an excess profits tax. The Act of 1942 slashed the personal exemption in half and reduced the lowest marginal tax rate from 24 per cent to 10 per cent. In 1944, the marginal tax rate on incomes over $200000 peaked at a historic maximum of 94 per cent, with about 60 per cent of the labour force paying some income tax. For the first time, lower-income workers, especially those in industrial sectors, began paying income tax. However, despite this radical restructuring of the federal income tax levy: 'Most Americans thought the federal income tax was fair. Even among the hardest hit group – those who thought they would have difficulty paying – two-thirds felt the tax was fair'.[63]

The social cohesion brought on by the World War II effort did not extend beyond the end of the war. The struggle of the Republicans to protect the wealthy from the income and estate taxes, that extends back to the debate over the lapse of the Civil War income tax, suddenly found an audience in the broad base of the population now paying income tax. The subsequent history of federal government tax policy captures the differential impact that institutional characteristics of the checks and balances in the US democratic process imposes on policy decisions. In 1946, the Republicans made tax cuts a central plank in the party platform for the elections of that year and 'with this banner won a massive electoral victory and finally took control of the Congress'.[64] In contrast, at this time President Truman was worried about maintaining budget balance and wanted to retain the tax rates. Though the Republicans passed three tax cut bills that were vetoed by Truman, the eventual override of the veto in 1947 was for a bill that portends the need to include 'exceptions, special rules and individual allowance' to get tax bills through Congress. Over time, this has contributed to the design of a long and complex US federal tax code.[65]

The pressure for income tax limitation peaked in 1951, shortly after the beginning the Korean War, propelled by passage of the Revenue Act of 1950 and the Excess Profits Tax Act of 1950, legislation that introduced large tax increases and reversed the post-World War II trend toward income tax cuts. The peculiarities of the American democracy are illustrated by the subsequent inability of Eisenhower to pass broad tax rate cuts, despite controlling both houses of Congress and having such tax limitations as a central part of the Republican platform. With Eisenhower, there begins a 'quiescence of the tax issue for the following decades'.[66] This quiescence began to unravel in the late 1960s when the substantial increase in the combined federal, state and local taxation burden came up against the decline in real incomes due to economic slowdown induced stagflation, oil price shocks and the increasing burden of the Vietnam war.[67] Significantly, the bulk of the 98 per cent increase in the combined tax burden for an average family between 1953 and 1974 was not due to federal taxation, which rose only 34 per cent, but rather to the increases in other taxes which were much greater: 77 per cent for local property tax, 150 per cent for state property tax, 436 per cent for payroll tax, and 533 per cent for state income tax.[68]

Proposition 13, the 1978 amendment to the California state constitution rolling back assessments to 1976 levels and restricting the maximum amount of any annual tax increase on real property to not exceed 2 per cent unless the property was sold, is a fitting symbol of the dramatic overhaul of the tax systems in the US and 'a huge set of remarkably diverse countries' that took place in the 1980s.[69] This proposition appears in California, the state that elected Ronald Reagan as a two-term governor. Reagan was able to tap into the anti-tax sentiment that was a key element in the election of Reagan as US President in 1980. The proposition was passed in the year prior to Margaret Thatcher beginning her term as British Prime Minister. It was Thatcher and Reagan who became perceived leaders of the neoliberal revolution that underpins the process of globalization. This revolution has taken somewhat different forms across countries. In the US, the Economic Recovery Tax Act of 1981 that cut taxes an average of 25 per cent, and the 1986 Tax Reform Act, were epic in massively lowering income tax rates, first increasing and then reducing tax expenditures and, in the 1986 Act, paying for these increases with increased corporate tax rates. Though the plan was to reduce spending, the Reagan tax reductions and other fiscal measures were ultimately paid for largely through increased borrowing.

While Reagan was able to incur substantial increases in the federal deficit, this was less of an option for Margaret Thatcher. 'If the overall burden could not be reduced, at least the rich, whose increased superfluity would, in [Thatcher's] view, have the greatest effect on the overall health of the economy, should be relieved of much of their crushing tax burden.'[70] With this in mind, the first budget of the Thatcher government in 1979 contained deep cuts in taxes for the wealthy and steep rises in taxes paid mostly by the poor. In 1980, the budget featured a further income tax rate decrease and a shredding of the death duties. And so it goes with further budgets, broadening the value-added tax (VAT), eliminating the investment income surcharge, abolishing the National Insurance surcharge on employers, further cuts in marginal income tax rates until the reforms of 1988 'that were unusually impressive in their unabashed effort to reduce taxes paid by the wealthy in Britain'.[71] It is an oddity that the most regressive Thatcher tax policy – a 1986 proposal for a poll tax to replace property taxes as the method for local funding – was a contributing cause of riots that broke out, leading to the eventual removal of Thatcher as British Prime Minister.

GLOBALIZATION AND RISE OF TAX COMPETITION

What is the Globalization Thesis?

Globalization is a multifaceted process that has produced profound alterations in the financial, economic, social and political landscape of the modern world.[72] Even if the political and societal implications of globalization are ignored, untangling one thread of the globalization process especially important to the wealthy – the rise and impact of capital tax competition between national jurisdictions – requires understanding the interconnection with other threads, such as the initiatives to ease restrictions on international capital flows and trade, the evolution of payments technology and changes in national tax regimes. With this in mind, it is useful to consider the odd empirical conclusion reached by a number of studies on the capital tax competition thread: 'The weight of the evidence leads to the unanticipated impression that international capital mobility may be unrelated (or even positively related) to capital taxation.'[73] Aligned against this optimistic perspective on globalization are the pessimistic supporters of the 'globalization thesis'. This thesis has been summarized as:[74]

[G]lobalization in the form of increased international trade and capital mobility presents governments with a serious dilemma: it increases the demands on them to provide social insurance and public goods at the same time as it undermines their ability to finance this spending. Citizens want their governments to help them compete and feel secure in the global economy; but globalization makes it more difficult for governments to play this role because it constrains their ability to tax capital . . . this argument [is] commonly referred to as the globalization thesis.

The debate over capital income taxation divides those who are pessimistic about the domestic political consequences of globalization and those who believe that governments still have substantial room to manoeuvre in the global economy.

Fallout from globalization, in the sense of a significant expansion in multilateral trade and payments, appears at various points in history. For example, there was a well-defined period of globalization from the last quarter of the 19th century up to World War I, centred on London as the world's financial capital. Similarly, the Italian city states were the focus of the globalization associated with the revival of trade and payments during the Renaissance. Each period of globalization has different consequences that depend on the relevant political, social and economic landscape. Though there are certain points of commonality with earlier globalization periods, the modern globalization process has taken place against a backdrop of a substantial increase in federal taxation and spending authority following World War II, financed by a dramatic increase in personal and, to a lesser extent, corporate income taxes. Given this, roots of modern globalization can be traced to the signing of the General Agreement on Tariffs and Trade (GATT) in October 1947 that aimed for substantial reduction of tariffs and other trade barriers and the elimination of preferences, on a reciprocal and mutually advantageous basis.

The GATT was successful mostly in removing trade restrictions, especially tariffs, on a wide range of industrial products and services. The success of the GATT stimulated a range of regional multilateral agreements, the most notable being the evolution of the European Common Market into the European Union (EU) and passage of the North American Free Trade Agreement (NAFTA). The GATT text was incorporated into the next multilateral round of globalization with the establishment of the World Trade Organization (WTO) in 1995, following the Uruguay Round of negotiations that culminated in the signing of the Marrakesh Agreement by 123 nations in April 1994. The WTO provides an institutional framework for dispute resolution, the regulation of trade and the negotiation of new trade agreements. Since the Doha Round was initiated in 2001, the WTO has been struggling to find a resolution to protectionist barriers in the agricultural sector provided by farm subsidies, marketing boards and the like. A subtle feature of the globalization thesis is that much of the increased trade stimulated by the GATT and WTO is touched by publicly traded limited liability corporations that generate increasingly difficult-to-tax capital income.

Against this backdrop, there is the general empirical claim that international capital mobility is not significantly impacted upon by the level of capital taxation. This positive view of globalization argues that instead of a race to the bottom in capital taxes, there is a non-zero market equilibrium distribution of capital taxes where countries with 'excessive' capital taxes lose revenue to those with 'generous' capital taxes, resulting in an eventual convergence of tax rates over time. In effect, the constraints that increased international capital mobility impose on taxation are not severe. However, this perspective ignores the theoretical claim – increasingly supported by empirical evidence – that this lower equilibrium level of capital taxes will result in an increased burden on labour income to cover the tax shortfall, with increasing inequality (skewness) in wealth and income distributions as an outcome. In addition, there will be a differential impact of domestic institutions on the national responses to globalization: 'According to this "varieties of capitalism" line of thinking, globalization has ushered in a new era of "divergent reconfiguration" in the varieties of national capitalism.'[75] The implication is that there is unlikely to be a one-size-fits-all solution to dealing with the implications of globalization for addressing the increasing inequality in wealth and income through tax reform.

Avenues of International Tax Competition[76]

International tax competition is a multifaceted problem involving a variety of taxes and regulations that impact upon both capital and labour. Though the focus has often been on the impact of globalization on the movement of capital taking advantage of differential corporate income tax treatment, individuals also can and do relocate legal residence from high personal tax to low personal tax jurisdictions. The movement of capital and labour to avoid and evade taxes and government regulations is not new. For example, the displacement of Bruges by Antwerp as the focal point for Northern European trade in the 16th century was propelled by favourable tax and regulatory treatment of foreign traders made available in Antwerp. International tax competition is one piece of a much larger puzzle connecting increasing wealth and income inequality with the equity and efficiency of government revenue policy. The arguments supporting the globalization of capitalism are consistent with an ideological perspective traceable to Enlightenment thinkers such as Boisguilbert and Adam

Smith. From this perspective, it is not clear whether international tax competition is undesirable a priori.[77] The ultimate objective is, somehow, to use tax reform to democratically and efficiently alleviate the growing inequality in income and wealth while capturing, if possible, the economic gains from the global expansion of trade and payments.

Recognizing that equity capital shares in corporate entities, limited partnerships and the like represent a considerable fraction of the wealthiest individuals' assets, the contribution of globalization to wealth and income inequality is, arguably, largely associated with the easing or elimination of restrictions on the movement of capital. As such, there are three distinct avenues associated with 'catching capital', taking inequitable advantage of international tax competition: capital in portfolios seeking to avoid or evade capital gains tax by moving funds offshore; capital in transnational corporations seeking to avoid corporate income tax and, to a lesser extent, sales taxes and regulations; and finally, there is the capital attracted by foreign direct investment incentives that allow for 'round-tripping' to evade and avoid both personal and corporate taxes.[78] In an economy that is closed to the world, taxing corporate incomes is relatively straightforward. However, when companies operate in a variety of taxing jurisdictions featuring different methods of assessing tax, the problem becomes more than complex. In turn, 'the scope for tax arbitrage depends crucially on the legal rules governing the taxation of cross-border activities and . . . the intensity of tax arbitrage varies greatly across different taxes'.[79]

The different legal environments governing corporate and personal tax play a key role in determining the impact of international tax competition and the government reactions to the associated tax arbitrage activities. For example, US citizens are assessed income tax based on citizenship, not residence. This requires the payment of taxes on global income, wherever that income is generated. Consequently, US-owned corporations are technically required to pay US taxes on all profits, whether originating from US operations or abroad. In contrast, Canadian citizens are assessed tax based on residency, not citizenship. Canadian citizens who are non-residents for tax purposes are not assessed tax on income earned outside Canada. Difficulties such as the risk of double taxation arise when two countries aim to tax the same income or profits, raising the complexities of offset in the tax treaties that are yet another aspect of the globalization process. This problem is not new. The three general principles currently used to guide the resolution of international taxation complications, especially double taxation, were initially developed in the 1920s under the auspices of the League of Nations.[80]

The first principle of international taxation is that corporate tax is to be paid 'at source' to the national government where the corporate income is generated. For example, if a US corporate entity owns a Columbian coffee producer then it is appropriate for Columbia to levy tax on the income generated there. As evidenced in the early English income tax, this method of taxation at source is rooted in 19th century tax laws which imposed different 'schedular' tax rates on various sources of income such as wages, rents and dividends. Source-based taxation is sensible for a situation where a corporation owns a branch plant or office in a foreign country for purposes of producing and selling goods or services only in that country. That simple 'branch plant' model of taxation is undermined when the branch plant is involved in exporting goods from the foreign country back to the controlling parent corporation for sale in the domestic country or, even more complicated, to a distribution network owned by the parent corporation in another foreign country. How and where do the profits of the branch plant get taxed? The ability for the controlling parent corporation to shift profits to a lower-tax jurisdiction through internal transfer pricing decisions creates obvious practical difficulties for tax authorities.

Difficulties such as tax arbitrage through transfer pricing leads to the second principle of international taxation coordination: 'arm's length pricing'. This requires the various entities involved in the production or distribution of goods and services within the branch plant model to calculate profits as if the various entities were unrelated. In the coffee example, the Columbian coffee producer would compute profits as if it the coffee were sold at the applicable – for example, world – market price. In turn, if the American parent imports the coffee produced by the Columbian entity then it is required to calculate profits as if the coffee were purchased at the applicable market price for that coffee. While the arm's length pricing model worked reasonably well for the decades when the bulk of production was in countries with relatively similar tax structures, such as with the branch plant network of American corporations in Canada, globalization has facilitated the shift of production to low-tax jurisdictions in the emerging economies, substantively expanding the ability of corporations to implement tax arbitrage strategies arising from transfer pricing and related discretionary decisions.

The third and final principle of international taxation with roots in the League of Nations framework was the practical use of bilateral, as opposed to multilateral, agreements to resolve the problems of double taxation. The upshot is that, since the 1920s, there have been over 3000 bilateral tax treaties implemented that require source-based taxation and arm's length pricing and provide some measure of relief against double taxation, for example, by using foreign tax credits in calculating taxable income. Unlike the multilateral approach to trade reflected in the GATT and WTO, the various bilateral agreements 'differ in a myriad of specific ways'.[81] This had little import during the decades from the Great Depression until the 1960s, when profits from foreign operations accounted for a small fraction of corporate profits; for example, roughly 5 per cent of US corporate profits during this period:

> The situation started changing in the 1970s, but slowly. It is only in the 21st century that a surge in international investments brought the problems to the frontlines. Globalization is back on a broader scale than in the late 19th and early 20th century, and the choices made by the League of Nations are coming back to haunt the tax authorities.[82]

Globalization and Tax Reform in the 21st Century

Writing at the turn of the 21st century, the eminent economist Edward Feige made the following prescient observation:[83]

> Technological innovations in finance and communications have internationalized financial activity and created a virtual worldwide commerce. Institutional adaptions to these radical changes may ultimately require some form of global financial architecture. Today's taxation schemes are based on personal income, corporate profits and expenditures, generated within national borders. However, massive reductions in transactions costs render these borders increasingly porous. Capital mobility, transfer pricing, offshore tax havens, tax competition, Internet commerce and the creation of global equity exchanges make it more and more difficult to identify and assess the national origins of income and profits to tax them. Taxation on global scale offers a technological solution, but the politics of taxation and fiscal sovereignty remains an essentially national matter.

Having identified the problem, Feige went on to propose an outside-of-the-box 21st-century solution, an Automated Payment Transaction tax, to replace:

> the present system of personal and corporate income, sales, excise, capital gains, import and export duties, gift and estate taxes with a single comprehensive revenue neutral Automated Payment Transaction (APT) tax. In its simplest form, the APT tax consists of a flat tax levied on all transactions. The tax is automatically assessed and collected when transactions are settled through the electronic technology of the banking/payments system. The APT tax introduces progressivity through the tax base since the volume of final payments includes exchanges of titles to property and is therefore more highly skewed than the conventional income or consumption tax base. The wealthy carry out a disproportionate share of total transactions and therefore bear a disproportionate burden of the tax despite its flat rate structure. The automated recording of all APT tax payments by firms and individuals eliminates the need to file tax and information returns and creates a degree of transparency and

perceived fairness that induces greater tax compliance. Also, the tax has lower administrative and compliance cost.

Such seemingly impractical outside-of-the-box tax reform proposals that aim to retain the basic capitalist structure of globalization implicitly reveal much more than intended about the profound ideological issues associated with the increased wealth and income inequality that has accompanied the global spread of capitalism.

Clearly, the single Automated Payment Transaction tax would not be able to replace the current tax system and eliminate the need to file tax returns. This is not realistic; another example of an interesting but impractical solution. Rather, the APT poses the questions: will raising enough government revenue to address increasing inequality of wealth and income require outside-of-the-box, non-status quo approaches? In the face of the multifaceted aspects of globalization, are such solutions consistent with democratically addressing the apparent increasing wealth and income inequality in modern capitalist society? In the context of answering such questions, recommendations for reforming taxes on the wealthy need to have two essential features: the ultimate objective of reducing wealth and income inequality within and, hopefully, across countries; and the necessity of using some form of democratic process to affect required changes. Focusing on such questions avoids the distressing existential quandary that accompanies the likelihood that there are no solutions: that wealth and income inequality will continue to persistent and, likely, increase; and that the wealthiest are too influential to allow democratic solutions to emerge.

Concern about the implications of globalization for restructuring of tax systems is not new. More than a quarter of a century ago the influential public policy economist Sven Steinmo observed that: 'The world economy has undergone astounding changes since the 1970s: it has, in a word, globalized. Such globalization is bringing about dramatic restructuring of tax systems throughout the world.'[84] Looking back on the dramatic tax policy changes in various countries around the world, Steinmo correctly recognized that these tax reforms were aimed at redistributing the tax burden 'downwards', a consequence of 'the argument for social justice [being] overwhelmed by the argument for economic growth'. In a globalizing world, growth depended on international competitiveness and, according to a certain ideological perspective, 'a successful capitalist class' is needed to provide the capital required to fund this growth. Portending the assessments of future scholars, Steinmo recognized that this approach depends on 'that class's willingness to use and invest . . . in the domestic economy'. Two 'salient features of the changing world economy' that undermined the validity of the restructuring of tax systems have been 'the increasing mobility of capital and the growing flexibility of production technologies'.[85]

The predicament of rethinking wealth and taxes in a globalizing world revolves around why and how tax and trade reforms were implemented that have resulted, perhaps unexpectedly, in increasing wealth and income inequality. Going back to Aristotle, the 'tyranny of the majority' inherent in the democratic process is expected to put constraints on the growth of such inequality. Yet, tax and regulatory reforms accompanying globalization have enhanced the ability of the wealthy to reduce, avoid and evade taxes and for corporations and other 'legal persons' to shift profits to low-tax offshore jurisdictions. Comparing the 'soak the rich' social taxation of the New Deal with the increasing downward redistribution of the tax burden that has continued since the reforms of Reagan and Thatcher is revealing of two profoundly different ideological perspectives on issues of social justice and political economy. Yet, whatever the ideology, the search for fairness requires reforms aimed at tax avoidance and evasion. As the history of government revenue assessment and collection amply demonstrates, evasion and avoidance of tax is a systemic and difficult-to-address problem. Modern multilateral initiatives against immense tax evasion and avoidance by the wealthy, such as the US Foreign Account Tax Compliance Act (2010) (FATCA) and the EU Base Erosion and Profit Shifting (BEPS) project (initiated by the OECD/G20) aimed at the financial institutions involved in the international transfer of funds for wealthy free riders, illustrate the difficulties in achieving multilateral solutions against a backdrop of bilateral tax treaties and financial secrecy laws in the tax haven countries.

Fuelled by multilateral trade agreements and removal of barriers to international capital flows, increasing wealth and income inequality has accompanied the dramatic economic, financial and technological progress that globalization has produced.[86] Unanticipated impacts of the globalization process on the broad-based income tax have produced perverse opportunities for wealthy free riders to exploit. In conjunction with globalization, the legal basis for much of the observed inequality is associated with a pillar of modern capitalism: the 'realization principle' treatment of capital income. This principle has encouraged the transformation of tax revenues based on wage income, taxed when earned at personal rates, into (long-) deferred tax revenues associated capital income that is taxed at lower capital gains rates when (if) realized. Against this backdrop, there is substantial risk that the current state of wealth and income inequality will be carried forward to future generations by failing to reform death taxes for the wealthiest. Having identified key issues that need rethinking, Part

II of this book examines potential tax regime changes that could address increasing income and wealth inequality arising from the complicated relationship between wealth and taxes.

NOTES

1. See, for example, MacMullen (1959) or Burton (2004).
2. As discussed in Smith et al. (1890).
3. Ashton (1956) for England, White (2004) for France, and Butcher and Dick (1993) for South East Asia.
4. In addition to debunking the common claim that there was a stock market in ancient Rome, Poitras and Geranio (2016) give details on tax farming in the late Republic.
5. Bang (2008, p. 213).
6. Included in the useful studies of the *catasto* are Calkins (1991), Martines (1988), McLean (2005) and Brucker (1993). More general contributions that also touch on the *castato* include Tilly (1992) and Webber and Wildavsky (1986).
7. Brucker (1993, p. 11).
8. McLean (2005, p. 644).
9. Ibid.
10. The definitive scholarly contribution on the assault on privilege by Louis XIV is McCollim (2012).
11. Johnson (2006) discusses the gradual evolution of the tax farms into the General Farms.
12. McCollim (2012, Ch. 1).
13. Ibid.
14. See Gross (1993).
15. McCollim (2012, p. 42).
16. McCollim (2012, p. 191).
17. McCollim (2012, Ch. 1).
18. Gross (1993, pp. 82, 83).
19. Gross (1993, p. 83).
20. Boisguilbert, quoted in Gross (1993, p. 84).
21. Hont (2015, p. 118).
22. Hale (1985, p. 386).
23. See Cave and Coulson (1965, p. 362) for more detail.
24. Mitchell (1951, p. 111).
25. Jewell (1972, pp. 89–90).
26. The sale of corporate charters was not limited to the towns. The Crown was also involved in the sale of corporate charters to regulated and joint stock companies, such as the regulated Company of Merchant Adventurers and joint stock British East India Company. As with the towns, the granting of a Royal Charter was accompanied not only by a cash payment but also by other duties that would be specified in the charter; see Poitras (2016, Pt II).
27. Hale (1985, p. 386).
28. Ibid. This source also lists other relevant sources for the early use of 'ability to pay'.
29. See Hale (1985, p. 387). The origins of English parliamentary democracy can be traced to the need to hear appeals about taxes and the like (e.g., Jewell, 1972, p. 91).
30. Hale (1985, p. 388).
31. Over time, the 'aid on moveables' was expanded to include tax on land, buildings and the like. An interesting example is the English 'window tax', introduced in 1696 and repealed in 1851, that resulted in the bricking up of windows to reduce the tax burden. A similar tax was imposed in Scotland, Ireland and France.
32. Kennedy (1913, pp. 42–3).

33. From this were born the juries of assessment which travelled to North America in the 17th century and which are the very recognizable ancestors of the contemporary local board of assessors (Jewell, 1972, pp. 109–10; Mitchell, 1951, p. 63).
34. Hale (1985, p. 389).
35. Kennedy (1913, p. 20).
36. Hale (1985, p. 389).
37. Seligman (1895, p. 16).
38. Hale (1985, p. 390).
39. Seligman (1895, p. 48).
40. Seligman (1895, pp. 54–80).
41. Benson (1965, p. 19).
42. Cox (1919) is still a useful source on the time line of the English income tax during the 19th century. Seligman (1914 [1911]) is the definitive work on US, English and French income taxes for this time period until the 20th century.
43. O'Brien (1988, p. 1). In terms of percentage share of national income appropriated as taxation, O'Brien (1988, Table 2) estimates an increase from 3.4 per cent at the time of Charles II to 18.2 per cent at the end of the Napoleonic Wars.
44. 'Tax evasion, corruption and frauds on the revenue were pervasive throughout Britain (and Ireland was not taxed from London until 1817). But no historian reading parliamentary and departmental enquiries concerned with the collection of customs and excise duties in Scotland and other regions distant from the metropolis could doubt that the ratio of sums collected to the legal liability for taxes varied considerably across the country' (O'Brien, 1988, p. 5).
45. Emory (1965, p. 288).
46. Emory (1965, p. 289).
47. As quoted in Cox (1919, p. 42).
48. Cox (1919, p. 43).
49. O'Brien (1959, p. 260).
50. O'Brien (1959) is still an essential source of these records and the source of the following summary.
51. O'Brien (1988, p. 267).
52. Material on the pre-history of the 16th Amendment is provided in *Harvard Law Review* (1909). Baack and Ray (1985) is a more complete recent account of the process leading to passage of the 16th Amendment.
53. Baack and Ray (1985, p. 608).
54. Seligman (1914 [1911], p. 435).
55. Ibid.
56. Paine (1791).
57. Senator Sherman in the debate over retaining the Civil War income tax, as quoted in Seligman (1914 [1911], p. 464).
58. This has implications for the subsequent contributions of Henry George, especially George (1882 [1879]).
59. As quoted in Seligman (1914 [1911], p. 591).
60. Steinmo (1993) is a useful source on historical developments in the US, UK and Sweden during most of the 20th century.
61. Thorndike (2009, p. 30).
62. FDR, quoted in Thorndike (2009, p. 40).
63. Campbell (2009, p. 54).
64. Steinmo (1993, pp. 136–7).
65. Steinmo (1993, p. 138).
66. Campbell (2009, p. 58).
67. By impinging on managerial cash compensation, this decline in economic activity may also have been a contributing factor to the rise of contingent equity compensation for executives combined with share buybacks.
68. Campbell (2009, p. 61).

69. Steinmo (1993, p.156). For further detail on Proposition 13 see https://www.califor niataxdata.com/pdf/Prop13.pdf.
70. Steinmo (1993, p.172).
71. Ibid.
72. The precise definition of 'globalization' is elusive. For example, in reviewing sociological contributions, Kellner (2002, p.285) observes that: 'today's world is organized by accelerating globalization, which is strengthening the dominance of a world capitalist economic system, supplanting the primacy of the nation-state with trans-national corporations and organizations, and eroding local cultures and traditions through a global culture'. In turn, Kellner also provides an alternative explanation for globalization theory that argues: 'the key to understanding globalization is theorizing it as at once a product of technological revolution and the global restructuring of capitalism in which economic, technological, political, and cultural features are intertwined. From this perspective, one should avoid both technological and economic determinism and all one-sided optics of globalization in favor of a view that theorizes globalization as a highly complex, contradictory, and thus ambiguous set of institutions and social relations, as well as one involving flows of goods, services, ideas, technologies, cultural forms, and people.'
73. Swank (2002, p.247). Similar results and references to related studies can be found in Hays (2003) and Stewart et al. (2006).
74. Hays (2003, p.80).
75. Hays (2003, p.83).
76. For earlier surveys of the scholarly literature on tax competition, see Wilson (1999) and Oates (2001). More recent surveys are available in Genschel and Schwarz (2011) and Dietsch (2015), sources that provide numerous recent references to the substantial literature that has emerged on tax competition.
77. Edwards and Mitchell (2008) are representative of this view: 'As globalization advances, individuals and businesses are gaining greater freedom to work and invest in countries with lower taxes. That freedom is eroding the monopoly power of governments and forcing them to reform their tax systems and restrain their fiscal appetites.'
78. 'Catching capital' is a reference to Dietsch (2015).
79. Genschel and Schwarz (2011, p.339).
80. Clausing (2009) provides more detail on the development of these principles. In the late 1950s, the general League of Nations principles were formalized by the Organisation for European Economic Co-operation, a precursor of the OECD, into a model treaty of international taxation. This model has subsequently evolved in the current OECD model tax convention, a non-binding agreement among OECD (and some non-OECD) countries used to structure bilateral tax treaties and to resolve disputes. It is understandable that Europe is the source of the initiative for such a model treaty. The small size and multiplicity of countries in Europe made the problem of how to fairly tax without significantly impeding economic growth an ongoing and historical concern.
81. Zucman (2014, p.124).
82. Ibid.
83. Feige et al. (2000, p.473).
84. Steinmo (1993, p.156).
85. Steinmo (1993, p.158).
86. The *New York Times*, 29 April 2017, provides a fitting illustration of poverty amid riches in New York City, a global destination for the wealthiest with some of the most expensive real estate in the world. In discussing the opening of the Cary Leeds Center for Tennis and Learning in Crotona Park in the Bronx, the *New York Times* reports that: 'Some 30000 children live within walking distance of Crotona Park, 3000 of them in homeless shelters.'

PART II

Rethinking Taxation of the Wealthy

4. Public economics of taxing the wealthy

> The subject of every State ought to contribute towards the support of the government, as nearly as possible, in proportion to their respective abilities; that is, in proportion to the revenue which they respectively enjoy under the protection of the State.
>
> (Adam Smith, *Wealth of Nations*, 1776, Vol. 2)

EQUITY, EFFICIENCY AND DISTRIBUTIVE JUSTICE

Concepts of Tax Equity

Taxes, in some form, have been present since the beginnings of civilization. As Daniel Defoe, Benjamin Franklin and many others have observed, the only certainties in life are death and taxes. In turn, the system and methods employed to raise taxes are not only of economic and administrative interest. Rather, the evolution of social decisions made to arrive at a particular amount and distribution of the tax burden reflects the moral values of a given society about fairness and justice.[1] In the liberal democracies, basic moral values descended from the contributions of Enlightenment thinkers regarding individual natural rights that inspired the American and French revolutions and are enshrined in documents such as the American Constitution. While there are general moral values that are shared by the various liberal democracies, such as the right to life, liberty and the pursuit of happiness, these shared values are augmented by specific constitutional and societal constraints imposed in each such country that impact upon tax policy. Against this backdrop, there is an implicit, strongly held assumption that democratic equality of voting rights will lead to pressure for equitable distribution in wealth and income. As it turns out, the relationship between democracy and economic inequality is decidedly more complicated.[2]

Justice and fairness in modern analysis of tax policy, especially for income and consumption taxes, is usually synthesized into two general and sometimes conflicting concepts: horizontal equity or 'net benefit', and vertical equity or 'ability to pay'.[3] While these notions of justice and fairness are useful for considering the whole tax base, horizontal and vertical equity alone are insufficient when applied to the narrow group of wealthy individuals and households. Included in this narrow group are 'the wealthiest', 'a select, extraordinarily affluent class who rely on an army of high-priced accountants and higher-priced lawyers to shield enormous amounts of money from the tax authorities'.[4] The wealthiest also exercise substantial influence over the national political arena where decisions about income tax and other taxes are made. As Thomas Paine and many others have claimed, the inter-generational transfer and concentration of wealth pose a serious potential risk to the democratic process, 'being one of the principal sources of corruption at elections'.[5] Globalization has added an additional layer of opaqueness to the traditional devices used by the wealthy to avoid income taxes, such as: income splitting among several taxpayers; transmuting wage income into deferable capital gains taxable at lower rates; shifting income from one year to another using the 'realization principle' and other devices; utilization of trusts and foundations; and realizing income in non-taxable form.

A variety of approaches have been used, with varying degrees of success, to distinguish between the vertical and horizontal equity concepts as rationales for using the tax system to redistribute resources. Specifically, conceived as charging for the net benefits provided by society, horizontal equity explicitly considers the positive-sum connection between tax revenue and expenditure: taxes paid need to (loosely) correspond with benefits received from government and, in some presentations, from being a member of society. Though useful for theoretical tax policy analysis, precisely how the complex bundle of goods and services provided by the government – such as national defence or the protection of contracts and property rights provided by the courts – is to be apportioned voluntarily across taxpayers is difficult to determine. In contrast, conceived in egalitarian terms of the ability to pay, vertical equity takes a coercive, negative-sum approach by giving less consideration to the goods and services provided by the government. However, while ability to pay is commonly associated with vertical equity and the requirement that those with higher income and wealth bear a larger portion of the tax burden, it also implicitly imposes horizontal equity on those with equal ability to pay. Viewed differently, horizontal equity addresses 'local inequality' and vertical equity deals with 'global inequality'.[6]

Concern with horizontal and vertical equity in the assessment of income tax policy is long-standing. The intellectual history reveals various sources of conflict between these goals. Much of the complexity in various national tax codes is ostensibly due to provisions aimed at alleviating disparities that arise. For example, an early version of the alternative minimum income tax was proposed in 1960 by United States (US) Senator Russell Long (Democrat, Louisiana) to address: 'concern about the inequity and complexity of our tax structure, particularly with regard to individuals in the upper-income brackets. A study of individuals in high-income brackets shows two things: Some taxpayers do not pay nearly enough; others pay too much'. The evidence quoted by Long is illustrative:

> Of the 1000-odd returns with adjusted gross income exceeding $500000 in 1959, about 90 paid effective rates lower than 20%, while about the same number paid rates above 65%. Of the 37 returns with 'amended gross income' exceeding $5000000 in that year, six paid no tax and six paid more than 50%.[7]

Many exceptions aimed at capital income in the tax codes of the US and other countries to address horizontal equity for the wealthy go well beyond broad-based deductions available to less-than-wealthy wage and salary earners: the personal exemption, charitable contributions, possibly mortgage and other interest, pension income and contributions, dependent children and medical expenses.

Tax Efficiency and Optimal Taxation

What do the 'gurus of economics' have to say about taxing the wealthy?[8] In the landscape of the intellectual attention space, academic contributions from economists on tax policy theory have tended to dominate those from other disciplines. Claiming the intellectual high ground sustains the prominent role that economists with appropriate ideological predisposition have in the political arena where actual tax policy is implemented. Against this backdrop, the illusion of an 'optimal' tax policy is difficult for economists to resist. Closer inspection reveals normative optimal tax theory that involves solving for the properties of a tax system chosen to maximize a social welfare function, somehow defined, subject to a set of constraints. At this point, economists tend to move quickly past the complex issues of distributive justice embedded in the specification and practical applicability of a specific social welfare function. In general:

> The literature on optimal taxation typically treats the social planner as a utilitarian: that is, the social welfare function is based on the utilities of individuals in the society. In its most general analyses, this literature uses a social welfare function that is a nonlinear function of individual utilities. Nonlinearity allows for a social planner who prefers, for example, more equal distributions of utility.[9]

An important commonly used alternative is a social welfare function that is linear in individual utilities.

Using this general analytical structure, optimal tax theory has generated a variety of theoretical results about tax policy that provide ample ammunition for the wealthy and, especially, the wealthiest to argue for tax policies that seemingly underpin increasing wealth and income inequality. Such results are not new, appearing initially with 'A Contribution to the Theory of Taxation' by Frank Ramsey in 1927. This contribution is structured as:[10]

> a given revenue is to be raised by proportionate taxes on some or all uses of income, the taxes on different uses being possibly at different rates; how should these rates be adjusted in order that the decrement of utility may be a minimum? I propose to neglect altogether questions of distribution and considerations arising from the differences in the marginal utility of money to different people; and I shall deal only with a purely competitive system with no foreign trade.

Ramsey derived theoretical results connecting optimal tax policy to the elasticity of the demand and supply schedules for goods and commodities, generally concluding that when taxing commodities, those with the least elastic demand or least elastic supply be taxed the most.[11] Similarly, Ramsey provides the first of a long line of results from optimal tax theory regarding the taxation of savings: that is, 'income-tax should be partially but not wholly remitted on savings'.[12] Recognizing that Ramsey was dealing with a tax system not yet heavily reliant on income taxes, it is not surprising that goods consumption and commodity production were central features of the 'optimal taxation' results. It is with contributions by the likes of J. Mirrlees, A. Atkinson, J. Stiglitz, P. Diamond and others during the 1970s that optimal tax theory took its contemporary form.[13]

Optimal taxation theory has produced a multitude of results. A number of these contributions deal with the relaxation of specific assumptions that underpin an influential early work of James Mirrlees (1971), 'An Exploration in the Theory of Optimum Income Taxation'. Specifically, these assumptions include: limited ability to shift income across years; no differences in tastes, family size and composition; social welfare that is a function of individual utilities; no possibility of migration; and the costs of administering the optimal tax is negligible. This is problematic for the case of taxing the wealthy, where income shifting is common, enhanced ability to migrate allows a favourable country or state domicile to be used for tax purposes, and costs of detecting evasion are significant. Despite this, consider the following recent listing of 'eight general lessons suggested by optimal tax theory':[14]

1. Optimal marginal tax rate schedules depend on the distribution of ability.

2. The optimal marginal tax schedule could decline at high incomes.
3. A flat tax, with a universal lump-sum transfer, could be close to optimal.
4. The optimal extent of redistribution rises with wage inequality.
5. Taxes should depend on personal characteristics as well as income.
6. Only final goods ought to be taxed, and typically they ought to be taxed uniformly.
7. Capital income ought to be untaxed, at least in expectation.
8. In stochastic dynamic economies, optimal tax policy requires increased sophistication.

Allowing for some variation due to different contexts for results gleaned from different studies, many of these theoretical results, such as (2) and (7), are more than obviously biased toward reducing marginal tax rates for the wealthy and, especially, the wealthiest. It seems that the implications of globalization and wealth and income inequality are not substantively incorporated in the 'general lessons' from optimal tax theory.

This raises a quandary: why does the theory of optimal taxation produce results that are seemingly slanted in favour of the wealthy? The answer to this question has been explored by various eminent public finance economists such as Joel Slemrod. While admitting that, 'The theory of optimal taxation has . . . generated several useful insights about the relationships between assumptions about the set of tax instruments available to the government, the structure of the economy, and the objectives of tax policy', Slemrod finds that:[15]

> optimal tax theory is incomplete as a guide to . . . critical issues in tax policy. It is incomplete because it has not yet come to terms with taxation as a system of coercively collecting revenues from individuals who will tend to resist. The coercive nature of collecting taxes implies that the resource cost of implementing a tax system is large. Furthermore, alternative tax systems differ greatly in the resource cost of operation. Differences in the ease of administering various taxes have been and will continue to be a critical determinant of appropriate tax policy.

While Slemrod is concerned about the whole tax system, when focused on the wealthy individuals able to employ international tax accountants and corporate lawyers to avoid and in some cases evade taxes, 'the resource cost of implementing a tax system' is especially large. As such, compliance costs and the ability to assess and collect taxes are essential barriers to rethinking taxes on the wealthy in an era of globalization.[16] This observation suggests a traditionalist approach to the profoundly difficult questions surrounding what taxes and how taxes can be assessed to address increasing wealth and income inequality.

It is unfortunate that the essence of the early theoretical contribution by Mirrlees on optimal taxation – that taxes are necessarily distortionary if allowance is made for differences in ability to generate income – provided essential support for a key proposition of neoliberal supply-side economics: 'A stiffer tax rate intended to raise more revenue, to reduce the public debt, and boost the capital stock, might be counterproductive through a chilling effect on the activity being taxed or some other taxed activity.'[17] This macroeconomic efficiency hypothesis is unfortunate, because it deflects attention from the essential relationship between tax policy, the measurement of economic inequality and inter-generational equity. Continuing a theme in fiscal policy stretching back to David Hume (1711–76), the eminent Nobel Prize winning economist Edmund Phelps has observed: 'the present generation gains nothing from tax-financing its government spending in whole or in part instead of borrowing. If there is a gain from tax-financing it must accrue to the next generation.'[18] This is especially relevant to the optimal taxation of inter-generational and inter-jurisdictional wealth transfer, an issue that is relevant primarily to taxing the wealthy.

Writing in 1979, just prior to the most important steps in the globalization process, Phelps makes an insightful observation about optimal taxation theory being 'applicable only to the world as a whole and only when acting in a cooperative spirit. The national economics of public finance in one country among other nations goes quite a bit differently as long as international fiscal coordination is lacking.' More specifically, Phelps makes the prophetic observation:

> Until the tax loophole of international migration of capital and labor is effectively closed, a single country cannot unilaterally achieve inter-generational equality of social welfare within its own borders, taxing future generations when they have natural advantages for the benefit of the present generation, for much the same reasons that the poor cannot achieve equality with the rich within generations.

With this backdrop, it follows that a world of perfect capital and labour mobility 'would be a world incapable of justice in the absence of international cooperation' and, contrary to the trend to globalization, the assumption of 'perfect immobility' has underpinned the direction that optimal taxation theory has taken since Mirrlees.[19]

Different Perspectives on Distributive Justice[20]

One limitation of optimal tax theory is the reliance on a narrow conception of distributive justice embedded in a specific utilitarian social welfare function. If those emphasizing a central role for distributive justice in the determination of tax policy are considered, the landscape of contributions on tax policy extends well beyond the narrow confines of economics. Political philosophers, in particular, have dedicated considerable effort to identifying and exploring a range of possible approaches to distributive justice, often under the rubric of 'social justice'.[21] These approaches include: egalitarianism, where the goal is for all adult individuals to have roughly the same distributive shares; libertarianism, where the goal is that individual freedom and property rights are paramount; cosmopolitanism, where 'the fundamental unit of moral concern is the person, and that all persons are moral equals regardless of where they happen to be across state boundaries',[22] and prioritarianism, where the goal is to maximize a non-linear social welfare function, with utility of the worse-off counting for more than those who are better off. Prioritarianism is related to perhaps the most debated approach to distributive justice in political philosophy: the Rawlsian difference principle.[23]

While such divergent philosophical concepts of distributive justice are of interest in academic debate over the general design of tax systems, when attention focuses solely on comparison of the few wealthy with the many others not so privileged, the phenomena of distributive justice are more transparent, though still not adequately resolved. The complications that globalization poses for tax fairness and distributive justice still confound the various available approaches even when focusing only on those at the top of the wealth and income distributions. In particular, while the failing of the highly influential *A Theory of Justice* (1971) by John Rawls to account for implications of globalization can be rationalized by observing that the main features of globalization were largely in the future when that text was written, when he did address the burgeoning literature on globalization, instead of extending Rawlsian distributive justice across countries as dictated by cosmopolitans, Rawls advanced *The Law of Peoples* (1999). This text advances principles of justice to govern international relations that 'do not concern themselves with the distribution of income and wealth per se, but instead presuppose the existence of separate societies within which distributive principles do apply'.[24]

Though cosmopolitans would like to apply the distributive justice concepts from *A Theory of Justice* on a global scale, this was not the approach used by Rawls in *The Law of Peoples*.[25] In other words, 'the laws and institutions of the United States should be designed in such a way as to maximize the position of the worst-off Americans, and the laws and institutions of Bangladesh should be designed in such a way as to maximize the position of the worst-off Bangladeshis'.[26] According to Rawls, 'justice does not require that the worst-off Bangladeshis should be as well-off as the worst-off Americans . . .

the principles of distributive justice impose no constraints at all on the distribution of income and wealth between the United States and Bangladesh or among citizens of the two countries'. When applied to the wealthy, the failings of this approach are apparent. The wealthy benefit significantly from the impact of globalization on the ability to move large amounts of funds across boundaries using financial intermediaries. Globalization enhances the ability to choose the tax domicile of capital assets. In addition, many of the wealthy who benefit indirectly from such globalization also own multiple properties in various political jurisdictions, leaving considerable flexibility in choosing a 'flag of convenience' for tax purposes. Precisely how the *Law of Peoples* deals with this situation is unclear.

An alternative to the traditional emphasis on distributive justice is to place emphasis on commutative justice.[27] Distinction between these two different ethical norms for justice follows from distributive justice focusing on the achievement of equitable outcomes, while commutative justice 'ascribes qualities of justice to end results solely on the ground that they are the consequences of a procedure that is inherently just'.[28] With roots in contributions by the classical liberal Friedrich Hayek (1899–1992), the commutative justice approach 'treats individual freedom of choice as a primary ethical objective'.[29] In practice, commutative justice is a central feature of neoliberal approaches that emphasize the importance of individual liberty and the coercive character of tax policy. Of specific interest, contributions by the American economist James Buchanan (1919–2013) recommend constitutional tax limitations and emphasize that the political-bureaucratic process may prove incapable of securing ethically desirable redistribution. As reflected in constitutional tax initiatives such as the successful Proposition 13 (1978) in California, such constitutional approaches to justice in tax reform reveal the importance of subtle and not so subtle differences in the constitutional structure of democratic societies and the ability of the wealthy and, especially, the wealthiest to influence the political-bureaucratic process.

In the US first-past-the-post two-party democracy:

> government policies need not reflect commonly held views of the citizenry . . . securing a majority on any given issue may result in 'logrolling' or the use of 'side payments' that ultimately run counter to otherwise accepted distributive objectives. Under these or similar circumstances it is reasonable for individuals to seek constraints on the political process to protect against certain outcomes rather than to insure that the government has the capability to achieve some elusive distributive 'ideal', even if that ideal is widely accepted.[30]

The potential for the wealthiest to influence such a process is well known. By contrast, in constitutional monarchies such as Canada and the United

Kingdom (UK) that use a first-past-the-post electoral system with multiple parties, voting along strict party lines means that a majority government does not have to engage in logrolling to achieve passage of legislation. There are less checks and balances, and the government of the day has more centralized power than in the US, allowing the implementation of substantive tax changes with greater scope and legislative speed. This process can, and often does, provide greater scope for the wealthy to influence tax policy. This illustrates that there is no one-size-fits-all democratic solution for reforming taxes on the wealthy. As such, rethinking wealth and taxes needs to account for how constitutional differences in the democratic process across taxing jurisdictions interact with the ability of the wealthy to influence the formation of tax policy. Such interactions can take place at all levels of government, using different methods to obtain influence.

Neoliberalism, Globalization and Distributive Justice[31]

Increasingly, commonly used methods of taxing the wealthy are an outcome of the modern neoliberal approach to organizing economic activity in a global capitalist system.[32] It is difficult to ignore the rise of neoliberalism starting in the 1980s in the political sphere, and subsequent observations of increasing wealth and income inequality. This begs the question: what is neoliberalism, and how is this approach to public policy relevant to globalization and taxing the wealthy? Exploring the history of neoliberalism reveals two distinct periods. Prior to the 1970s, neoliberalism 'was used primarily to signify a category of economic ideas that arose in the 1930s–60s, associated with the Freiburg Ordoliberalism school, the Mont Pelerin Society, the work of Friedrich Hayek and the counter-Keynesian economics of the Chicago School'.[33] In Germany, 'some elements of this "proto"-neoliberalism were influential in the making of the *Wirtschaftswunder*, or economic miracle, of West Germany's postwar "social market economy" attributed to its Minister for Economics, Ludwig Erhard'. In turn:

> By the early 1980s, neoliberalism was used in a very different way, as it came to describe the wave of market deregulation, privatization and welfare-state withdrawal that swept the first, second and third worlds. It then went on to expand accretively as a concept to signify not just a policy model, but a broader political, ideological, cultural, spatial phenomenon. By the early 1990s, neoliberalism had become elevated to an epochal phenomenon and was often used as loose shorthand for a prevailing dystopian *zeitgeist*. This has led to characterizations of neoliberalism as 'capitalism in its millennial manifestation' . . . a revolutionary turning-point in the world's social and economic history.[34]

Over time, neoliberalism has evolved from being 'an esoteric term', used scarcely, and more or less only by economists, to become a widely used term in other social sciences, 'except in economics where it has disappeared ... neoliberalism has come to be featured in so many different contexts and theoretical containers that it shoulders an inordinate descriptive and analytical burden in the social sciences'.[35] To avoid the semantic confusions created by a multitude of interpretations, accept that 'neoliberalism' is an economic philosophy claiming that self-regulated 'free markets' are the most efficient approach to solving the economic and social problems confronting modern society. Put differently, governments should seek to minimize interference with markets by removing protectionist barriers to trade, privatizing government-owned enterprises and liberalizing the movement of capital between countries. Though such ideas have a long historical pedigree, this interpretation traces the proximate intellectual origins of neoliberalism in the US to the 1970s and contributions by economists such as Milton Friedman and James Buchanan, backed by political philosophers such as Robert Nozick.[36] The neoliberal period in economic theory encompasses the emergence of monetarism, supply-side economics, public choice theory, the rational expectations hypothesis and real business cycles. In the US, neoliberal ideas have been actively promoted by influential think tanks such as the American Enterprise Institute, the Heritage Foundation and the Hoover Institution. Similar think tanks appear in Canada, for example the Fraser Institute; in the UK, for example the Adam Smith Institute and Institute of Economic Affairs; and in Australia, for example the Institute of Public Affairs.

Recalling that neoliberalism employs the ethical values of commutative justice, while the traditional utilitarian approach that underpins optimal tax theory employs a restricted form of distributive justice, provides an opportunity to recall a quotation by J.M. Keynes:[37]

> the ideas of economists and political philosophers, both when they are right and when they are wrong, are more powerful than is commonly understood. Indeed the world is ruled by little else. Practical men, who believe themselves to be quite exempt from any intellectual influences, are usually the slaves of some defunct economist. Madmen in authority, who hear voices in the air, are distilling their frenzy from some academic scribbler of a few years back. I am sure that the power of vested interests is vastly exaggerated compared with the gradual encroachment of ideas.

While neoliberal defenders and advocates of the free market emphasize the connection between personal liberty and wealth creation, considerably less emphasis is given to the connection between free markets, the rise of globalization, and the increasingly unequal distribution of wealth and income. As for the global spread of neoliberalism and free markets, this required much more than the scribbling of a defunct economist or 'the spontaneous result of market forces, but [required] political decisions and diplomatic compromises that produced a liberal structure that enabled national and global markets'.[38] Following on initiatives that originated after World War II, such as the Marshall Plan, the US has led the charge for successive rounds of trade and capital account liberalization. This was partly aided by the US Congress delegating responsibility for trade negotiations to the executive branch. The General Agreement on Tariffs and Trade (GATT) was replaced with the far more effective World Trade Organization (WTO), a regime that significantly expanded the global reach of free markets to include China, the former USSR and a variety of Third World markets.

Proponents of the neoliberal agenda for globalization make great claims about the success of the programme: 'These changes [that produced trade liberalization] catapulted the world, in just 40 years, from an age of poverty, autarchy, insecurity, and political fragility to an era of globaliza-tion, poverty alleviation, strong institutions, and peace between the great powers.' For proponents, the US played a role in providing an 'invisible hand' for this process:[39]

> None of this would have been imaginable without American power deployed at the service of liberal ideas. It is tempting to believe that the hard and soft power advantages the United States enjoyed within its Cold War coalition can continue to provide the essential substructure for a prolonged and effective functioning of markets on a more global scale. An abiding commitment to liberal ideas, including effective national governance and strong multilateral institutions, can extend the gains from collaboration and consolidate norms of global behavior. In the process, US power could become the 'invisible hand' injecting ideas, political capital, and security into the system.

Accompanying the neoliberal shift toward deregulating markets has been a competition-driven, cost-reducing trend toward producing in lower-wage locales with weaker environmental, consumer product and job safety regulations. These trends have been combined with an erosion of collective bargaining and participation in labour unions, reducing labour costs in high-wage countries; and a reduction in effective tax rates for capital income and the like that benefit the wealthy. In contrast to the 'regulated capitalism' that emerged in the period from World War II to the rise of globalization starting in the 1980s, neoliberalism has not spread uniformly. Some nations have adopted neoliberalism wholesale, while others have resisted specific aspects.

Missing from this common missive about neoliberalism is the impact of globalization on the tax base of individual countries. Basic concepts such as the distributions of wealth and income lose meaning in a world where capital is mobile and freedom of movement and domicile for the wealthy is relatively unrestricted. When the wealthy own and live in properties in various jurisdictions, what does the concept of residency for tax purposes mean?[40] When the production of family income is domiciled primarily in a lower-income tax jurisdiction and spent in a higher-income tax jurisdiction, what is the appropriate method of determining and collecting the tax owing? When large amounts of capital can be situated within anonymous corporations and trusts, operating in numerous jurisdictions with domiciles in countries of tax convenience, how is the capital income tax burden in a specific country to be determined? Widespread use of immigrant investor programmes and other methods fast-tracking immigration of the wealthy facilitate the ability to avoid and evade personal income taxes. Such questions and observations illustrate that traditional ethical quandaries concerning application of distributive or commutative justice norms in determining tax policy lose practical meaning when confronted with globalization.

THE PROGRESSIVE INCOME TAX

Early History of the US Income Tax[41]

Working on the presumption that knowledge about income tax policy is a cumulative process, it follows that insights from previous debates about the income tax will have been incorporated, encompassed and extended by current knowledge. However, tax policy is made by institutions populated by individuals with free will creating an ever-changing context where knowledge is recreated in real time. In this process, insights from past intellectual history of income tax policy can be lost. The masterful study by Edwin Seligman, *The Income Tax: A Study of the History, Theory and Practice of Income Taxation at Home and Abroad*, initially published in 1911 with a second edition in 1914, is an excellent case in point.[42] While the first edition was written with the objective of contributing to the debate over passage of the 16th Amendment in the US, the second edition is significant due to the addition of an Appendix, 'The Law of 1913', which deals with details of actual legislation that was passed by the US Congress and ratified by the states. In addition to providing a definitive history of the income tax in England, France, Germany and other countries up to 1911, Seligman also gives a detailed account of the history of federal and state income tax plans in the US. Appearing at a time of profound changes in the US tax code, Seligman provided scholarly discussion of fundamental issues surrounding passage of the 16th Amendment.

One relatively undiscussed issue in debate over the 16th Amendment was the progressive or graduated rate structure. As this has been a central feature of income tax policy since the inception of the income tax, Seligman observes:

> The consideration of tax rates involves not only the question of exemption, but that of graduation. It is significant that the principle of progressive taxation evoked almost no discussion. The legitimacy of the theory was taken for granted, and in the few cases where it was mentioned, it was assumed to be a corollary of the theory of ability to pay. This shows the development which has taken place since the discussion of the law of 1894. In considering the question of graduation, only two difficulties confronted the framers of the bill. The one was how to make a workable system of progressive taxation harmonize with the administrative methods employed; the other, how to oppose with success the demands of the radicals.

This relatively unwavering support for a progressive rate structure was, nonetheless, tempered by voices that called for limitation on taxation of the wealthy. As reflected in the Congressional record, support for limiting the highest marginal rate was expressed by members of the Senate Finance Committee that considered the initial income tax rate structure introduced in 1913. Specifically, speaking at a time when the great fortunes of the Rockefellers, Mellons, Carnegies and the like weighed heavily on radical attitudes, Senator Bristow maintained a position to trust in 'the American people' to limit possible future rate increases on the wealthy:

> I am not worrying about where we are going to stop [increasing income tax rates on the wealthy]. I believe the American people are capable of self-government. I believe their purpose is to do what is right to every citizen. The American people, as a whole, would not do an injustice to a rich man any quicker than they would to a poor man . . . I would rather trust the honesty of the American people as a whole in dealing with a rich man, than to trust a good many rich men in their dealings with the American people. If there is any prejudice in this country against the rich, it is because the rich have not been just in their dealings with the public. There is no fundamental prejudice in the Anglo-Saxon race against property or the rights of property. It is the very basis upon which every Saxon nation has been built [*sic*] in the history of our civilization. Yet here in this, the most enlightened nation of all in my opinion, we are afraid to enter upon a system of taxation which England has been following for years, because, forsooth, the American people may confiscate the property of their well-to-do citizens. Such a suggestion is abhorrent to me . . . In endeavoring to work out this amendment, I have tried to be conservative and just, so that no man could say it was a radical measure, and no man has declared here that it was an unjust

measure. The only objection to it has been from those who were afraid that in the future somebody else might do an injustice.[43]

Similarly, the influential Senator Williams stated in the record:

> I realize another thing: No honest man can make war upon great fortunes, per se. The Democratic party never has done it, and when the Democratic party begins to do it, it will cease to be the Democratic party and become the Socialistic party of the United States; or better expressed, the Communistic party, or Quasi-Communistic party of the United States . . . The war that an honest man makes upon accumulated wealth must be a war upon the manner in which the wealth was accumulated . . . I am not going to attempt to make this bill a great panacea for all the inequalities of fortune existing in this country; nor would it do any good if we did, because we would be doctoring the symptoms, and not the cause of the disease.[44]

Despite the perception and claims of modern writers, the notion of tax limitation that is central to the Buchanan commutative justice approach to tax policy appears in debates over the introduction of the 16th Amendment.

It is difficult to avoid making comparison between the dramatic wealth inequality that had emerged at the beginning of the 20th century with the increasing wealth and income inequality at the beginning of the 21st century.[45] Seligman captures received opinion leading up to passage of the 16th Amendment on the need to introduce an income tax as the best method to get the rich to share the 'public burden':

> Everywhere we meet the growing complaint that great wealth does not bear its share of the public burden. If, then, the tariff, as it actually exists, imposes too large a share of the burden on the expenditure of the poorer classes, and if the state and local revenue systems do not succeed in reaching the abilities of the more well-to-do classes, the argument becomes exceedingly strong in favor of some form of tax which will redress the inequality . . . Under existing conditions in the United States the burdens of taxation, taking them all in all, are becoming more unequally distributed, and the wealthier classes are bearing a gradually smaller share of the public burden. Something is needed to restore the equilibrium and this something can scarcely take any form but that of an income tax. Without prejudicing the question whether it should be a state or a federal tax, it is difficult to escape the conclusion that some form of income taxation is needed to redress existing inequalities.[46]

Such observations pose a quandary: if the income tax was initially introduced to alleviate perverse wealth inequality, what has happened in the interim to undermine this objective? Why is increasing inequality at a time of 'great wealth' no longer considered a 'social bad' that needs redress?

Haig–Simons Income and the Realization Principle[47]

From the beginnings of the income tax, difficulties of defining income have been a central feature of debates on tax policy. Just prior to the massive ramp-up in income taxes brought on by World War II, there appeared a monumental scholarly effort in tax policy by Henry Simons in 1938, *Personal Income Taxation: The Definition of Income as a Problem of Fiscal Policy*. Recognizing previous contributions stretching back to Georg Schanz in 1896, Simons advances a definition of income that is 'generally considered by most tax scholars to be the ideal definition of income' if distributional equity is the objective.[48] The definition employs the accretion concept of income, where income is defined as the sum of consumption and wealth accumulation ($Y = C + \Delta W$). In the US, this approach to defining income was first introduced by Robert Haig in 1921, which produces the modern eponym 'Haig–Simons income'.[49] Haig wrote that income is 'the increase or accretion in one's power to satisfy his wants in a given period in so far as that power consists of (a) money itself, or, (b) anything susceptible of valuation in terms of money. More simply stated, the definition of income which the economist offers is this: Income is the money value of the net accretion to one's economic power between two points of time.'[50] By focusing on the point in time when the power to satisfy wants is increased, not necessarily the point in time when the wants are actually satisfied, Haig included savings in income even though they had not yet been consumed.

In the Simons definition, income takes a more precise form, as the: 'algebraic sum of (1) the market value of rights in consumption and (2) the change in the value of the store of property rights between the beginning and end of the period in question'. Simons also noted that income 'is merely the result obtained by adding consumption during the period to "wealth" at the end of the period and then subtracting "wealth" at the beginning' ($Y = C + \Delta W$). The eminent public finance economist John Head recognized that the impetus for the Simons definition was a reaction 'against the subjectivism and indeterminacy of traditional ability-to-pay theories, including the sacrifice doctrines'. Significantly:

> Simons emphasized the need for precision and measurability in the basic equity concepts of tax reform theory. After allowing a strictly limited role for benefit-related levies, *the fundamental objective of taxation is seen as the reduction of inequality*; the tax load should be distributed in such a way as to promote a just distribution of income.

The basic logic of the Simons definition is that 'the broadest and most objective income concept provides the base for the most nearly equitable levies'. This leaves the question of 'the precise degree of progression to be determined by explicit resort to an ethical evaluation of the existing distribution of income'.[51]

While Simons recognized the obvious potential conflict between the fundamental goal of equity and other possible policy objectives, especially the related goals of capital formation and production efficiency, globalization confounds the application of the Haig–Simons definition of income. Writing at a time of well-defined national boundaries and substantial restrictions on international capital mobility and trade, globalization was not a concern to Simons. In the modern case, where income is earned and wealth stored in a variety of tax jurisdictions, the broadest income measure would capture worldwide income; but which tax jurisdiction is entitled to what share of the income generated? Is equality to be measured within taxing jurisdictions or is some global measure the objective? The problem is made more complex when income and wealth are associated with corporations, trusts and other legal entities which are more readily relocated to favourable taxing jurisdictions than individuals who are subject to citizenship, residency and other restrictions. Against this backdrop, with the possible early exception of the Canadian Report of the Royal Commission on Taxation (the Carter Commission) issued in 1967, the Haig–Simons approach to defining income for tax purposes has received no more than minority support in various rounds of tax reform associated with the era of globalization.[52]

Because the Haig–Simons approach to defining income for tax purposes is explicitly aimed at the objective of an equitable distribution of income, deviations from this definition in practice are motivated by other objectives than distributional equity. In particular, motivated by capital formation and production efficiency concerns, the single largest deviation from the Haig–Simons definition of income is the 'realization doctrine', where the increase in wealth is not subject to tax until a property or asset is sold, gifted (absent step-up or carry-over basis) or otherwise disposed of.[53] In practice, all countries in the world of global capitalism use the realization principle, not the accrual principle, to tax increases in equity capital wealth. It is well known that much of the wealth of the wealthiest individuals, such as Bill Gates, Warren Buffet, Steve Zuckerberg, Elon Musk and Steve Bezos, has not been taxed because the bulk of the wealth holding is in common stock of specific corporations. In other words, the wealthiest are permitted to defer tax on accumulating capital wealth indefinitely, while many of the less wealthy can only accumulate wealth by making savings from after-tax income. Even for those less-than-wealthy who generate Haig–Simons income increases from tax-deferred changes in wealth, such changes pale into insignificance in comparison to the size of their wage income. In contrast, the wealthiest can generate the bulk of Haig–Simons income from tax-deferred increases in the value of equity capital (wealth) holdings, and not from traditional wage income.[54]

If Haig–Simons income is the theoretically correct approach to defining income for an ideal income tax system if distributional equity is the objective, it follows that mark-to-market (accrual) accounting of ΔW is needed for practical implementation of the Haig–Simons definition. It is commonly claimed that eliminating the realization principle in favour of Haig–Simons mark-to-market accounting for appreciation (and depreciation) in equity claims, real property and the like raises various potential problems. These problems include: difficulties in determining the fair market value of changes in wealth, especially for assets that are not amenable to public trading; and possible liquidity problems associated with having to pay tax on accrued asset value increase before enough cash flow is available, either from sale of the asset or from income generated by the asset. However, where the wealthiest are concerned, in most cases the bulk of wealth market value can be accurately determined. In particular, much of the wealth of the wealthiest is located within corporate entities, hedge funds, trusts and the like, where mark-to-market accounting is already in use for various items.[55] The confusing inconsistency in the determination of income for corporate and personal tax purposes is illustrated by the treatment of executive incentive stock options and the like, where mark-to-market accounting is required for purposes of determining reported earnings in the public filings for publicly traded corporations, at the same time as the realization principle is applied to the income that is paid to the executive receiving the contingent equity claim.[56]

Complications associated with the realization principle have received substantial, if misconceived, attention from academic economists. In opposition to the liquidity and valuation concerns arising with the accrual principle, one complication associated with the realization principle is the encouragement to accelerate capital losses and to defer capital gains, resulting in suboptimal liquidation decisions. Complex provisions in some income tax codes have been introduced to avert the possibility that capital losses can be used to substantially reduce current taxable income concurrently with tax on capital gains being deferred. Another complication is the so-called 'lock-in' effect where the ability to defer the tax on a capital gain encourages the owner of an asset to defer selling the asset, even though there may be alternative assets that have a higher before-tax return. This results in distorted capital asset pricing – typically resulting in higher prices for assets, such as stocks, that have experienced significant price appreciation – as well as inefficient portfolio allocations. Various theoretical recommendations that aim to imitate an accrual principle

---

BOX 4.1   SELIGMAN ON TAX EQUITY

Writing at a time where dramatic change in the tax code was being propelled by
increasing wealth and income inequality and a regressive tax structure, Edwin
Seligman was a strong proponent of the income tax. Seligman (1914 [1911]) provides insight that seems germane to optimal taxation theory:

> Amid the clashing of divergent interests and the endeavor of each social class to
> roll off the burden of taxation on some other class, we discern the slow and
> laborious growth of standards of justice in taxation, and the attempt on the part
> of the community as a whole to realize this justice. The history of finance, in other
> words, shows the evolution of the principle of faculty or ability to pay – the prin-
> ciple that each individual should be held to help the state in proportion to his
> ability to help himself.
>   . . . Granted that in some more or less rough way an endeavor is made, almost
> from the beginning, to apportion public burdens in accordance with the presumed
> capacity of individuals or classes, the problem arises as to how the capacity to
> bear this burden is to be measured. Even where it is difficult to recognize any
> conscious attempt on the part of government to carry this principle into practice,
> and even where actual fiscal institutions represent more or less thinly disguised
> efforts of the dominant economic class to roll the burdens on the shoulders of the
> weak, – even here it is rare to find a cynical disregard of all considerations of
> equity; and even here a more or less successful effort is made to clothe the hard
> facts of economic oppression in the garb of some specious explanation. Thus,
> whether it be actually realized or not, it is possible to interpret the successive
> stages of fiscal development in terms of an attempt to enforce various criteria of
> ability to pay.

To provide historical context, recall that the 'income tax' Seligman was endorsing
was narrowly focused on the wealthiest Americans.

---

outcome while retaining the realization principle have been proposed to
remedy these complications.[57]

Though not without interest, such analysis of the realization principle
ignores the fundamental reason for using Haig–Simons income: distributional equity (Box 4.1). There is an implicit misconceived assumption that
assets will at some point be sold, and if sold, that tax will be paid in the
appropriate jurisdiction. The contingencies that assets will not be sold or
that tax implications will be shifted to a low-tax jurisdiction are not considered. Recognizing that many of the wealthy and, especially, the wealthiest have ownership stakes in companies that, in many cases, will not be
sold, the realization principle serves as a linchpin for increasing inequality
of wealth. Insofar as ownership also confers ability to generate income
from an increasing stock of untaxed assets, the realization principle also

contributes to increasing income inequality. In such cases, the realization of capital gains is expected to occur at death, leading to consideration of the various avenues available for the wealthy to further avoid tax on increased wealth. Depending on the country, possible avenues include estate tax exemptions, carry-over basis and sophisticated use of trusts and foundations. The problem of valuing non-traded and difficult-to-value assets raised against using the accrual principle now becomes an argument in favour of accrual, to prevent the wealthy from declaring a self-serving realization on such assets if sold.

Agenda for Progressive Taxation

The *Agenda for Progressive Taxation* (1947) by the Nobel Prize winning economist William Vickrey (1914–96) was an important and thoughtful contribution to the debate surrounding commencement of the income tax, around the middle of the 20th century, as a major source of US government revenue. Writing some 45 years later, Vickrey observed: 'Since the publication of the *Agenda* in 1947, remarkably little of its recommendations have seen implementation, while in spite of sporadic moves toward "simplification", the bulk of the internal revenue code and regulations has increased explosively.'[58] The *Agenda* appears at a time of subtle change in the focus of tax reform concerns. Instead of zeroing in on contributions of the wealthy to government revenue, expanding the income tax base to include non-wealthy taxpayers introduced a general shared interest with the wealthy of reducing the income tax burden. Over time, 'cutting taxes' became a central theme in right-of-centre political platforms that conflate tax reductions applicable largely to the wealthy with reductions that largely benefit the non-wealthy taxpayer. Much of the progressive insight provided in the *Agenda* that relates directly to the role of taxation in increasing inequality of wealth and income has been ignored.

The *Agenda* is clear on the implications of the realization principle and the favourable treatment of capital gains. In addition to finding serious defects in the treatment of gift and estate taxes in the US tax code, a key feature of the *Agenda* was aimed at correcting inequities associated with the treatment of capital gains: 'More controversy has raged over the treatment of capital gains, and more varied and illogical treatment has been given to them than any other form of income'.[59] As for subsequent, more recent suggestions by 'optimal tax' proponents that capital gains not be taxed, the *Agenda* observes: 'Although it has been observed in season and out that capital gains of one kind or another should be excluded from taxable income, no method of doing this that does not involve gross discrimination, hairline distinctions, and opportunities for avoidance has been devised'.

While the *Agenda* gives support to the theoretical notion of capital income taxation using Haig–Simons income where capital income would be taxed on an accrual basis instead of when realized, the *Agenda* recognizes obvious practical difficulties of determining the change in asset value when 'there is room for considerable disagreement as to just what accrued income is'.

It is not surprising that the *Agenda* was concerned with difficulties relevant to implementation of a broad-based income tax, largely failing to account for features that have since become important contributors to wealth and income inequality. For example, among the problems created by the graduated income tax rate structure identified in the *Agenda* was the discrepancy in tax paid for those with variable income streams, such as those working on commissions, farmers subject to weather and pests, sellers of a large asset, those who do not work every year, and so on. Compared to those on relatively constant salaried income, over some years the variable income stream would be disadvantageous by assessing tax on annual rather than lifetime income. Consequently, Vickrey suggested 'cumulative averaging' of income as a solution for a range of problems created by 'divergences between income defined for federal income tax purposes and an income tax base that in the author's opinion would be both neutral and equitable'.[60] As such, cumulative averaging could be adapted to adjusting the adverse income tax implications of the realization principle for the non-wealthy taxpayers in the tax year in which the accumulated value of a large asset was realized by a sale that forced the individual into a higher tax bracket. The current situation relevant to the wealthy and wealthiest where unrealized capital gains increase dramatically could not have been anticipated.

With the *Agenda* begins what is 70 years and counting of debate over issues identified with achieving the goal of broad-based progressive taxation.[61] As such, the *Agenda* can be used to benchmark the progress that has been made over that time as it relates to progressively taxing the wealthy. Shortly after the appearance of the *Agenda*, the famous British economist Nicholas Kaldor (1908–86) revived the equity argument for an expenditure or consumption tax over an income tax.[62] This perspective on progressive taxation has a long lineage, stretching back to Hobbes's *Leviathan* and John Stuart Mill's *Principles of Political Economy*.[63] As the legal scholar Alvin Warren observes, this debate over the distributional fairness of the income tax compared to a consumption tax skirts the issue of taxing the wealthy:

> The argument that the consumption tax is to be preferred as a matter of fairness has generally involved a comparison of the core ideas of the two taxes – income and consumption. Wealth – the third traditional candidate for taxation on the

basis of economic resources – has typically been left out of the comparison on the ground that whatever considerations would support wealth taxation can best be taken into account by enacting a tax on wealth or transfers of wealth, and that those quite distinct considerations should not obscure the direct comparison of the income and consumption taxes on equity grounds.[64]

This suggests a bifurcated tax system, where horizontal equity would be achieved by reduction in more easily avoided income taxes replaced by increased use of harder-to-avoid, largely *ad valorem* consumption taxes. In turn, vertical equity would be addressed with increased taxes (transfers) targeted at the upper (lower) tails of the wealth and income distributions.

From the beginnings of the broad-based income tax, numerous inequities were apparent. In the *Agenda*, Vickrey considered four general problems in detail that arise in using income taxes as a broad-based source of tax revenue: non-money income, items given special treatment, deductions, and capital gains and losses. Though these potential sources for inequity have implications for taxing income of the wealthy, the impacts of 'solutions' differ substantively depending on the wealth and income of the taxpayer. Over time, numerous adjustments have been made to specifics of the broad-based income tax in different countries to deal with such perceived inequities for both the wealthy and the less-than-wealthy. However, because the wealthy generate income in various ways not applicable to the less-than-wealthy, adjustments to income tax rules primarily for the wealthy do not attract the scrutiny that broad-based measures attract. Similarly, the complexity of income generation by many of the wealthy requires complex rules to address concerns. The upshot is considerable dispersion in the details of income tax implementation across countries. Even though most countries have evolved income tax rules that feature favourable treatment of income items generated by the wealthy, the ability to disperse income and wealth across countries provides additional avenues for the wealthy to avoid and evade income tax.

Despite being the backbone of national government revenue generation, there is no one-size-fits-all approach to implementing a broad-based income tax. Some countries have opted for less complex, if potentially less equitable, implementation to facilitate tax compliance. In Canada, for example, there is no tax assessed on income from gifts or inheritance, but capital gains typically are to be realized before a gift or inheritance is transferred. There is also a federal sales tax introduced in 1991 to ease the burden on the income tax to raise government revenue. By contrast, by foregoing a federal sales tax, the US places greater reliance on a federal income tax that has considerable complexity, to address perceived problems of inequity. The difficulty of this task has created serious political problems for the progressive income tax. By the mid-1990s, William Archer, Chairman of the House Ways and Means Committee from 1995–2001, repeatedly expressed his desire to 'tear the income tax out by its roots and throw it overboard'.[65] This perspective was captured in 1998 when the House of Representatives voted 219 to 209 in favour of the Tax Code Termination Act that would have seen the federal income tax terminated at the end of 2002, to be replaced by some unspecified new federal tax. In 2003, the legal scholar Steven Bank observed: 'current [US] federal income tax is too complex, too easily evaded by the wealthy, and too likely to distribute the burdens of taxation to the people least able to bear it'.

THE DEBATE ON CAPITAL INCOME TAXES

More on Optimal Taxation of Capital Income

Starting with Irving Fisher and Nicholas Kaldor, a long line of eminent academic economists have recommended eliminating the tax on capital income.[66] Based on the proposition that consumption is the most appropriate foundation for broad-based taxes, such theoretical claims are seemingly at odds with the objective of distributional equity and stifling the increase in wealth and income inequality. Building on the earlier work of the seminal public finance economist Arnold Harberger, the influential economist Martin Feldstein makes the following observation about the cloudy state of debate on the taxation of capital income:

> Although economists have long discussed the pros and cons of eliminating the tax on capital income, the subject remains clouded in confusion. As a result, there is no valid estimate of the welfare cost of the current method of taxing capital income. Similarly, the likely magnitude of the gain from reducing the rate of capital income tax through such reforms as the integration of the corporate and personal income taxes remains unassessed.[67]

The claim that elimination of capital income tax is 'optimal' reached a peak in the 1980s with theoretical contributions by Judd and Chamley.[68] Follow-on theoretical contributions claim to demonstrate that the elimination of capital income tax result is robust to relaxing certain key assumptions of the optimal taxation model.

In contrast to those academic economists claiming optimality on efficiency and social welfare maximization grounds for the elimination of capital income taxes, there is a collection of contributions that adopt the basic optimal taxation model to arrive at different conclusions regarding capital income taxes. The renowned contribution by Atkinson and Stiglitz in 1976 on the difference between direct and indirect taxation demonstrated that, under common assumptions about the utility function of individuals with identical tastes (separability between leisure and all other commodities), it is optimal to tax only labour incomes, negating the need to impose differential tax rates on different commodities. In exploring the validity of such results, Feldstein finds:[69]

(1) A reduction in the rate of tax on capital income which is compensated by a rise in the rate of tax on labour income or consumption would necessarily increase personal saving.

(2) To achieve economic efficiency, taxes should be levied on consumption or labour income but not on capital income.

(3) A capital income tax has an annual welfare cost or excess burden only to the extent that the (compensated) annual supply of savings responds to the net rate of return.

(4) Although not taxing capital income might increase economic efficiency, it would violate the fundamental principle of horizontal equity that individuals with the same income should pay the same tax.

While (4) does recognize conflict between efficiency and horizontal equity in the debate over capital income taxes, Feldstein and other economic gurus apparently dismiss, on theoretical efficiency grounds, practical vertical equity concerns that plague the connection between increasing inequality of wealth and income and the need to address capital income taxes.

From this capital income tax elimination consensus among one group, various prominent and not-so-prominent academic economists also using optimal taxation models have produced a variety of results that invalidate the zero-capital income tax result. One group emphasizes 'tight borrowing constraints' and 'uninsurable idiosyncratic income risk' to produce a model solution with a positive capital income tax. Another group employs 'life cycle models' to demonstrate that the optimal capital income tax is different from zero 'if the tax code cannot explicitly be conditioned on the age of the household'.[70] These efforts do not directly address the appropriate size of the optimal capital income tax, relative to the optimal labour income tax. Recognizing that the widely cited Atkinson and Stiglitz result depends on consumers having the same preferences for consumption, some contributions focus on the implications of introducing various types of heterogeneity. Different preferences for saving – via the selection of the discount rate in a separable utility function – and differences in earnings ability due to differences in skills, are common sources of heterogeneity. With such heterogeneity, it is possible to show theoretically that: 'introducing a savings tax on high earners or a savings subsidy on low earners increases welfare, regardless of the correlation between ability and discount factor'.[71]

Granted that the bewildering blizzard of seemingly contradictory results on the optimal taxation of income tends to undermine confidence in the results of a given study, consider some recent results using a 'realistically calibrated life-cycle model in which households face borrowing constraints and idiosyncratic income risk'.[72] In such a model, the optimal capital income tax is 'significantly positive at a rate of 36 percent'. In combination with such a capital income tax, a 'progressive' labour income tax is, to a first approximation, 'a flat tax of 23 percent with a deduction of $7200 (relative to a GDP [gross domestic product] per capita of $42 000)'. The rationale given for this specific tax structure to be optimal is that, in life cycle models with endogenous labor supply, 'it is typically optimal to tax labor at different ages at different rates'. Given that age-dependent labour income taxes are not available, a positive capital income tax allows the government to achieve the same impact as a progressive labour income tax. As is conventional in optimal tax models, the social welfare function is *ex ante* the expected lifetime utility 'of a newborn in a stationary equilibrium'.[73] The problem for the policy-maker in this variant of the optimal tax model is to trade off tax distortions on labour supply and capital accumulation decisions. As with virtually all theoretical optimal taxation model results, no direct attention is given to the practical implications for the tails of the wealth and income distributions, or that globalization could undermine the applicability of the results to real-world situations.

Set against the increasing wealth and income inequality that has accompanied globalization, it is difficult to avoid the perception that much economic theorizing on optimal tax policy lies in the realm of rhetoric; a study in how academic economists persuade each other and policy-makers. The rhetorical conversations involved are found in journals, monographs and textbooks. In some instances, knowledge claims are presented in the rhetoric of hypothetical deductive models that can be described as metaphorical analogies between, say, accumulation of wealth, income budgets over time and marginal tax rates. In other cases, the knowledge claim is presented in the rhetoric of empirical findings, one of many possible readings permitted by the data. In the spirit of McCloskey (1985), the extensive academic literature on optimal tax policy begs an obvious question: 'What is the point of promoting prior convictions dressed up as findings?' The answer, seemingly, is that theoretical methods of persuasion, using the metaphor of the model combined with an authoritative style to suppress alternative stories, can be effective tools for promoting efforts to reduce or eliminate taxes on capital income that, ultimately, benefit the wealthy and contribute to increasing wealth and income inequality.

Defining Capital Income

Taxes on differing types of capital or capital income are ancient. For example, the Romans imposed taxes on the booty that conquering armies repatriated to Rome.[74] However, it is not until the introduction of the broad-based income tax that the modern concept of 'capital income' emerges. In turn, closer examination of modern capital income taxes begs important questions that are suppressed in conventional 'optimal taxation' models. Specifically, these questions include: what is capital? How is capital income differentiated from labour income? Is a flat tax appropriate for the various types of capital income? When does a capital income tax proxy for a tax on wealth or capitalized income? Such questions are not new. However, the historical context is essential to understanding the connection between what is 'capital' at a given point in time, the political structure that exercises control over capital, and the tax system that generates revenue for government activities. For example, in rudimentary, communal prehistoric societies, capital was scarce and often held in the form of livestock or storable food stuffs. In such societies, where there was limited trading and the needs of government were small, graduated poll taxes – precursors of the tithes (Roman *decumae*) – were appropriate.[75] The concept of wealth or capital income tax is vaguely related to grazing fees (Roman *scriptura*) that would be assessed on the amount of livestock capital.

On the definition of capital, the famous economist, Irving Fisher (1867–1947), quoted a precursor political economist, Nassau Senior (1790–1864), as saying: 'Capital has been so variously defined, that it may be doubtful whether it have any generally received meaning'.[76] A conventional modern distinction is to identify equity capital and debt capital, which are typically given different tax treatments. However, until the 20th century, there was considerable lack of clarity in definitions of 'capital', and references to equity in relation to capital were concerned with application of the 'law of equity' to legal situations involving owners of the 'capital stock'. Fundamental disagreements about the definition of 'capital' prior to the introduction of the broad-based income tax are captured in the academic debate between the Austrian economist Eugen Böhm-Bawerk (1851–1914) and Irving Fisher at the end of the 19th century about the relation between capital and interest.[77] The modern usage of 'equity' and 'equity capital' as distinct from 'debt' and 'debt capital' emerged haphazardly from this debate, providing some clarity to the confusing collection of definitions. The evolution of the accounting profession and the expanded usage of accounting terminology also contributed to this clarification.[78] In turn, it is the treatment of equity capital in modern tax codes that has fuelled the spectacular rise of more than a few of the wealthiest.

Modern income tax codes make a fundamental distinction between income from debt and from equity capital, a distinction that is integral to rethinking wealth and taxes. In modern usage, reference to 'capital' can be identified with the balance sheet relationship where (the right-hand side) *Assets = Liabilities + Equity* (the left-hand side). In this context, *Assets* represent the physical capital, financial and, possibly, the intangible capital that generate the net cash flows for the firm, household or individual.[79] In turn, the *Assets* are financed by a combination of debt obligations (*Liabilities*) and equity capital (*Equity*). In modern times, this distinction between the sources of financial capital given by the right-hand side of the balance sheet is well defined in commercial law. Legally, debt capital is comprised of contractual obligations defined by indenture contracts, mortgages, and the like; while equity capital depends on the specifics of the ownership structure. For example, many of the largest modern commercial operations possess a large and permanent stock of physical assets that is financed by the pooling of equity capital from many owners. Such operations are often, though not exclusively, organized as limited liability corporations for which modern corporation law provides essential characteristics of the legal environment. Significantly, modern tax codes make a sharp distinction in the treatment of income from debt capital and equity capital.

Beyond this basic accounting classification of capital into equity and debt lies a bewildering array of distinctions that impact upon tax status of equity capital, again with different treatment in modern income tax codes.[80] A variety of legal structures – corporations, companies, partnerships and trusts – are available that differ on corporate status, fiduciary duties and limited liability.[81] In particular, a traditional partnership lacks both corporate status and limited liability, with tax implications and fiduciary duty for the business entity flowing through to the partners. In turn, there are a number of alternative 'flow-through entities' that possess limited liability but lack corporate status. In the US, included in this group of flow-through entities without corporate status are the limited liability company, the limited liability partnership and the limited liability limited partnership. In turn, the S corporation is a flow through entity with corporate status. Finally, there is the C corporation which has traditional corporate taxation at the entity level with taxable dividend payments at the owner level given favourable tax treatment to offset the implications of double taxation. A dramatic change in equity capital organization in the US occurred during the 1990s following a 1988 Internal Revenue Service (IRS) ruling that accepted the flow-through status of the modern limited liability company first introduced in Wyoming in 1977.[82]

Against this American backdrop, there is generally a more restricted variety of equity capital structures available in other countries. Whereas 'LLC' in the US refers to a limited liability company, this flow-through entity is not common in other countries, where 'LLC' typically refers to a limited liability corporation. In the UK and various other countries, 'LC' refers to 'limited company', with 'PLC' referring to an LC that is also publicly traded and 'Ltd' used to designate a private limited company. In Canada, flow-through entities appear as limited partnerships, investment trusts and income trusts. Seeking to compare such Canadian entities with those used in other countries such as Australia and the US, the Canadian Department of Finance has observed: 'the tax system and tax treatment of flow through entities varies by jurisdiction; therefore, direct comparisons with Canada are difficult to make', also observing that other countries impose restrictions on the ability to use flow-through entities.[83] For example, following a 1981 tax decision, most trusts in Australia were treated as corporations for tax purposes. Circa 2008, flow-through entities in Australia were only available for venture capital. In a major about-face announced on Halloween 2006, the Canadian government eliminated the tax advantages of the flow-through aspect of income trusts.[84] And so it goes, a veritable buffet of legal structures for high-priced lawyers and accountants seeking to use the tax treatment of equity capital to enable legal tax avoidance by the wealthy.

Capital Income Taxes in Practice

Moving from the heights of tax policy theory to practical implementation of government revenue assessment and collection finds academic economists descending from the intellectual high ground to be replaced by lawyers, accountants and investment bankers.[85] Together with financial institutions, such professionals and experts sell 'tax avoidance schemes to corporations and wealthy elites ... [that] have facilitated a skewed distribution of income of wealth'.[86] Many (if not all) such schemes involve capital income, in some fashion. Unlike the economists who are keen to display and promote academic results, this group of professionals occupies the intellectual high ground mainly to sell expertise and, as such, are not keen to engage in the production and distribution of knowledge about the practical aspects of tax policy that are the bread and butter of those providing such professional services. The less that is widely known about the complexities of the tax code, the more valuable are such expert services. What is known about the use of capital income provisions by the wealthy to avoid and evade taxes? In addition to a variety of studies scattered throughout the academic literature, and technical advice from practitioner-focused journals, some significant legal proceedings and whistle-blowing events have revealed where the tentacles of globalization were employed to avoid and evade taxes on capital income.[87]

It is important not to overstate the role of globalization in the wealthy free rider using personal and capital income tax provisions in bilateral and multilateral agreements to escape taxes. In many cases, there are ample avenues for domestically avoiding such income taxes. Even though less than half of all corporations pay income tax, there is accumulating evidence that the emergence of pass-through entities such as S corporations and LLCs has been a significant factor in reducing taxes on the wealthy in the US.[88] The implications of these fundamental equity capital structure changes for income and wealth inequality in the US has been addressed in a study by the US Treasury:[89]

> 'Pass-through' businesses like partnerships and S-corporations now generate over half of US business income and account for much of the post-1980 rise in the top-1% income share. [Using] administrative tax data from 2011 to identify pass-through business owners and estimate how much tax they pay ... present[s] three findings. (1) Relative to traditional business income, pass-through business income is substantially more concentrated among high-earners. (2) Partnership ownership is opaque: 20% of the income goes to unclassifiable partners, and 15% of the income is earned in circularly owned partnerships. (3) The average federal income tax rate on US pass-through business income is 19%, much lower than the average rate on traditional corporations. If pass-through activity had remained at 1980's low level, strong but straightforward assumptions imply that the 2011 average US tax rate on total US business income would have been 28% rather than 24%, and tax revenue would have been approximately $100 billion higher.

Such results require considerable reflection. For example, what are the implications of 20 per cent of pass-through entity income going to 'unclassifiable partners'? It is significant that these results are obtained from US administrative tax data and do not capture some unknown amount associated with substantial activities that could take place offshore or occur as unrealized capital gains.

Examining taxes paid by US corporations, the evidence for increasing use of pass-through entities to reduce taxes on business income is puzzling. According to the Government Accountability Office, in each year from 2006 to 2012, at least two-thirds of all active corporations had no federal income tax liability:

> Larger corporations were more likely to owe tax. Among large corporations (generally those with at least $10 million in assets) less than half – 42.3 percent – paid no federal income tax in 2012. Of those large corporations whose financial statements reported a profit, 19.5 percent paid no federal income tax that year.

The reasons given why profitable corporations may have paid no federal tax in a given year include: 'the use of tax deductions for losses carried forward from prior years and tax incentives, such as depreciation allowances that are more generous in the federal tax code than those allowed for financial accounting purposes. Corporations that did have a federal corporate income tax liability for tax year 2012 owed \$267.5 billion'.[90] Again based on evidence from federal tax returns, these results also require considerable reflection. At this point, the complexity of complexities that is the US federal income tax code needs to be deciphered to interpret the seemingly conflicting results for corporations and pass-through entities.

In contrast to the US, the situation regarding flow-through entities in Canada is less complicated and illustrates the importance of differences in the national context and, perhaps more importantly, how rapidly a subtle change in tax policy for firms can be adopted. The most successful Canadian variant of the flow-through entity was a trust structure – the unit trust, income trust or business trust – which was more or less eliminated by the federal Conservative government on Halloween 2006 by voiding the income tax advantages of such entities. While such trusts technically did initially possess unlimited liability, de facto the trusts did not require such status, as unsuccessful firms would be wound up prior to their assets being exhausted. In the few years prior to the Halloween massacre, the legal situation was gradually being clarified, with changes in legislation in some provinces giving limited liability to income trust investors. While such flow-through trust structures were used to hold financial investment assets for many years prior, the impetus to expanded use for a range of businesses came initially from the physical assets in the oil and gas sector. In search of additional capital to continue exploration activities, firms would sell a producing well with a predictable decline rate to a non-operating trust. The trust would then own the producing well and flow-through the netback to the unit holders, paying a management fee for well maintenance and marketing but avoiding tax at the business level. The largest of such entities in the oil and gas sector was the non-operating Canadian Oil Sands Trust (since purchased by Suncor) that owned over one-third of the Syncrude oil sands project in northern Alberta.

This initial oil and gas trust structure received a Revenue Canada tax ruling in late 1985 permitting flow-through status to a non-operating so-called 'royalty trust', Enerplus Resources Fund (now operating as Enerplus Corp.) that facilitated an initial C\$9 million initial public offering of units.[91] The transition to recognition of operating business trusts as flow-through entities by Revenue Canada started in 1995 with an oil and gas business trust, Enermark Income Fund (merged with Enerplus Resources fund in 2001). However, it was not until after the collapse of the

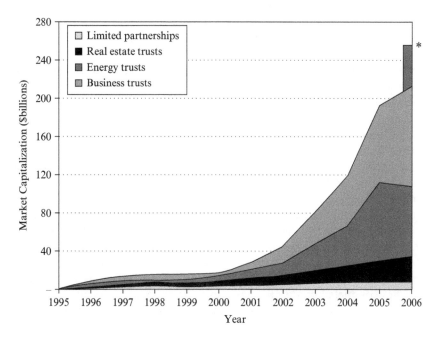

Note: * Conversions to trusts announced in 2006, not yet implemented.

Source: Minister of Finance, Backgrounder News Release, 20 October 2006.

Figure 4.1 *Market capitalization of publicly traded Canadian flow-through entities, 1995–2006*

dot.com bubble in 2000 that investment bankers turned to business trust conversions as a mechanism to generate business in lean times (see Figure 4.1). Under direction of the federal Liberal government the conversion of corporations into business trusts expanded dramatically to include, in addition to dog food companies, pipelines and timber companies, such varied entities such as Boston Pizza, A&W, Sleep Country, Sterling Shoes and Second Cup. From 73 listed trusts in 2001 with market capitalization of C$22 billion, by September 2006 there were 255 listed trusts worth over $200 billion. At the peak of the income trust frenzy, major Canadian corporations such as Bell Canada, Telus and Royal Bank were actively considering converting to income trusts to avoid corporate taxes.[92]

The avalanche of conversions from Canadian corporations to income trusts ended abruptly on Halloween 2006 when the newly elected Conservative government eliminated the income tax advantages of conversion. As these capital income tax reduction-driven conversions typically resulted in increases in market capitalization of from 10 to 20 per cent, it seems likely that conversions from corporations to pass-through entities in the US would have a similar capital income tax reduction-driven value increase.[93] The seemingly odd outcome where a business-friendly federal government makes such a drastic action against conversions that benefit the owners of equity capital is explained by the subsequent move by the Conservative government to reduce federal corporate tax rates. In addition to the weak governance organization of the non-operating trust structure, the move on corporate tax rates is more in line with the global trend toward capital income tax competition for corporations. Having a uniquely Canadian pass-through structure, such as the income trust, would make it more – not less – difficult for Canadian businesses to raise capital in international markets. In turn, even the US, with the highest statutory corporate tax rate in the Organisation for Economic Co-operation and Development (OECD) other than Japan (prior to the Trump tax cuts), has proven vulnerable to the migration of equity capital to lower-tax jurisdictions facilitated by globalization. In any event, as compliance studies conducted by the IRS have revealed, pass-through entities such as the S corporation are significant sources of non-compliance in income tax reporting in the US.

It is revealing to consider the implications of the differing treatment of flow-through entities in Canada, where the tax advantages of such entities over limited liability corporations has been more or less eliminated, and in the US, where the use of flow-through entities expanded substantively due to inherent marginal income tax rate advantages. The Office of Tax Analysis estimated a $100 billion loss in 2011 in federal government tax revenue due to the election to file as S corporation instead of the higher marginal tax rate C corporation.[94] With passage of the Tax Cuts and Jobs Act of 2017 (P.L. 115-97), there has apparently been an upsurge of 'many S corporations considering whether to convert to a C corporation to take advantage of the lower [income tax] rate'. The adjustment in marginal tax rates since 2017 combines with other potential advantages of the C corporation to reverse the tax management implications of legal structure choice: use of accrual accounting rather than cash accounting of the S corporation; enhanced ability to add shareholders and transfer shares; enhanced oversight from securities regulators, and so on. The most signifi-cant disadvantage of the C corporation is the double taxation of dividends that has exacerbated a perverse preference for share buybacks, fuelling the increase in wealth and income inequality.

NOTES

1. The considerable literature on the connection between justice, fairness and tax policy, sometimes referred to as normative tax theory, is reviewed in Duclos (2006) and, for earlier studies, in Birch (1988).
2. See, for example, Timmons (2010).
3. Recent evolutions of these general approaches to normative tax theory include optimal tax theory, and the constitutional approach of Buchanan and Brennan (1980), who provide constitutional arguments for the limitation of taxes.
4. Porter (2016, p. 117), discussing Zucman (2015).
5. The quote is from Thomas Paine, *Rights of Man* (1791) made in connection with the need for 'progressive tax'.
6. This approach is reflected in Duclos (2006, p. 1080).
7. Hufbauer (1966, p. 189). Anderson (1985) discusses the horizontal equity of the income tax.
8. '[G]urus of economics' is a veiled reference to the 1999 book by Bernard Maris, *Lettre ouverte aux gourous de l'économie qui nous prennent pour des imbeciles* (Open Letter to the Gurus of Economics Who Take Us for Idiots). Maris was among the victims of the attack against the *Charlie Hebdo* magazine in Paris on 8 January 2015. Maris is known by historians of economics, with several essays on Keynes and economic methodology (in French).
9. Mankiw et al. (2009, p. 148). Similar descriptions can be found in various sources (e.g., Diamond and Saez, 2011). The long, protracted debate over the feasibility of a (Samuelson–Bergson) social welfare function, given results such as Arrow's Impossibility Theorem, is another feature of optimal tax theory that casts doubt on the general validity of potential policy prescriptions.
10. Ramsey (1927, p. 47).
11. A recent example of this approach is Dowd et al. (2015).
12. Ramsey (1927, p. 59).
13. The list of contributions here is considerable. Specific seminal papers that are typically recognized include Mirrlees (1971), Diamond and Mirrlees (1971) and Atkinson and Stiglitz (1976). An early insightful application of optimal taxation theory to the problem of determining the optimal use of direct versus indirect taxes is provided by Atkinson (1977).
14. Mankiw et al. (2009, p. 148). The list provided is not fully comprehensive. For example, Bastani et al. (2013) find substantial welfare gains to switching from age-independent to age-dependent income taxes. In addition, Mankiw et al. (2009) provides only a crude description of the results of 'dynamic' public finance – for example, Golosov et al. (2006) – and does not explore the distinction between the 'micro' and 'macro' approaches to optimal taxation identified by Golosov et al. (2011).
15. Slemrod (1990, p. 157).
16. Extending the optimal tax model to incorporate globalization, Landier and Plantin (2017) explicitly recognize that: 'Affluent households can respond to taxation with means that are not economically viable for the rest of the population, such as sophisticated tax plans and international tax arbitrage'. The theoretical model demonstrates that attempting to implement progressive taxation can result in regressive taxes due to 'high migrations of wealth'. Brunner et al. (2013) is another recent contribution to a growing number of scholarly studies on the impact of including opportunities for tax evasion in the traditional optimal taxation literature. Brunner et al. demonstrate that a comprehensive tax system, involving a combination of inheritance tax and progressive income tax, in combination with a tax on commodities, is 'optimal'. Though the impact of globalization is ignored, as is conventional in such studies, it is intuitive that globalization enhances, rather than reduces, the need for a comprehensive tax system.
17. Phelps (1979, p. 680).
18. Phelps (1979, p. 681).

19. Phelps (1979, pp. 691–2). Among the relevant contributions by David Hume is the 'Essay on Public Credit'.
20. For the uninitiated, practical issues associated with the various approaches to distributive justice are captured by Slemrod and Bakija (2000).
21. Representative studies of the social justice perspective include Bonus (1982), Spragens (1993) and Cirillo (1984). Scholarly studies considering social justice on a global scale include Brock (2008) and Nayar (2008).
22. Boran (2008, p. 1).
23. The importance of Rawls to political philosophy is captured by Scheffler (2008, p. 68): 'Rawls elevated the concept of justice above other important political ideas such as liberty, law, equality, power, rights, obligation, security, democracy, and the state, and gave it a privileged place on the agenda of contemporary political philosophy. It is testimony to Rawls's influence that justice – especially "distributive," or economic, justice – has remained a central preoccupation of political philosophers ever since'.
24. Boran (2008, p. 2).
25. Selg (2012) provides a radical democratic perspective on Rawls.
26. Scheffler (2008, p. 69).
27. This is not the only possible alternate approach to 'fairness' or justice in tax policy. For example, Green (1984) provides a religious perspective on the ethics of taxation.
28. Gordon (1980, p. 89); see also Birch (1988).
29. Specifically, Hayek (1976) makes the argument that distributive or social justice is meaningless as an ethical guide in a large-group environment if individual freedom is a primary ethical consideration.
30. Birch (1988, p. 1007).
31. Kotz (2015) argues that neoliberal capitalism is now in decline.
32. Venugopal (2015) discusses the various interpretations given to 'neoliberalism', arguing that: 'neoliberalism has become a deeply problematic and incoherent term that has multiple and contradictory meanings, and thus has diminished analytical value'. In turn, there are various general interpretations. Specifically, neoliberalism can be interpreted 'as a given doctrine, revealed by its key thinkers and articulated in canonical texts. This would involve rereading these texts to extract authentic interpretations and deeper meaning, uncovering the provenance and trajectory of those ideas, contextualizing the circumstances in which they arose and documenting the lives and travails of the key thinkers . . . For example, Raymond Plant's study of the neoliberal state is based on the writings of Friedrich Hayek, Michael Oakeshott and Robert Nozick. Ha-Joon Chang describes neoliberalism was "born out of an unholy alliance between neoclassical economics and the Austrian-Libertarian tradition"' (Venugopal, 2015, pp. 166–7).
33. Venugopal (2015, p. 168).
34. Ibid.
35. Venugopal (2015, pp. 169–70).
36. Nozick (1973) provides a summary of the political philosophy on distributional justice. Mezzetti (1987) examines the connection between Rawls and Nozick. See also Gordon (1980).
37. Keynes (2018 [1936], Ch. 24, Sec. V, p. 340).
38. Oppenheimer (2008, p. 1).
39. Oppenheimer (2008, p. 2). Other positive examples abound, for example Micklethwait and Wooldridge (2001).
40. This question highlights an important difference between the US, which assesses tax based on citizenship, and almost all other countries, such as Canada, that assess tax based on residence.
41. The historical discussion of the income tax concentrates mostly on the US, if only because the history of income taxes in Canada follows a similar path. Prior to World War I, Canada sought to avoid taxing income, as was the case in the US and the UK, ostensibly to make Canada an attractive location for immigrants. Despite this, the income tax was first introduced in 1917 to pay for the considerable expenses being

incurred in World War I. The debt and fiscal situation following World War I was dire enough that the government was not able to eliminate the income tax. Smith (1993) documents the changes from World War II to the early1990s. Much as in the US, the income tax on individuals grew rapidly as a share of gross domestic product (GDP) following World War II. Circa 1946, 16 per cent of individuals filed income returns; by 1992, the figure had risen to 69 per cent, and it has stayed in this range until the present. Though income tax rates did not rise significantly between 1946 and 1971, a 70 per cent increase in the price level and an 84 per cent increase in real per capita GDP resulted in individuals being moved significantly up the rate schedule. 'Direct taxes on persons [mostly income tax] rose from 7% of personal income in 1946 to 17% in 1971' (Smith, 1993, p. 1055). Tax reforms in 1972, 1981 and 1987 flattened individual income tax rates and broadened the brackets. Although the maximum marginal rate was reduced three times between 1972 and 1987 for those with the highest incomes, average personal income tax rates rose significantly for most taxpayers with average or above-average incomes. Decreases in top marginal rates and flattening of the rate structure since 1971 have raised concerns about whether the personal income tax is progressive enough to meet income distribution goals. Much of the heavy lifting for the income equality objective is now taken up by transfer payments and tax expenditures for individuals, such as refundable goods and services tax (GST) credits and child tax benefits, that have appeared since 1971. 'There is evidence that although income before the personal income tax and transfers has become *less* equally distributed since1971, income after the personal income tax and transfers was *more* equally distributed in 1993 than in 1971. In view of the current heavy reliance on the personal income tax in Canada and the "flat tax" debate in both Canada and the United States, it seems unlikely that the personal income tax will contribute significantly to any increase in income equality in the future. In any case, if greater equality in income distribution is a goal, expenditure policies are likely to be more effective than tax policies as a means of achieving it' (Smith, 1993, p. 1055).

42. Building on the scholarly *Progressive Taxation* (2nd edn, 1908), Seligman was already a leading authority on taxation prior to the appearance of *The Income Tax*. In addition to covering the historical background on the income tax, Cox (1919) discusses developments in other countries around the time the 16th Amendment was passed.
43. Seligman (1914 [1911], pp. 690–91).
44. Seligman (1914 [1911], p. 691).
45. The dramatic wealth inequality in the US at the beginning of the 20th century witnessed the rise of various social movements inspired by the highly influential work by Henry George, *Progress and Poverty* (1882 [1879]).
46. Seligman (1914 [1911], pp. 640–41).
47. Shakow (1986) and Alm (2018) provide useful recent commentary on the prospects for Haig–Simons income as a basis for an implementable ideal tax system.
48. Hanna (2000, p. 125).
49. Wildasin (1990) argues that Haig is more appropriately classified as a proponent of an expenditure tax.
50. Haig (1921, p. 7); see also Hanna (2000, p. 126).
51. Head (1970, p. 198).
52. In addition to Head (1970), useful commentary on the Carter Commission is provided by Musgrave (1968), Carter (1968) and Head (1972). As Shakow (1986, p. 1113) observes: 'An accrual tax system offers many advantages; that is the reason the proposal never dies. Unfortunately, the accrual system has never attracted a large group of adherents because its twin problems of valuation (How can all assets be valued every year?) and liquidity (How can taxpayers pay taxes if they do not sell their assets?) have never been solved.'
53. The long legal history of the realization doctrine in the US traces back to *Eisner vs. Macomber* 252 US 189 (1920) that involved the constitutionality of imposing income tax on a pro rata stock dividend. In declaring that a stock dividend is not realized income,

the US Supreme Court concluded that taxation of unrealized gains was not authorized by the 16th Amendment (e.g., Zelenak, 2010). In ruling that the taxation of stock dividends was unconstitutional as a tax on unrealized appreciation, the Court made explicit reference to the non-taxable accumulation of earnings within a corporation that is not paid out as dividend. Since *Macomber*, there have been various cases loosening requirements for whether a gain is realized for income tax purposes. For example, in *Commissioner vs. Glenshaw Glass Co.* 348 US 426 (1955), the Court ruled that a treble damage award in an anti-trust case was taxable income; the Court shifted the definition of income from the source of the gain, as in *Macomber*, to whether there had been an increase in wealth – more consistent with a Haig–Simons definition of income.

54.   Some sources consider the income earned by an owner of a company due to increases in the value of company shares to be part of wage income (e.g., Bankman and Weisbach, 2006). This is a legitimate complication regarding the classification of wage income or capital income. However, Haig–Simons avoids this issue of income sources by classifying income uses as either consumption or additions to wealth.

55.   Inability to do mark-to-market accounting for privately held companies and the like as a reason for adhering to the realization principle is a red herring. As demonstrated in Finnerty (2002), there is a sophisticated accounting methodology in place to value privately held flow-through entities. Toder and Viard (2016) is a recent study recommending the use of mark-to-market accounting for shareholders as a route to reducing the US corporate income tax rate to 15 per cent.

56.   An important instance of the differential use of mark-to-market accounting appears with (re)valuations under International Financial Reporting Standards (IFRS) accounting, where mark-to-market is used, and US Generally Accepted Accounting Principles (GAAP) where assets are carried at cost until sold. Similarly, accounting rules for derivatives such as Financial Accounting Standard (FAS) 133 introduced in 1998 reveal the host of complications that can arise when mark-to-market accounting for derivative positions is used in combination with assets carried at cost. Adkins (2016) makes the following observation: 'The rules regarding the taxation of stock options and restricted stock are complex. With respect to [incentive stock options] (ISOs), the treatment of disqualifying dispositions and the impact of ISOs on the alternative minimum tax are especially complex. For nonqualified options, the tax treatment is relatively straightforward. Complexity abounds with respect to restricted stock, especially in regard to whether a section 83(b) election should be made. It is important for executives to understand these tax rules in order to maximize the after-tax value of equity-based compensation.'

57.   Studies that explore adjustments to the realization principle to imitate the accrual principle include Auerbach (1991), Bradford (1995), Land (1996) and Sahm (2008). A recent survey is provided in Sahm (2009).

58.   Vickrey (1992, p. 257). In the context of emerging economies, Weller and Rao (2010) argue that progressive income taxes 'are associated with greater income equality and a higher likelihood of countercyclical fiscal policies'.

59.   Vickrey (1947, p. 164).

60.   Blough (1948, p. 671).

61.   For a recent contribution on 'progressive taxation' reforms, see Diamond and Saez (2011). As illustrated by Harrod (1930), analysis of progressive taxation was advanced well prior to the appearance of the *Agenda*.

62.   The original source is Kaldor (1955).

63.   Hobbes (1676) and Mill (1849). Seligman (1914 [1911], p. 11) refers to Hobbes, Jean Bodin (1530?–96) and Sir William Petty (1623–87) as proponents of expenditure as the best test of ability to pay, 'a system of taxation that no one could escape'.

64.   Warren (1980, p. 1081).

65.   As quoted in Zelanak (2010, p. i).

66.   An example of an optimal capital taxation model, Vogelgesang (2000) 'studies the effects of agent heterogeneity on optimal capital income taxation' to find 'conditions for the

optimality of zero capital income taxes in a multiperiod model with heterogeneous agents'. As it turns out the theoretical results demonstrate that 'the sign of the optimal capital income tax rate does not depend on the extent of inequality in goods endowments and productivities each by itself, but on a measure of inequality in their joint distribution'.

67. Feldstein (1978, p. S28).
68. Judd (1985) and Chamley (1986).
69. Feldstein (1978, p. S30).
70. Conesa et al. (2009, p. 26). This source also provides references for the studies involved.
71. Diamond and Spinnewijn (2011, p. 54).
72. Conesa et al. (2009).
73. Conesa et al. (2009, p. 27).
74. This connection between the Romans and capital references the etymological origins of 'capital'; see Poitras (2016, Ch. 1).
75. Assessed on a producing unit such as a farm, the *decumae* or 'tenth' was related to the fraction of the unit's produce that was paid in tax. Hence, the *decumae* was progressive, because those with higher product would make a larger absolute payment. The *decumae* would be lower when output was deficient in a given year, and would capture 'excess profits' in times of abundance and high produce prices.
76. Fisher (1896, p. 510).
77. See Poitras (2016) for relevant references to Böhm-Bawerk (1970 [1891]) and Irving Fisher (1896, 1904). Fetter (1900, 1907) provides a helpful review of the debate.
78. Modern accounting standards issued by accounting entities such as the Financial Accounting Standards Board (FASB) in the US, or the International Accounting Standards Board, are replete with references to 'equity'. For example, in 1990 the FASB issued a discussion memorandum, 'Distinguishing between Liability and Equity Instruments and Accounting for Instruments with Characteristics of Both', to clarify issues associated with the increasing appearance of 'hybrid' equity (debt) securities with debt (equity) features.
79. This is a notional approach aiming to provide a connection with historical notions of capital. In accounting practice, there are numerous other items also included on the assets side of the balance sheet, such as goodwill and accounts receivable, that do not qualify as either physical or intangible assets.
80. Tax status of debt owned by individuals is typically straightforward: an individual owning debt typically pays tax on interest payments at the individual's marginal tax rate. There is some variation across countries in the capital gains treatment of interest on zero coupon debt where interest cumulates and is paid at maturity.
81. Jacobson (2001) discusses the impact of fiduciary duties on the choice of equity capital organization.
82. Murdock (2001) traces the early history of the limited liability company in the US to statutes for partnership associations enacted by some states in the early 1800s. The American Bar Association (ABA) (2011) provides discussion surrounding a prototype for a limited liability companies Act designed to correct deficiencies in previous versions stretching back to November 1992 when the ABA drafted a 'Prototype Limited Liability Company Act'. Though all the states had adopted LLC laws by the end of 1996, in 1997 the IRS repealed the so-called 'Kintner' regulations that were a significant limitation on the drafting of LLC legislation by classifying business entities into partnerships or corporations for tax purposes. This resulted in further changes in state LLC legislation. The IRS replaced the Kintner regulations with a 'check-the-box' classification scheme. The many states that subsequently amended LLC Acts have resulted in the LLC becoming 'the fastest growing form of business and investment entity'. States amend LLC Acts 'frequently to deal with emerging issues such as single member LLCs, series within an LLC, shelf LLCs, subsidiary style LLCs, conversions, and domestications' (ABA, 2011, p. 117).
83. See Canadian Department of Finance (2008). As an example of how constitutional factors impact tax policy, observe that an important element in the decision by the

Canadian federal government to effectively eliminate the tax benefits of flow-through entities for all but real estate investment trusts was the incidence of tax gains and losses across provinces. The loss of corporate income tax revenue in resource-producing provinces, especially Alberta, coincided with an increase in personal income tax in the provinces with larger populations, Ontario and Quebec, where the bulk of taxable unit trust distributions were paid.

84. The relevant history of Canadian income trusts is discussed in Poitras (2011, pp. 669–76).
85. The complicity of professionals in tax evasion and aggressive tax avoidance using offshore transactions is documented in various studies from different perspectives. In providing a critique of such expert services, economists such as Balafoutas et al. (2015) emphasize factors such as the hidden costs of such expert services; sociologists such as Harrington (2012) emphasize the socio-economic costs; and accountants such as Sikka (2015) question the ethics of accountancy firms involved in such practices.
86. Sikka (2015, p. 46).
87. Included in the scattering of useful academic studies are Alstadsæter and Kopczuk (2014), Hanlon et al. (2015) and Donohoe et al. (2015). Examples of practitioner contributions include Brackney (2015), Lofft et al. (2012), Jacobson (2001) and Davis and Ko (n.d.).
88. See, for example, Hodder et al. (2003) and Erickson and Wang (2007).
89. See Cooper et al. (2015, p. 91).
90. Government Accountability Office (2016).
91. The use of different terms to refer to the Canadian federal tax authority is due to a bureaucratic renaming process associated with a succession of government reorganizations. From 1927 until the introduction of the Federal Identity Program in 1970, the federal tax authority was referred to as the Department of National Revenue. In 1970, the name 'Revenue Canada' was substituted, and used until 1999 when another government reorganization created the Canada Customs and Revenue Agency, which lasted until 2003 when customs enforcement was relocated to Canadian Border Services Agency and the Canadian Revenue Agency (CRA) became the government entity responsible for collecting income and other federal taxes.
92. The actual flow-through for a business trust was not transparent. A rough description is accomplished by viewing the business as borrowing from the non-operating trust and using the cash flows from the assets owned by the business to pay the (possibly variable) interest on the borrowing. As such, the payment to the unit holder would be treated like a net interest payment – that is, at full marginal rates – and the distributions would be fully deductible against corporate taxes. In order to obtain Revenue Canada approval, most of the income generated by the asset or business was required to be paid out. Because the trust was conceived to be a passive entity, the evolution of the model to include business trusts attempted to restrict such entities to passive ownership. However, this did not happen in practice and it was possible for a unit trust to incur a tax liability on 'active' profits. The tax advantage to using such Specified Investment Flow-Through (SIFT) trusts over corporations was eliminated by the federal Conservative government on Halloween 2006. Similar to limited liability partnerships in the US, Canadian unit trusts were publicly traded.
93. Based on a US sample comparing takeovers of S corporations and C corporations, Erickson and Wang (2007) report tax-driven premiums in the same range (12–17 per cent).
94. See Cooper et al. (2015).

5. Taxing the wealthy across jurisdictions

> We maintain that if a state is to avoid the greatest plague of all – I mean civil war, though civil disintegration would be a better term – extreme poverty and wealth must not be allowed to arise in any section of the citizen-body, because both lead to both these disasters. That is why the legislator must now announce the acceptable limits of wealth and poverty. The lower limit of poverty must be the value of the holding. The legislator will use the holding as his unit of measure and allow a man to possess twice, thrice, and up to four times its value.
>
> (Plato, *The Laws*, Book V)[1]

PROPERTY, CONSUMPTION AND LOCAL CONTROL

Evolution of the Property Tax

Among the defining events in the history of Western civilization were the fiscal reforms of Augustus starting in 27 BC that mark the transition from the Roman Republic to the Empire.[2] With regard to taxation, these reforms restored – sometimes magnificently – control to the provinces, under the direction of the governor, at the expense of the *publicani* situated in Rome. The theme of local versus centralized control of fiscal policy in general, and taxation policy specifically, has played out in a variety of different venues over the centuries. In the modern era of broad-based income taxes, national governments have captured and administered a significant component of aggregate tax revenue. Initially introduced as an all-out initiative to pay for the war effort, the expenditure component of modern fiscal policy has evolved dramatically since the end of World War II, yet national government programmes continue to comprise a large component of total government spending. Tax revenue is raised by a national taxing authority from the individuals, households and businesses situated in localities, and then returned to those localities to fund various programmes in a somewhat haphazard fashion that often does not typically reflect the relative contributions to national tax revenues from the different localities.

What are the prospects for shifting the income tax burden, largely administered by national governments, to taxes administered at the state/provincial or local level? It is well known that taxes on immovable assets, especially real estate, are decidedly more difficult to avoid and evade. Luxury taxes, licences and user fees on items such as high-end automobiles and yachts can also be effectively assessed at the local level. Of course, providing more local control over tax assessment and collection would likely change the aggregate composition of government expenditures. If localities in the US were responsible for raising the bulk of tax revenue and then redistributing some agreeable portion to the federal government, how much support would there be for the more than 50 per cent of discretionary spending by the federal government on defence? On the other hand, property values and luxury consumption differ substantively across local jurisdictions, raising questions about how enhanced tax revenue would and could be redistributed. Diversity across localities could potentially allow the wealthy to have more, not less, influence over the assessment of taxes, thus exacerbating, not alleviating, increasing wealth and income inequality.

Being one of the oldest types of tax, the property tax has taken many forms over the millennia.[3] Recognizing that 'no understanding of the tax will suffice that does attempt to recapture its tangled history', a useful, if rough, breakdown of the development in the English-speaking countries is to distinguish the medieval period of feudal and corporate obligations; the pre-modern period, stretching from the introduction of the 'aid' in England at the beginning of the 13th century as 'the chief form of national direct taxation until the advent of the income tax in 1799';[4] and the modern period, which begins with the 1799 introduction of the income tax in England and continues, in some fashion, to the present.[5] Though the relative contribution of property taxes to government revenue diminished significantly throughout the 20th century, it is in the English-speaking countries where the property tax has retained the largest, albeit still smaller, role. As such, it was the earlier English property tax that was transplanted to the North American colonies and elsewhere in the British Empire. The philosophical structure of this tax was heavily influenced by important 17th and 18th century English intellectuals representing upper-class views, such as John Locke, William Petty and Thomas Hobbes. All were of the view that property is a poor basis for taxation.

A central feature of the upper-class argument promoted by Locke, Petty, Hobbes and others was that property ownership was not substantively connected to the benefits – somehow identified – received from the government. This perspective is consistent with the well-known position of Locke that 'the great and chief end of men's uniting into commonwealths is the preservation of their property'.[6] For Locke, the property tax was not an appropriate tax base because the unequal distribution of property meant that a large majority of the population would not pay the tax. As with Hobbes, a tax that does not reach the great majority of the citizenry will not compel them to understand and support the public order. Only if the citizen is conscious that the government is delivering some private benefit will there be such understanding of the support. To be conscious of the private benefit, the citizen must be reminded; every day if possible. A citizen who largely escapes taxation – 'whether he is a miser whose gold is hidden from the assessor, or a poor man who owns nothing – is getting a free ride and learning a dangerous lesson. However, both must eat and therefore buy food; both can be compelled to pay taxes on whatever they consume.' As Hobbes observed: 'when the impositions are laid on those things which men consume, every man pays equally for what he uses' (Hobbes, 1676, Pt II, Ch. 30).[7]

Being a fervent proponent for introduction of a United States (US) federal income tax and the 16th Amendment, Seligman was at pains to make a strong case against the property tax, recognizing that:

> In theory the system of state and local taxation is calculated to reach the respective abilities of the property owners; but in practice, as has repeatedly been pointed out, the general property tax has broken down completely; and, especially so far as personal property is concerned, the wealthier classes stand from under.[8]

Seligman proposes a number reasons for the 'breakdown of the general property tax in state and local taxation'. Specifically, the methods of assessing personal property:

> gives rise to the most striking abuses and the most shocking injustice. The efforts on the part of tax-reformers to bring about a change in the law have heretofore failed, very largely because of the perfectly explicable feeling on the part of the great mass of the voters that the wealthier classes, with their great ownership of personal property, should in some way be made to bear their share of the burden.

This scathing indictment of the property tax needs to be seen in context: 'It was not until shortly before the middle of the nineteenth century that the local taxes, or rates, as they are called, were limited to real estate.'[9]

Being a strong proponent of ability as a basis for tax assessment, Seligman felt that the desire to reach the abilities of property owners was 'laudable', but 'strict enforcement of the local property tax has turned out to be a dire failure'. The subsequent claim that introduction of income taxes on 'the wealthy classes' would be an impetus to reform of the local property tax is a striking illustration of the importance of context. In effect, in arguing strongly for the income tax, Seligman is envisioning the use of income tax to reach the wealthy, while a reformed property tax would be the centrepiece of local government revenue:

> If now the average citizen could see that the wealthier classes were actually subject to some form of income taxation, even if they paid this tax to the state or to the federal government, rather than to the local government, the opposition to a reform of local taxation on sound lines would very largely disappear, and it would doubtless be far easier to effect a readjustment of the entire fiscal system without the present complications of a general property tax.[10]

In making this statement, Seligman is speaking as a leading academic Progressive. In proposing the use of multiple taxes instead of a single tax, as well as seeking to place public finance on a more 'scientific' base, Seligman represented a substantive evolution of Progressive thought from the ideas and reform proposals that had initially inspired the Progressive era.[11]

Progress and Poverty

That Henry George (1839–97) still has a dedicated following over 140 years after the initial publication in 1879 of his most influential work, *Progress and Poverty: An Inquiry into the Cause of Industrial Depressions and of Increase of Want with Increase of Wealth; The Remedy*, speaks to the power of the message.[12] This message is reflected in the dedication to this work (and this book): 'To those who seeing the vice and misery that spring from the unequal distribution of Wealth and Privilege, Feel the possibility of a higher social state, and would Strive for its attainment'. In contrast to Seligman, a professor at Columbia University through his entire career, George cut his teeth in journalism and the school of hard knocks. Though his writings inspired various reform movements during the Progressive era, given the subsequent development of the income tax, it is most appropriate to refer to George as a populist and early Progressive era leader. The power of the message is revealed again and again in *Progress and Poverty*. For example:

> This association of poverty with progress is the great enigma of our times. It is the central fact from which spring industrial, social, and political difficulties that perplex the world, and with which statesmanship and philanthropy and education grapple in vain . . . not to answer is to be destroyed. So long as all the increased wealth which modern progress brings goes to build up great fortunes, to increase luxury and make sharper the contrast between the House of Have and the House of Want, progress is not real and cannot be permanent. The reaction must come.[13]

Recognizing that passage of the Sherman Anti-Trust Act was some years in the future, an important theme in *Progress and Poverty* is that monopoly and privilege are at the root of the economic and social problems, persisting despite the rapidly advancing technology of that time. George argues that this is and has been the case in every society in which monopoly and privilege have appeared.[14]

Writing prior to the introduction of the income tax in the US, the problem of increasing poverty at a time of prosperity inspired Henry George. Though *Progress and Poverty* would be considered to have socialist leanings in modern times, many of the tax reform proposals would now fall into the conservative or libertarian mould. For example, George maintained: 'anything that tends to make government simple and inexpensive tends to put it under the control of the people'. To this end, George advocates the 'principle of ideal taxation':

> the tax must not over-burden or discourage production; it must be easy and cheap to collect; it must be 'certain' in the sense of not facilitating evasion by taxpayers or official corruption in the tax-collection process, and it should bear equally on people and not unduly advantage or disadvantage some people.[15]

In order to best achieve an ideal tax system, Henry George is today most remembered for his proposal of a single tax on land as the most expedient route to an 'ideal' tax system. On efficiency grounds George was opposed to 'manifold taxes', raising revenue using different types of taxes such as income tax, inheritance tax, excise tax and sales tax that discouraged production. Again, on efficiency grounds of discouraging production, the tax on land was not to include a tax on buildings or other improvements on the land.

Recalling that George was a populist and not an academic, the substance as opposed to the method of presentation requires attention. For George, land is a monopoly and the landowner has appropriated that land from the common stock, excluding others from the using that land. George argued that natural justice permits taxing someone who takes land from the 'common stock', but it is not just to tax the exertions of labour.[16] It is a land tax that meets all necessary criteria of an ideal tax: easy to collect, hard to avoid, simple and clear. The obvious objection advanced as early as Locke and Hobbes, that a land tax bears disproportionately only on the landowning class, is met by a natural-justice argument: in acquiring ownership of the land, landowners had appropriated the land from the common stock. Because it is the community that gives land value, because land prices rise as the community grows, it is naturally just for landowners to be taxed for the benefit of the community. At the time, *Progress and Poverty* was highly influential, spawning a single-tax movement and providing a strong message for Progressives and reformers. Over time, George also influenced many utopian thinkers, across the political spectrum. More recently, the single-tax idea has been adopted by purveyors of right-wing utopias.[17]

Among the more recent tax experts who have sought to bring George into the modern era was the eminent Columbia University economist C. Lowell Harris (1912–2009). For Harris, 'land deserves a prominent place in a tax system for reasons articulated long before tax evasion became a recognized problem'.[18] While George argued that land should be the only tax base, Harris recognized that a single tax would not finance all government expenditures in the modern era. However, placing increased taxes on land values would raise substantially more revenues, permitting reductions in other taxes. For Harris, this would necessarily involve reducing property taxes on buildings and machinery. With some caveats, land is a productive resource that is not diminished by the taxes imposed. Extracting a tax payment for ownership of land does not reward the landowner in the same fashion as payments the landowner makes towards the labour and physical capital needed to use the land for profitable production. As distinguished from the value of buildings, the bulk of land value arises from past and present community development, not from the efforts of past and present landowners. Non-payment of tax means that the government can take back the land, instead of having to attach financial assets or income. Harris felt that the variety of good reasons for using land as a tax base cumulated into an impressive total, even before recognizing the merit and uniqueness of the land tax among government revenue sources as being evasion-proof.

Rethinking Land and Property Taxes

'The power to tax should ideally be situated at the level of government that best reflects the reach of the benefits provided and the burdens imposed.'[19] If correct, such seemingly practical statements imply that local governments, and the property tax, should have a greater role in the raising the revenues needed to support government services. Instead, higher levels of government typically raise more revenue than the constitutionally mandated benefits provided, and then reallocate the extra funds raised to lower levels of government. If the evidence that income tax evasion and avoidance are systemic, and a significant contributing factor in rising wealth and income inequality, why do land taxes or property taxes play a relatively minor role in the government revenue mix? The conventional academic rationale for taxing land is clearly stated by the influential economist Larry Summers:

> Distortions are minimized by taxing bases that are least responsive to taxation. Land is the classic example of a factor inelastic in supply and therefore non-distortionary to tax, though taxing land raises other issues. In any case, modern governments require far more revenue than is feasible to obtain from land taxes alone.[20]

While the property tax may have difficulty addressing vertical equity at the national level, such sweeping statements ignore the intimate connection between property tax, horizontal equity and vertical equity at the state/provincial and local level.

Leaving aside substantive questions associated with how much revenue that property or land tax could raise, an ideologically easy, and inadequate, answer regarding the limited use of such taxes compared to income and sales taxes is to reference public opinion toward the property tax. Reviewing opinion surveys conducted by seemingly reputable testing firms, the American Enterprise Institute (AEI) reports that, although the question is not asked regularly, surveys suggest that 'the local property tax is now seen as more onerous than the federal income tax'. For example, a Kaiser/NPR/Harvard poll taken in February–March 2003 reports that 36 per cent of those surveyed felt local property tax was the tax disliked the most, followed at 29 per cent by the income tax. Consistent with an ideological perspective that promotes the benefits of tax reduction, the American Enterprise Institute claims: 'Gallup shows a substantial jump since the late 1980s in the proportion of people mentioning the local property tax as the worst or least fair tax. In their April 2005 poll, 42 percent gave that response. Twenty percent said the federal income tax was the worst tax.'[21] As with poll results in general, such results are subject to a range of potential biases, such as characteristics of the population being sampled; composition of responses and non-responses; structure, order and type of questions asked; and the influence of subjective interpretation that goes beyond the objective results provided.[22]

How much objective content do such survey results possess? Being little more than talking points, such results do not explore the possible reasons that the property tax is disliked. Casual consideration of the myriad of property tax regimes in various US states, counties, townships, and the like reveals a heterogenous combination of reasons why this type of tax could be disliked. It would be useful to know the geographical distribution of responses. For example, due to implementation of Proposition 13, the cumulative impact of limitations on increases in property tax rates and assessments in California has produced a situation where longer-term property owners pay lower taxes, based on assessments that reflect historic property values, while newer owners pay higher property taxes based on more recent property values. Specifically, Article XIIIA uses 'acquisition value' to determine property tax. This involves property being reassessed to reflect current appraised value when there is new construction or a change in ownership. Two general exemptions to acquisition value reassessment are available: for principal residence exchanges by persons over the age of 55, and for transfers between parents and children. It is ironic that Proposition 13 – introduced to deal with property tax implications of rapidly rising property values – has produced sometimes dramatic disparities in property taxes imposed on similar pieces of property. The constitutionality of these disparities was affirmed in *Nordinger vs. Hahn* (505 US 1 1992) which upholds the use of acquisition value to determine property tax.

Like 'the wealthy', the notion of 'the property tax' is a fiction. There is a vast array of property tax regimes in the US featuring differences in: assessment methods and number of years between assessments; property tax exemptions; limits on assessment and property tax increases; and provisions for expenditure limitations and revenue rollbacks.[23] Depending on the jurisdictions, assessors can be appointed or elected, and assessment cycles determined at either the local or the state/provincial level. In addition to real estate, property could also include other types of tangible real property. It is difficult to briefly summarize all potential sources of inequity in local property taxes in the US. There are many complications, due to municipalities having limited tax autonomy, improper land valuation and poor tax administration, and possible substantial differences between commercial versus residential and rural versus urban valuations. Significantly, there is both logical and empirical evidence that the *ad valorem* property tax structure is regressive.[24] Accepting that regressive taxes are generally disliked, this can be rectified by making the property tax progressive, with higher-valued properties paying a higher marginal tax rate. This raises the complicated issue of property value assessment.

The variety of government units in the US with direct or indirect ability to raise property tax revenue is illustrated by the US Census Bureau's 2017 Census of Governments. There were 90 075 local governments in the United States, up slightly from 90 056 in 2012. Local governments included 3031 counties, 19 495 municipalities and 16 253 townships tasked with a range of 'general purposes'. In addition, there were 38 542 special districts and 12 754 independent school districts tasked with specific functions. State and local governments rely heavily on the tax revenue derived from property taxes, often the largest source of revenue for local governments and some state governments. In the US, the collection of both state and local property taxes is authorized in 37 states, with property taxes comprising more than 50 per cent of all local tax revenue. Only nine states raise 60 per cent or less of revenue from property taxes. For property tax assessment at the county level, local assessors determine property value according to standards set by state law. Though other assessment methods are used, assessment based on market value is most common. Property assessment cycles are based on standards set by the state government. Assessing practices in and across many local jurisdictions can result in properties with equal market value paying significantly different levels of property tax for the same level of local government services.

To benchmark the bewildering array of local assessment processes in the US, consider the market value-based assessment process in British Columbia (BC), a jurisdiction where there are no limits on property tax rate increases, assessors are appointed not elected, and assessments are done on a province-wide basis. Market value assessment was introduced in 1974 with the creation of the independent BC Assessment to provide uniform and fair property value assessments across the province.[25] Passage of the Assessment Authority Act (1974) reconciled 'almost 100 years of inequities, commissions, and official government reports into BC's property assessment and valuation process'. The proximate impetus for the creation of BC Assessment was 'a rising incidence of serious equity grievances, and pressure by property owners and the public sectors'. In creating the independent property assessment authority, the BC provincial government required: 'This Authority must be independent of taxing functions (either municipal or provincial) and its control must be such as will result unmistakably in complete independence.' Currently, BC Assessment provides online access to all assessments. These assessments can be used to appeal against a specific assessment based on objective criteria such as equity across comparable properties. The upshot is that ability to arrive at comparably equitable market value assessments of property values across taxing jurisdictions is not, per se, a valid reason for arguing against increased reliance on property tax to address vertical equity at the national level. However, the bewildering array of property tax systems used to raise local government revenue indicates that it is impractical to expect more than the possibility of property tax achieving horizontal equity at the local level.

Migration and the Tiebout Hypothesis

Some essential features of the market value assessment process in BC have significant implications for the equitable use of the property tax by local jurisdictions in the US and elsewhere. Specifically: (1) an annual market value assessment is done by professional, independent assessors; (2) assessments are done on a province-wide basis; and (3) there is an assessment appeal process based on objective criteria. The region over which assessments are conducted is particularly important, to mitigate the impact of inter-jurisdictional migration, a crucial consideration for wealthy free riders seeking to avoid property taxes.

Such migration is at the core of 'the most significant article on the theory of state and local public finance . . . the seminal paper by Charles Tiebout' in 1956.[26] The so-called Tiebout model is multijurisdictional where independent local governments provide 'a wide variety of expenditure and tax policies, and perfectly mobile consumers reveal their preferences for local public goods through their choice of residential community'.[27] The subsequent 'Tiebout hypothesis' demonstrated that, under specific theoretical assumptions, the provision of local public service would be efficient. 'The Tiebout model has formed the basis of a vast number of subsequent articles in the state and local public finance literature and has also been very influential in urban and regional economics.'[28] Extension of the Tiebout model to international migration by the wealthy is an appealing possibility.

In an era of globalization, the Tiebout model has implications well beyond local public finance. Specifically, this model is the first step in a long line of studies on tax competition culminating in tax competition between national governments for corporate income tax revenue and foreign direct investment. Examining potential efficiency problems associated with competition for capital by local governments, and writing prior to the emergence of the main thrust of globalization, the important American local public finance economist Wallace Oates described problems with the Tiebout hypothesis:[29]

> The result of tax competition may well be a tendency toward less than efficient levels of output of local services. In an attempt to keep taxes low to attract business investment, local officials may hold spending below those levels for which marginal benefits equal marginal costs, particularly for those programs that do not offer direct benefits to local business.

More precisely, local governments will supplement conventional measures of marginal costs with costs arising from 'the negative impact of taxation on business investment. These additional costs might include lower wages and employment levels, capital losses on homes or other assets, and reduced tax bases.'[30] Consequently, the presence of these costs reduces public spending and taxes to levels where:

> the marginal benefits equal the higher marginal costs. Oates's conclusion that this behavior is inefficient rests on the idea that when all governments behave

this way, none gain a competitive advantage, and consequently communities are all worse off than they would have been if local officials had simply used the conventional measures of marginal costs in their decision rules.[31]

A common theme in public finance in the 21st century is the downloading of expenditure burdens onto local governments. Such downloading is both direct and indirect. For example, a reduction in funding provided by higher levels of government for welfare programmes indirectly increases the burden on local governments to deal with an increasing homeless population. Given that property taxes are a reliable source of funding, this begs the question: would the introduction of progressive taxes applied to residential real estate be optimal compared to *ad valorem* taxation? Studies that have addressed this question using optimal tax models have found that 'when consumers differ in their tastes, differential tax treatment of housing and its subsidization to the poor may indeed become desirable'.[32] Recognizing that local government expenditures are usually visible, such as police and fire services and schools, how would increasing local control of a larger portion of government revenue through increased use of property taxes, consumption taxes and user fees at the expense of revenue raised by higher level of governments work in practice? Would the inefficiencies associated with internal migration of the wealthy to claim residence in lower-tax jurisdictions undermine the ability of local government to capture revenue from wealthy free riders and tax evaders? Similarly, is property tax capable of reaching the accumulation of wealth in equity capital shares?

Would a shift from raising the bulk of tax revenue from income taxes and *ad valorem* sales taxes to property taxes and consumption taxes with progressive rates require a radical restructuring of the tax system? Though property is inelastic in supply, the wealthy, and especially the wealthiest, can migrate for tax purposes. Without detailed insight into reasons why the wealthy choose to live in a specific locale, it is unclear why those able to avoid income tax would not migrate from a locality that significantly increased taxes that were difficult to avoid. Even if inter-regional tax competition within national boundaries can be controlled, this still raises the spectre of a decidedly marked evolution in the substance of international tax competition. This, again, illustrates the difficulty of extrapolating results for the 'average' taxpayer to the select group of the wealthy and wealthiest taxpayers. While raising property tax, either absolutely or progressively, may alleviate revenue difficulties at the local level, significantly raising property and sales tax, either absolutely or progressively, does not get at the bulk of capital assets and income that underpin increasing wealth and income inequality.

TAXING THE WEALTHY AT THE NATIONAL LEVEL

For the impositions that are laid on the people by the sovereign power are nothing else but the wages due to them that hold the public sword to defend private men in the exercise of their several trades and callings. Seeing then that the benefit that everyone receives thereby is the enjoyment of life, which is equally dear to poor and rich, the debt which a poor man owes them that defend his life is the same which a rich man owes for the defense of his . . . Which considered, the equality of imposition consists rather in the equality of that which is consumed than of the riches of the persons that consume the same. (Thomas Hobbes, 1676, Part II, Ch. 30)

Taxing Expenditure and Consumption

Together with Locke, Petty and a variety of other upper-class English Enlightenment intellectuals, Hobbes argued for the replacement of property taxes, based largely on rack rents, with consumption taxes. In the US, the implications of relying heavily on consumption taxes – excise, customs, value added and sales taxes – came to a head with the debate over the 16th Amendment. As Seligman observed at the time:

Under existing conditions in the United States the burdens of taxation, taking them all in all, are becoming more unequally distributed, and the wealthier classes are bearing a gradually smaller share of the public burden. Something is needed to restore the equilibrium; and this something can scarcely take any form but that of an income tax.[33]

Over a century after passage of the 16th Amendment, the evolution of the income tax has again resulted in a situation where 'the wealthier classes are bearing a gradually smaller relative share of the public burden'. The increasing inability of governments to pay for the public burden with available revenue sources raises an essential question about the best route forward: can the income tax be reformed to address the horizontal equity for wealthy free riders and vertical equity for the wealthiest, or are other taxes required to close the funding gap? Due to practical limitations of the property tax as a broad-based source of revenue, governments have increasingly turned to more-difficult-to-avoid consumption taxes – especially excise taxes, sales taxes and value added taxes – despite the regressive character of such taxes.

Recognizing that 'more than 130 countries now impose significant value added taxes, and there is widespread reliance on excise taxes on gasoline and other commodities', the influential public finance economists James Hines and Larry Summers observe that: 'The popularity of expenditure taxes is due in part to their administrative and enforcement features and in part to their efficiency properties.' The advantages of consumption taxes in a globalizing world follows because expenditures 'have relatively clear geographic associations, reducing the potential for international tax avoidance and generally reducing the mobility of the tax base compared to alternatives such as personal income taxes or source-based business taxes including the corporate income tax'. Conceding that consumption taxes do not directly tax capital income, Hines and Summers make the conventional observation that consumption taxes indirectly tax capital income when such income is spent on goods and services. This has:

> the effect of taxing pure profits on capital investments while effectively exempting normal returns to saving. Heavy use of expenditure taxation in place of income taxation can carry serious implications for tax progressivity, since in practice many expenditure taxes have flat rates that make them much less progressive than income tax alternatives.[34]

With this in mind, is it possible to make consumption taxes progressive enough to alleviate increasing wealth and income inequality?[35]

Of course, there are a variety of possible approaches to taxing consumption progressively. For example, numerous locales impose little or no tax on items that are purchased by low-income families, such as basic foodstuffs. However, such exemptions have no impact on capturing tax revenue from the wealthy to alleviate increasing wealth and income inequality. Some argue that the introduction of new expenditure taxes can be used to offset changes in income taxes designed to address such inequality. However, the technical design of such taxes and the sweeping character of such reforms raise 'realistic questions about whether countries in practice are capable of enacting such sweeping reforms'.[36] Even if serious proposals to implement broad-based progressive consumption taxes could be implemented through adjustments to current taxes, without compensating adjustment to other taxes and expenditures, 'the most likely outcome of greater reliance on expenditure type taxation is reduced overall fiscal progressivity. Given recent changes in income distributions, governments may be dissatisfied with such an outcome and seek creative alternatives that permit fiscal progressivity to accompany sufficient revenue generation.'[37]

Taxing Wealth Accumulation Over the Life Cycle

A real risk of broad-based tax reform aimed at alleviating increasing wealth and income inequality is a potential disruption in the life cycle process of savings and accumulation. In abstract economic theorizing, the individual starts employment in the earlier part of the life cycle.

Typically, at this point the individual has accumulated only a limited amount of wealth.[38] Over a lifetime, the individual saves from a combination of after-tax disposal income and deferred-tax pension contributions. The resulting accumulated wealth is used to support a given lifestyle in retirement. Taxation of such wealth accumulated from after-tax income is inequitable double taxation: tax is being imposed on wealth that has been accumulated from income that has already been subjected to tax. Imposition of taxes on such wealth will also introduce inefficiencies arising from the encouragement of current consumption over saving, reducing the supply of capital available for investment. For the average taxpayer, much of this wealth will be held in the form of real estate: investment in the family home that has been paid for by taking out a mortgage early in the life cycle savings process, and gradually paying down the mortgage until the borrowing is fully paid off, usually late in the life cycle savings process. Supplementing such life cycle wealth accumulation is the objective of tax-deferred public and private pension plans such as Individual Retirement Accounts (IRAs) in the US, Registered Retirement Savings Plans (RRSPs) in Canada, Personal Pension Plans (PPPs) in the United Kingdom (UK) and Superannuation in Australia. The maximum tax deferred contribution limit of such government schemes reduces their relevance for the wealthy with other sources of wealth accumulation.

The famous economist Franco Modigliani, an important early contributor to work on the life cycle hypothesis, has observed that 'one of the most significant early results of the Life Cycle Hypothesis was to establish that, even in the absence of bequests, the mere fact that income dries up with retirement could generate, for the entire economy, an amount of (hump) wealth quite large relative to income'. Specifically, in a stylized life cycle of income and consumption where it is assumed that consumption is level through life, income is constant up to retirement and there is a 'stationary economy', the ratio of wealth to income would be equal to half the length of retirement. Back in the early 1950s when the life cycle hypothesis was introduced, this ratio was about the order of 5; that is, retirement age of 65 and life expectancy of 75. This theoretical estimate appeared to be supported by empirical evidence for the US that 'the ratio of private net worth to disposable income was of that magnitude, or, if anything, a little lower'. The implication was that the bulk of wealth might be acquired not by inter-generational transfers of wealth, but instead be 'accumulated from scratch by each generation, to be consumed eventually by the end of life'.[39] Though useful in macroeconomic models, such claims have little applicability to the 1 per cent and 0.1 per cent.

The life cycle model has a variety of implications for the aggregate stock of wealth, and consequently for attempts to use broad-based income and, especially, consumption taxes to rectify an increasingly unequal distribution of wealth and income. Perhaps the life cycle model provides a partial explanation for the empirical evidence on income and wealth based on demographics. Because in almost all Organisation for Economic Co-operation and Development (OECD) countries the number of individuals over 65 has grown relatively to those in younger age groups, the wealth distribution has become skewed due to a greater number of the older wealthy. Because retired individuals are often cautious about unpredictable expenses, dis-saving in retirement is not as significant as the life cycle model predicts, due to significant wealth dedicated to precautionary saving preparing for the possibility of living longer than expected or having larger-than-expected medical bills and other expenses associated with ill-health.[40] In addition, the amount of dis-saving in retirement could differ from predictions of the life cycle hypothesis due to the bequest motive. In any event, the life cycle model aims at savings behaviour and wealth accumulation in the aggregate economy. Implications of broad-based consumption and income tax reform derived from the life cycle model for the extreme value group at the top 1 per cent and 0.1 per cent of wealth and income distributions are unclear, at best.

Taxes on Consumption by the Wealthy

> We don't pay taxes. Only the little people pay taxes.
> (Quotation attributed to the 'Queen of Mean', Leona Helmsley (1920–2007))

Life cycle models and the like focus on the aggregate wealth, consumption and savings of an economy over time. Turning attention from aggregate properties of these specifics for the top 1 per cent and 0.1 per cent is revealing. 'By 2006, the thousands of US households whose net worth was $100 million to $1 billion had primary residences worth on average $16.2 million, and spent an annual average of $311 000 on cars, $182 000 on watches, $379 000 on jewelry, and $169 000 on spa services.'[41] Despite the obvious potential for progressive consumption taxes to tap this type of annual spending, debate associated with reforming the US federal income tax has instead focused on regressive flat taxes. There have been. at least three serious attempts to persuade the US Congress to adopt some form of a progressive consumption tax. In 1921, during consideration of the first post-World War I Revenue Act, Ogden Mills, a Representative from New York, introduced a bill to replace the income surtaxes with a 'graduated spendings tax'. A variant of this proposal appeared again in 1942 when Treasury Secretary Henry Morgenthau proposed combining a refundable wartime tax with a permanent graduated surtax on spending.

Finally, during a more recent round of radical tax reform proposals in 1995, Senators Sam Nunn, Pete Domenici and Bob Kerrey introduced a bill to replace the income tax with the Unlimited Savings Allowance ('USA') Tax.[42]

While prior rejections of a progressive consumption tax were in part a result of unique circumstances, there are several common themes. In each instance, opponents complained that the progressive consumption tax failed to reduce the complexity characterizing the income tax. Furthermore, proponents miscalculated the source of opposition to progressivity in the consumption tax by those supporting some form of federal consumption tax. In the 1995 attempt, those supporting a progressive consumption tax were not in agreement with other consumption tax proponents who were only committed to a flat rate sales tax. In addition, proponents underestimated the overall support for an income tax base by those who also supported graduated consumption tax rates. Instead of finding a compromise between the two positions, proponents of the progressive consumption tax alienated both those who favoured a tax with graduated rates and those who favoured a consumption tax. However, where the wealthy and the wealthiest are concerned, debate over the structure of a broad-based federal consumption tax fails to recognize the significant differences in consumption patterns. Middle-income individuals do not consume yachts, private jets, mansions on private estates, and the like.

The US is anomalous in failing to impose some form of consumption tax at the national level. Drawing on theoretical arguments that taxes should be imposed neutrally on all commodities at the same rate, there has been considerable support for the position that ideal consumption taxes are superior to ideal income taxes.[43] Such arguments underpin the 1991 introduction of the 'Goods and Services' tax in Canada and value-added tax (VAT) in various other OECD countries. Compared to the amount of tax revenue that can be raised from a broad-based consumption tax, potential revenue from taxes aimed at consumption patterns of the wealthy is relatively insignificant. However, such taxes can be an important tool in the battle to reduce increasing wealth and income inequality. Yet, to be successful such taxes need to be aimed at physical items that cannot be moved to or sourced from an offshore location to avoid the tax. While wealthy free riders can source income and assets to low-tax jurisdictions, there is usually little associated 'psychic income' from flaunting extravagant wealth and income in such jurisdictions. The wealthiest are compelled to seek status in locations such as Malibu or Park Avenue or Kensington or Deep Water Bay or Azabu, while the 'only-wealthy' must be content with Palm Springs or Point Grey or Knightsbridge or Orchard Street.

Taxes aimed specifically at the consumption patterns of the wealthy and the wealthiest can take various forms. Graduated vehicle licence and registration fees that depend on vehicle size, age and market value are used in many locales. However, there are few locations where such user fees are dramatic. One exception is Singapore, where a Certificate of Entitlement (COE) valid for ten years must first be obtained, through a public auction of a limited number of COEs, classified according to engine size. Though prices at such auctions can be more than S\$100 000, the May 2017 tender averaged over S\$50 000. Having obtained a COE, cars are subject to an additional registration fee that depends on the initial price (open market value) of the vehicle that can more than double the initial purchase price. This fee is augmented by an annual road tax and vehicle emissions fee. Additional COE and road tax charges apply for vehicles older than ten years.[44] 'Mansion taxes', recently introduced by the UK in 2016 on properties valued at more than £2 million, are another such tax. Such graduated taxes can take a variety of forms involving stamp duty – that is, transfer tax – or property tax. Given the penchant for the wealthy to own properties through companies or trusts, additional property tax assessments are required to prevent transfer tax avoidance by selling a company or restructuring a trust without having to transfer the property.[45]

Different Approaches to Death Taxes[46]

For the uninitiated, a 'death tax' refers to a tax that is associated with the death of an individual and subsequent disposition of the estate. Distinguishing between different death taxes depends on whether the estate of the decedent or the recipient of disbursements from the estate is responsible for paying the tax. Death taxes are ancient, with evidence for the imposition of some variant of such taxes appearing in cuneiform tablets of ancient Mesopotamia circa 2000 BC. A considerable portion of the *Digest* of Justinian is concerned with the intricacies of Roman inheritance law. Given the concentration of Roman wealth in perpetuating family units, the Emperor Augustus imposed a 5 per cent tax on property transfers as an effective inheritance tax.[47] The rationale for this tax was to provide a pension fund for old soldiers. The Senate consented to the imposition of this tax when Augustus suggested a land tax as an alternative. Though Augustus set a low exemption limit and did not distinguish between transfers involving direct relatives or strangers, these conditions were eased over time, with periodic bouts of tightening. If the adage that 'an old tax is a good tax' is correct, then death taxes certainly qualify as having the potential to alleviate increasing wealth inequality.

There are a variety of ways that death taxes are imposed. In many European countries, inheritance tax is imposed on those receiving funds from an estate. In other countries, such as the US, an estimate of the market value of the estate is calculated and a federal estate tax is assessed before funds from the estate are disbursed.[48] In still other countries, such as Canada, there is no estate or inheritance tax. Rather, death of an individual triggers a 'deemed disposition' of capital assets subject to capital gains tax. In other words, capital gains deferral using the realization principle ends with the death of the individual.[49] Significantly, as the same treatment applies to gifts of capital assets domiciled in Canada, there is no benefit in trying to circumvent deemed disposition at death by transferring the capital asset prior to death, though some deferment is possible with certain types of trusts. Compared to the complex system of gift and estate taxes in the US involving changing exemption levels, and the various subterfuges such as the Grantor Retained Annuity Trust used to circumvent these taxes, the Canadian approach achieves an important ideal taxation system goal: simplification. However, simplification alone is not enough for a taxation system to achieve the goal of reducing or eliminating wealth dynasties associated with the 0.1 per cent.

Despite a widely held perception in the US and elsewhere that Canada is a progressive country with socialist leanings, as evidenced in universal health care and severe restrictions on handgun ownership, in the realm of taxes on wealth there are a number of ways in which treatment of the wealthy and, especially, the wealthiest in Canada is more regressive than in the US and many other OECD countries. Three of the most important direct tax features that support such a claim are: sale of a primary residence is exempt from capital gains tax; there is no gift tax for recipients, irrespective of tax treatment of income associated with the gift donor; and deemed disposition of assets at the time of death can be mitigated with the use of trusts. Compared to the US prior to the Trump tax cuts, there is more favourable tax treatment of corporate income, and there are few effective controls over the transfer of income from low-tax jurisdictions into Canada. Recent raising of the federal estate tax exemption level in the US, as well as ongoing efforts to eliminate that estate tax, raise the obvious question of whether 'most households today would find it in their interest to oppose the more realistic reforms in which a consumption or income tax would be raised to compensate for decreased revenues from abolishing estate taxation'.[50] In contrast, possibly erroneous arguments against death taxes include sizeable compliance costs and discouragement of entrepreneurship suppressing economic growth.

What would happen if the US eliminated the estate tax? Currently, the Tax Foundation reports that the US has the fourth-highest estate or inheritance marginal tax rate in the OECD at 40 per cent; nearly three times the OECD average of 15 per cent. Despite this high tax rate, the US estate tax accounted for only 0.6 per cent per cent of total federal revenue in 2014, with the estate tax raising $19.3 billion (Office of Management and Budget figures) of total federal revenue of over $3 trillion. In 2008, the estate tax collected about $29 billion from fewer than 20000 estates; the wealthiest 1 per cent of the 2.5 million people who died that year. The ideological impetus of proponents arguing for and against elimination of the estate tax on efficiency grounds is reflected in a recent study, that finds:

> the effects of eliminating estate taxation crucially depend on what other tax instrument is used at the same time to reestablish fiscal balance. In the case in which, perhaps more realistically, the tax on total income were raised, the distortions coming from this small increase for all of the population erase almost all of the aggregate increase in total output coming from increased investment of the very rich who benefit from the elimination of the estate tax.[51]

Alternatively, it can be claimed on theoretical efficiency grounds that if 'wasteful' government spending is cut as a fraction of output to pay for the estate tax elimination, then aggregate output will increase. Such 'efficiency' arguments ignore the role of death taxes in achieving vertical equity.

Ultimately, debate surrounding death taxes is confronted with a fundamental philosophical question: is inheritance a natural right or a social privilege? If inheritance is a natural right, government has no claim to taxing an estate; as a social privilege, the imposition of some form of tax at death is justified. Answers to this long-standing question differ by time and location. For medieval aristocrats, inheritance of the manor estate and the associated feudal obligations was a birthright. This right was used to impose payment upon the death of a tenant for the right of the tenancy to pass to an heir. As some landlords were liable to make extortionate payment demands, this led to the eventual establishment by legislatures of uniform rates. In modern times this philosophical question can be reformulated as: is the wealth that is accumulated during a lifetime, either through work or investment that has been appropriately taxed, the sovereign possession of the deceased, to dispose of entirely without being subjected to double taxation? Or does society have some claim on the estate of a deceased person from having provided the markets, rule of law, the local and national security, and the enforcement that allowed wealth to be accumulated?[52] Such questions frame the debate in terms of the whole population. Reframing the context to focus on the increasing wealth inequality accruing to the 1 per cent and 0.1 per cent, claims to 'natural right' appear to have less substance and the 'social privilege' that attaches to such wealth accumulation gains credibility.

In many situations, the 1 per cent and 0.1 per cent have substantial tax-deferred capital income that has been accumulated by taking advantage of the realization principle. Unlike middle-class wage-earning citizens who object to having to pay additional, double tax to transfer wealth to relatives and friends, the argument that an estate tax represents double taxation for the 1 per cent and 0.1 per cent is decidedly misplaced. In the US, the wealthy can take advantage of the realization principle beyond death to defer tax on capital income and avoid estate tax by choosing a 'basis carryover regime' instead of an estate tax.[53] Across countries, there is ample evidence that the 1 per cent and, especially, the 0.1 per cent have been and are able, directly and indirectly, to transfer immense wealth to their children and others, significantly increasing the chance those individuals will also be among the wealthiest.[54] While this does raise profound questions about vertical equity, there are much deeper political and social issues involved. It is difficult to avoid the insight of Thomas Paine about the risk to democracy from the concentration of wealth. Has the democratic process become so corrupted that the path to alleviating increasing wealth and income inequality is unpassable?

TAX COMPETITION, TAX EVASION AND TAX HAVENS[55]

Globalization and Tax Competition[56]

Competition among different taxing jurisdictions is not new, and not restricted to competition between countries. The competition could be for alternative types of tax revenue – for example, personal tax, property tax or corporate tax – and competition could be inadvertent or intentional.[57] Where competition between countries is concerned, the competition is primarily for differing types of capital. In general, there are three types of competition, for: portfolio capital, which can involve both avoidance and evasion; profits of multinational corporations shifting from high-tax to low-tax jurisdictions via transfer pricing, tax inversion and the like; and foreign direct investment (FDI), involving the relocation of capital for real production activity and, sometimes, involving a type of evasion known as 'round-tripping' to obtain preferential FDI benefits.[58] Typically, the owners of portfolio capital do not relocate to the offshore jurisdiction, while multinational corporations have to at least give the appearance of relocating, and owners of FDI will often relocate for operational reasons. When the owner does not relocate, the competition involves 'poaching', if the owner does relocate then the competition is 'luring'. The appropriate approach to reforming taxes on wealthy free riders and the wealthiest differs depending on whether the owner of capital relocates.

Issues associated with tax competition depend on perspective. Small countries, such as Ireland, can and do set corporate income tax rates at a level able to attract capital from large countries with significantly higher tax rates. Canadian corporate tax rates have also adjusted downward, though whether this was done for reasons of tax competition is unclear. In contrast, prior to the Trump tax cuts, the statutory corporate income tax rate in the US was, with Japan, the highest in the world, and even the significantly lower effective marginal tax rates in the US were still higher than the statutory rates for most international competitors for corporate tax revenue. As the recent reduction of the corporate tax rate demonstrates, the US became increasingly unable to maintain an independent policy on taxation of capital income, including corporate income.[59] In particular, the US responded to countries with:

> territorial tax systems, under which the foreign source income of their multinationals is exempt from domestic taxation – in contrast to the US system under which such income is subject to a residual domestic tax . . . High statutory rates in the US exacerbated inefficiencies in the tax system, encouraged tax avoidance and evasion, and increased administrative and compliance costs. In addition, high statutory tax rates are especially harmful in the modem globalized economy, as they drive capital out of the country and create incentives for income shifting to lower tax jurisdictions.[60]

Implications of the dramatic reduction in the US corporate tax rates in 2017 are still in the 'work-out' phase.

Estimating the Extent of Avoidance and Evasion

The search for truth is an important theme in the story of globalization and reforming taxes on the wealthy and the wealthiest. By design, the complexity and opaqueness of schemes to legally avoid taxes are compounded by the necessity of secrecy and opaqueness in schemes for illegal tax evasion. The upshot is an absence of precise information on the extent of avoidance and evasion for individual countries. Though some sources attempt to provide precise quantitative estimates for the extent of manipulations and amount of funds involved in offshore tax avoidance and evasion activities of the wealthy, the veil of secrecy is difficult to penetrate. It is possible to piece together some useful information from disparate publicly available sources associated with leaks, information from investigations by entities such as the International Consortium of Investigative Journalists and the Tax Justice Network (TJN) and public prosecutions by tax authorities. For example, a 2012 estimate by the TJN claimed that the loss due to tax evasion and avoidance to governments in the European Union was

US$1.3 trillion. Similarly, the TJN estimates that 10 per cent of European wealth is held offshore, with estimated percentages for Latin America of 50 per cent and the Middle East at 70 per cent. The global wealth hidden in tax havens is estimated by the TJN at US$21–31 trillion.[61] There are a host of less precise estimates concerned with tax evasion and avoidance. Some sources estimate that more than 25 per cent of global offshore wealth is managed from Switzerland, with another 25 per cent from the UK, indicating the importance to tax avoidance and evasion by the wealthy of offshore financial accounts, shell corporations and trust structures. However, any attempt to determine the amount of avoidance requires a difficult-to-calculate amount of tax that would have been paid if the machinations of avoidance schemes had not been employed. Evasion amounts are even less accessible.

The important public finance economist Gabriel Zucman uses balance-of-payments data and corporate filings to demonstrate that US companies are shifting profits to offshore tax havens such as Bermuda, Luxembourg, and similar countries. Zucman finds evasion 'on a large and growing scale'. More specifically, 'about 20 percent of all US corporate profits are now booked in such havens, a tenfold increase since the 1980s. This profit-shifting is typically done within the letter of the law and thus would be best described as tax avoidance rather than fraud'. Quantifying the cost for US government coffers, Zucman employs 'the most recent macroeconomic evidence' to find that: 'Over the last 15 years, the effective corporate tax rate of US companies has declined from 30 to 20 percent, and about two-thirds of this decline can be attributed to increased profit-shifting to low-tax jurisdictions.' Wealthy individuals also use tax havens; Zucman opines that the wealthy sometimes use tax havens legally, for example 'to benefit from banking services not available in their home country', and 'sometimes' to illegally evade taxes. Recent changes such as the US Foreign Account Tax Compliance Act (2010) (FATCA) have sought, with some success, to curb the use of tax havens to facilitate tax evasion. However, 'the available evidence from Switzerland and Luxembourg, as well as systematic anomalies in the international investment data of countries, show that offshore personal wealth is growing fast and that the bulk of it seems to be evading taxes'.[62]

To provide some scale to the numbers involved, consider the US Treasury estimate of the major foreign holdings of US Treasury securities. Given the need to identify holders for book entry in order to make interest payments and the like, this data is relatively precise. In February 2016, after China (US$1.252 trillion) and Japan ($1.133 trillion), the third-largest holding ($361 billion) is in the Caribbean 'banking centres' (*aka* tax havens) of Bonaire, St Eustatius and Saba; the Bahamas, Bermuda, the Cayman Islands, Curacao, Saint Maarten and Panama. Following the combined holdings of the oil-exporting countries associated with the Organization of the Petroleum Exporting Countries (OPEC) ($281 billion), five of the next six are countries either typically identified as tax havens (Switzerland, Luxembourg, Hong Kong), or combined with tax havens (the $236 billion associated with the UK includes holdings in the tax havens of the Channel Islands and the Isle of Man), or a jurisdiction with favourable corporate and personal taxes, that is, Ireland (in fifth place with $255 billion). In contrast, France ($78 billion) and Germany ($80 billion) are well down the list. As these estimates are precise but only suggestive, the connection of such numbers to an aggregate value for tax avoidance and evasion is complicated. This problem is compounded dramatically when the funds involve corporate profits, trust income, hedge fund returns, and the like.

Schemes for Avoiding and Evading Taxes on Wealth

It is difficult to make sense of the numbers on tax avoidance and evasion without some understanding of the schemes employed (Box 5.1). If such schemes were easy to understand and execute, then there would be little need for the armies of high-priced lawyers and accountants who facilitate such schemes for the wealthy and, especially, the wealthiest, both directly on individual taxes and through taxes on surrogate corporate, trust and company entities. An integral feature of many, but far from all, schemes is the use of financial accounts, corporations, partnerships and trusts that, at some point, involve offshore tax haven jurisdictions. The public release of the 2.6 terabytes of data in the so-called Panama Papers in April 2015, leaked from the law firm Mossack Fonseca by an anonymous source, followed by the November 2017 leak of 1.4 terabytes of data in the so-called Paradise Papers, are the latest in a string of glimpses into the activities involved. Mossack Fonseca is located in the tax haven of Panama, but with branches in important global financial centres. The leak was massive, illustrating how law firms, financial institutions and accounting firms conduct such business on behalf of clients. The list of clients revealed involves heads of state and important government officials, Russian oligarchs, relatives of the Chinese Communist Party elite, Third World despots, celebrities, soccer stars and FIFA football executives, and other members of the ultra and almost-ultra rich. While embarrassing to those uncovered, the Panama Papers do not reveal whether the objectives of those involved were nefarious – to launder money, avoid sanctions and evade taxes – or for legal convenience of tax avoidance or other business activities.

In addition to the 2015 leak from Mossack Fonseca and the 2017

BOX 5.1   VICTORIA FAMILY CITED IN CRA CRACKDOWN ON TAX EVASION

[T]he Canada Revenue Agency [reports] that a wealthy Victoria family paid almost no tax over eight years related to an offshore tax 'sham' developed by a respected accounting firm . . . [B]ased on court documents, that Victoria's Peter Cooper and his two adult sons, Marshall and Richard, signed up in 2000 for a KPMG tax product in the Isle of Man that targeted 'high net worth' Canadian residents. Court documents show that the Cooper family paid little or no tax between 2002 and 2010, yet received almost $6 million from an off-shore company. KPMG, which is both a tax and auditing firm, says any money the Coopers received were 'gifts' and therefore non-taxable.

Reached at his home in Victoria, Marshall Cooper [says] he was unaware of Canadian tax laws when he emigrated from South Africa in the mid-1990s and used the best people for advice. KPMG is representing the Coopers in their appeal in tax court. KPMG declined to speak . . . because the matter is before the courts.

. . . The government says the CRA [Canadian Revenue Agency] audited more than 8600 international tax cases between 2006 and March 31, 2014, identifying more than $5.6 billion in additional taxes that are being collected. . . . The government adds that in the fiscal year 2013–2014, the CRA resolved $46 billion in outstanding tax debt and that the CRA received more than 10 000 offshore voluntary disclosures . . .

'The fact is that the expertise in the senior ranks of the CRA has been lost over the years', NDP [New Democratic Party] politician Rankin said. 'Endless cuts to the CRA budget have seriously eroded its capacity to go after complex international tax avoidance schemes like the one at issue.' Rankin said aggressive international tax planning must be met with equally senior, experienced auditors . . .

Green Party Leader Elizabeth May said tax havens and tax credits used by extremely wealthy individuals and corporations are unethical, inequitable and detrimental to Canada's economy . . . The CRA should be mandated to go after offshore accounts and use more forensic accounting . . . May estimates about $3 billion in additional tax revenues could be recovered annually by closing tax loopholes. 'This latest scandal underlines how negligent Canada has been' . . .

'KPMG is a very reputable firm; therefore, their [alleged] involvement in such a scheme surprises me', Liberal politician Kane said. 'While Liberals have promised to bring greater fairness to the tax system, we know that this fairness goes both ways.' . . . In 2013, the CRA obtained a judicial order demanding KPMG hand over the names of all the wealthy clients who set up shell companies in the Isle of Man but KPMG Canada is fighting that decision in federal court, the CBC [Canadian Broadcasting Corporation] reported. The CRA alleges in court documents that the KPMG tax structure was a 'sham' and hit the Cooper family with an order to repay millions in unpaid taxes and penalties . . . How much more money is sitting in offshore accounts that could be contributing to Canada's infrastructure, schools and hospitals? . . . 'Is the CRA pushing hard enough in court to get these names; this has been going on for eight years'. (Cindy E. Harnett, *Times Colonist*, 10 September 2015)[63]

Paradise Papers leak from the offshore legal firm Appleby and other sources, a number of other massive leaks and investigations in the last decade – many conducted by the International Consortium of Investigative Journalists – include: the 'Luxembourg leaks' detailing the tax rulings that facilitate Luxembourg as a tax haven; the Swiss financial institution UBS AG facilitating client offshore tax evasion; the Swiss banking arm of the global bank HSBC that is centred in London and Hong Kong facilitating client tax evasion; and Canadian and American partners of the international accounting firm KPMG marketing tax evasion schemes to clients. This list is far from complete. What is apparent is that the numbers are immense. An HSBC case from 2008 involved $100 billion in accounts; and in terms of government revenue loss as a percentage of domestic output, the greatest percentage losses occur in the poorer countries of the world. Due to the constantly changing legal environment, total tax losses cannot be estimated with any accuracy.

As for offshore tax avoidance by US corporations, a recent study by Citizens for Tax Justice and the US Public Interest Research Group Education Fund used Securities and Exchange Commission (SEC) filings to estimate that America's largest publicly traded companies are holding more than $2.1 trillion in profits offshore; the *Wall Street Journal* (16 September 2018) estimates $2.7 trillion; and the Trump administration claims $4 billion. If these cash hoards were repatriated there would be an estimated increase of $620 billion in US tax revenue.[64] The Public Interest Research Group (PIRG) study estimated that about 72 per cent of the companies on the Fortune 500 list of largest US companies by gross revenue operate subsidiaries in tax havens such as Bermuda, Ireland, Luxembourg and the Netherlands. At year-end 2014, the following companies had the largest offshore cash hoards: Apple ($181.1 billion) in three tax havens; General Electric ($119 billion) in 18 tax havens; Microsoft ($108.3 billion) in five tax havens; and Pfizer ($74 billion) in 151 subsidiaries, not all tax havens. Seeking to encourage repatriation of these funds, the Trump tax cuts feature a reduced corporate tax rate on transfer of 'old funds' and effectively no tax on 'new funds'. However, as of September 2018 only $465 billion had been repatriated.

Evasion and avoidance strategies depend on the tax codes of the specific jurisdictions involved. For example, many schemes aimed at the US take advantage of two aspects of the tax code: corporate profits are only subject to tax when returned to the US, while funds left offshore have deferred tax treatment; and lower tax rates on portfolio investments of foreign compared to domestic investors. In addition to US-specific issues, schemes that can be found across countries include: flexible transfer pricing by multinational companies with operations in different countries, and 'round-tripping' of foreign direct investment (FDI). Driven by a desire to encourage direct investment from foreign companies, many countries give preferential tax treatment to such direct investments compared to the same investment in plant and equipment by domestic companies. Evidence for such round-tripping is reflected by Cyprus being the largest FDI investor in Russia, and Mauritius being the largest source of FDI for India.[65] In countries that provide favourable tax treatment for portfolio investors as well as foreign direct investors, round-tripping of portfolio investments exploiting the secrecy of tax havens is also a source of evasion and avoidance.

A widely recognized case of a technology company exploiting transfer pricing is the \$2.4 billion in worldwide taxes saved by Google in 2014, that involved shifting €10.7 billion (\$12 billion) in international revenues to a Bermuda shell company in a scheme referred to as the 'Dutch Sandwich'. The sandwich involved a Google Dutch subsidiary, Google Netherlands Holdings BV. Google would move money from a Google subsidiary in Ireland to the Netherlands subsidiary and then move the funds back to a different Irish subsidiary which was physically based in Bermuda, a tax haven with no corporate income tax. This scheme allowed Google to achieve an effective tax rate on its international income at 6.3 per cent for 2015. A central feature of the scheme involved using transfer pricing to allocate profits to the geographies where profit was deemed to have been generated. The amount of these payments is supposed to be based on estimates of what similar transactions with an unrelated company would cost. Google attributes most of the economic value of its products to its research and development operations in the US and, in the case of its overseas sales, to its Bermuda-based Irish subsidiary, which holds the international licences for Google's intellectual property. At the end of 2015, Google's foreign subsidiaries were holding \$43 billion in cash.[66]

While the basic mechanics of corporate tax arbitrage are often relatively simple, in practical applications complex organizational structures may be the result. One example is IKEA, the furniture retailer. Most IKEA stores and production units are owned by INGKA, a holding company situated in the Netherlands which, in turn, is owned by the Stichting Ingka Foundation, a tax-exempt, not-for-profit organization dedicated to the promotion of 'interior design'. While the foundation structure can minimize the tax burden on corporate profits for IKEA, the use of the foundation prevents the founder of the company from tapping into funds held by the foundation. To get around this difficulty, IKEA stores pay a fee for using the IKEA trademark to a separate company, Inter IKEA Systems, owned by Inter IKEA Holding, Luxembourg, a tax haven. In turn, this holding company is owned by a trust located in the Netherlands

Antilles, another tax haven. Secrecy rules prevent the de facto ownership of the Antilles trust being revealed, but it seems likely that the beneficiaries of this trust are the family of IKEA founder Ingvar Kamprad.[67] In 2016, Ministers of the European Parliament accused IKEA of avoiding more than €1 billion in tax over the previous six years.

Of course, tax evasion and avoidance are not unique to corporations or the US. In 2008, for example, a series of tax investigations across Europe by national governments suspicious of tax evaders revealed a network of banks and trusts in Liechtenstein. The largest and most complex investigation ever initiated in the Federal Republic of Germany for tax evasion revealed that millions of euros, involving hundreds of German citizens, were funnelled into the LGT Bank and other banks in the tax haven of Liechtenstein. The objective was to exploit Liechtenstein-based trusts to evade paying German taxes. An *Agence France* article at the time quoted the German prosecutor as saying that these trusts 'have been created apparently only to evade paying taxes'.[68] Liechtenstein trusts are particularly amenable to tax evasion, due to the separation of financial assets from the identity of the owners of the trust. A specific feature of these anonymized Liechtenstein trusts is the ability for them to be revoked at any time, with assets in the trust then being returned to the anonymous owner. An added benefit of such trusts is the relatively low fees charged of 0.1 per cent of assets. This affair illustrates the difficulties of applying pressure on uncooperative tax havens such as Liechtenstein, Andorra and Monaco. In March 2014, European Union (EU) finance ministers were unable to implement sweeping reforms to fight tax evasion because of resistance from Luxembourg, another tax haven, preventing the unanimous agreement needed to pass the reforms.

Limiting Use of Trusts and Foundations[69]

A central feature of many evasion and avoidance schemes is the role played by both onshore and offshore trusts and, in some cases, foundations. There are various uses of trusts to avoid tax (Box 5.2). For example, consider the case of a wealthy individual seeking to immigrate to Canada. Instead of transferring offshore foreign capital assets into onshore domestic capital assets subject to Canadian capital income tax after immigration, it is possible for the settlor to use the assets to set up a trust for a family member beneficiary or other surrogate living in an offshore jurisdiction that has little or no tax. Payments from that trust will be exempt from Canadian tax as the income is being domiciled and taxed offshore. The income from the trust can then be gifted back to Canada without tax. Given the secrecy provisions associated with many offshore trusts, it

BOX 5.2 ULTRA-WEALTHY DODGE BILLIONS IN TAXES USING GRAT LOOPHOLE

A new Bloomberg report describes how billionaires have dodged an estimated $100 billion in gift and estate taxes since 2000, according to the lawyer who perfected the practice. The trick involves temporarily putting corporate stocks (or similar assets) into a 'Grantor Retained Annuity Trust' (GRAT), where the grantor gets the stocks back after two years, plus a small amount of interest, while any appreciation of the stock goes to the grantor's heirs tax-free. Because the initial gift has no inherent value (it's essentially a gift to oneself), there is no gift tax at the time the GRAT is set up. The loophole is that the appreciation of the stock that goes to the heirs is not subject to gift tax either. As a result, extremely wealthy individuals avoid billions of dollars in gift and estate tax.

This is what Sheldon Adelson did (to take just one example) when he put much of his Las Vegas Sands stock in GRATs when the stock had plummeted during the recession. Adelson knew that the stock was likely to rise significantly from that low point. If Adelson had simply given his heirs the stock, the gift tax would have applied to the value of the stock at the time it was given. Or if he bequeathed the stock upon his death, the estate tax would apply. But by using GRATs, neither the value of the stock at the time it was temporarily put into the GRAT nor the subsequent appreciation was subject to gift or estate tax . . . Many well-known figures, such as Facebook CEO Mark Zuckerberg, Goldman Sachs CEO Lloyd Blankfein and fashion designer Ralph Lauren, have set up GRATs to shelter their assets from gift and estate tax. Bloomberg estimates that Adelson, whose net worth is more than $30 billion, has already avoided at least $2.8 billion in US gift taxes using at least 25 different GRATs over time.

For his part, Adelson has not just sought to follow (or exploit) whatever law is on the books, but has actually taken an active role in trying to shape the law and the government that enacts it. In 2012, Adelson spent an astonishing $150 million to support conservative candidates and has said that he's ready to 'double' his donations to candidates going forward. Considering the billions that Adelson has at stake, this exuberant campaign spending may actually be a prudent investment if it works to preserve the GRAT loophole and the plethora of other massive tax breaks for the wealthy individuals embedded in the tax code.

To their credit, the Obama Administration has proposed to curb the use of GRATs by requiring that a GRAT have a minimum term of 10 years. As the Treasury explains, this would create some downside risk to using a GRAT because it increases the likelihood that the grantor will die before the GRATs paid out the appreciation to the heirs, at which point that appreciation would be subject to the estate tax. Unfortunately, this proposal has been brushed aside by Republicans who seek to eliminate the estate tax entirely and by some Democrats who are not enthusiastic about taking on a tax break used by the large campaign donor class. (Richard Phillips, Senior Policy Analyst at Center for Tax Justice, 20 December 2013, https://www.ctj.org/)

would not be possible for the CRA to trace the funds in the trust back to the immigrant. Unfortunately, trusts also play an essential legal role in the organization of pension funds, mutual funds and some commercial ventures, so restrictions on trusts aimed at curbing abuses may have unintended consequences for the many legitimate uses for trusts. There are also substantive differences in the use of trusts between common law and civil law countries.

Trust law is one of the more complicated legal and accounting specializations.[70] In general, a trust is a legal arrangement benefiting those wanting to privately structure their financial affairs or wanting to control assets without the tax and other implications of owning those assets. In Canada and most common law countries, trusts are created by written agreements – deed of trust settlements – that usually do not require registration (though the trustees often will register) and are valid upon signing. Recognizing that the wealthy and the wealthiest often create a family trust for estate planning and tax management purposes, such trusts provide privacy and asset protection. Because the trustee is technically the legal owner of the trust property, the trust is protected from bankruptcy and other judgments against both the settlor and the beneficiary. As the legal scholar Henry Hansmann observed: 'trust law allows the parties to the trust to partition off a discrete set of assets for separate treatment in relationships formed with creditors ... the trust provides flexibility in organizational structure unavailable under even the more liberal business corporation statutes'.[71] Trusts provide asset protection that can be stronger than the limited liability available to corporate shareholders.

Taking aim at the abuses and risks that trusts can facilitate, arguably the most egregious is secrecy, justified under the guise of privacy rights. In common law countries such as the US and UK, trusts can hold assets and engage in business, just like companies. Trusts used by the wealthy to hide assets in order to evade taxes are typically not subject to registration, allowing the settlors, beneficiaries and controllers of trust assets to be largely hidden from public scrutiny. In certain situations, such secrecy can facilitate a variety of financial crimes, including but not limited to tax evasion. Even in situations where trusts do have to register, complexity of the control structure can confuse tax authorities about the true source of controls and the benefits being distributed from the assets. For example, either the settlor or beneficiary could be an offshore anonymous trust. Reforms regarding registration of the beneficiary of a trust, which trusts should be registered and how to enforce registration are indicated, to prevent wealthy free riders from exploiting trust structures to evade and avoid income taxes, death taxes and property transfer taxes.[72]

As uncovered in a variety of high-profile cases involving tax evasion by the wealthiest, tax havens engage in the provision of trust structures that have been characterized as 'devious and illegitimate . . . allowing multiple subterfuges to defeat the laws of other jurisdictions'.[73] Whether in tax havens or elsewhere, careful consideration needs to be given to disallowing the creation of 'ownerless' assets generating cash flows without associated tax implications. More precisely, until assets have been allocated to a beneficiary, asset ownership and the associated tax implications needs to be attached to the settlor, not severed as allowed by current trust law. In addition, requiring trusts to be publicly registered as a precondition to be legally valid for tax purposes, and to be binding on third persons, is also indicated. Mechanisms for piercing asset protection that affects third parties outside the trust would aid the tax authorities in tracking down wealthy tax evaders. Unfortunately, globalization prevents any practical resolution within national boundaries, requiring international cooperation to affect reform. Otherwise, there is little to prevent the wealthy from continuing to move assets, and possibly residency, offshore to escape a reformed trust law. Unfortunately, the lucrative legal business associated with establishing and running trusts has created an environment where common law countries are engaged in competition to enhance the legal attractiveness of trusts to attract such business.

While the trust business thrives on anonymity provided to those setting up trust structures that are at times used for less-than-legal tax evasion purposes, even more troubling is the cynical business of using charitable foundations to facilitate tax avoidance by exploiting legal loopholes and lax oversight. The possible variations are considerable. The objective is to claim receipts for ethically questionable tax-deductible 'donations'. This can involve overvaluation of difficult-to-value donated assets, such as shares in privately held companies or artwork; donation of assets without transfer of control; and questionable use of donations for business purposes. For example, an investigation by the *Globe and Mail* (25 October 2018) of the Canadian Theanon Charitable Foundation discovered a cluster of related foundations set up by one law firm, many involved only in holding donated assets and transferring the assets between the related foundations to satisfy legal requirements to maintain charitable status. The *Globe and Mail* reported that some of the related foundations 'bankrolled multimillion-dollar projects – including for-profit businesses – supported by the law firm and its clients'. Tax returns obtained from Canada Revenue Agency legal actions against the foundations show that, in a few cases, assets or loan payments flowed back to the original donors or their private foundations.

Of course, Canada is not the only country involved in use of charitable foundations for tax avoidance purposes. The law firm involved in the Theanon Charitable Foundation is known to advise charities throughout the world, often receiving generous payments from the charitable entities for 'expert advice'. Though miniscule in comparison to various tax avoidance schemes involving other foundations, perhaps the most prominent involves the activities of the Donald J. Trump Foundation reported in the *Washington Post* (10 October 2016). The bulk of the charitable spending by this foundation involves the use of donations made by other individuals and charities, giving the appearance of charitable largesse by Trump when the source of the funds does not originate with Trump. In one instance, such a charitable contribution of $150000 was made to the Palm Beach Police Foundation that also rents a room at the Mar-a-Lago club owned by Trump for an annual gala. Cost of renting the room, reported in a 2014 tax filing, was over $274000. In another instance, the Trump Foundation was fined for making a political contribution, a prohibited activity for charitable entities. From this, it is apparent that some activities of foundations do not have either charitable aims or tax avoidance as the proximate objective.

From Voluntary Disclosure to FATCA and After[74]

Tax authorities in various countries have not sat idly by while the wealthy and the wealthiest have been avoiding and evading taxes. From the US Offshore Voluntary Disclosure (OVD) Program to the OECD Financial Action Task Force on Money Laundering (FATF) to the multilateral Mutual Administrative Assistance on Tax Matters Convention and the Global Forum on Transparency and Exchange of Information for Tax Purposes (GFTEITP), there has been a myriad of unilateral, bilateral and multilateral efforts to stem the bleeding and capture tax revenues from wealthy tax evaders.[75] Included in these efforts are a barrage of government reports, legislative actions and international agreements. Many of these initiatives recognize that in the problem of tax evasion in the 21st century, financial institutions and international tax experts are playing a fundamental role. A multitude of whistleblowers and legal cases reveal the fundamental role of financial institutions such as UBS, LGT and HSBC, legal firms such as Mossack Fonseca and Appleby, and accounting firms such as KPMG, in facilitating the activities of wealthy tax avoiders and, in some cases, tax evaders. However, despite recent legislative efforts such as the US Foreign Account Tax Compliance Act (FATCA) introduced in 2010 and related multilateral efforts by the OECD, a complex structure of trusts and shell corporations located within a network of tax havens combine with rapid international funds transfer to pose a complex and frustrating challenge to those dedicated to limiting the machinations of wealthy tax evaders.[76]

The attack on wealthy tax evaders has been waged on a variety of fronts. In the US, faced with increasing, arguably overwhelming, evidence of wealthy tax evaders exploiting the advantages provided by globalization, starting in 2003 the IRS unilaterally introduced the first of various offshore programmes that provide incentives for taxpayers to disclose funds in offshore accounts and to pay delinquent taxes, interest and penalties. The Government Accountability Office (GAO) reports that, as of December 2012, the Internal Revenue Service (IRS) had collected over $5.5 billion in revenue from taxpayers participating in the OVD programmes, collecting some 39 000 disclosures, many receiving reduced penalties and a lower risk of criminal prosecution.[77] The first of the OVD initiatives, offered in 2003, was small but creative and related to an offshore credit card project that the IRS starting pursuing in 2000. In this initiative, the IRS served 'John Doe' summonses on major credit card companies seeking records on foreign bank accounts. Unfortunately, the three-year statute of limitations for tax assessment meant that by the time the IRS had gathered enough information to generate files for IRS revenue agents, most cases were not capable of prosecution. In 2003, this programme evolved, with the IRS announcing the Offshore Voluntary Compliance Initiative (OVCI) in order to get taxpayers to come forward and clear up their tax liabilities. The 2003 OVCI resulted in $75 million in taxes paid by taxpayers who participated.

Three key elements led to a substantial expansion of the OVD programme in 2009: the change in control of the US government from Republican to Democrat in the 2008 election; the erosion of government revenue brought on by the financial crisis of 2008–09; and the extent of offshore tax evasion involving Swiss bank accounts at UBS being revealed. Faced with compelling whistleblower evidence of tax evasion, the US government more-or-less forced UBS to name US clients, eventually charging UBS with 'conspiring to defraud the United States by assisting account holders in evading the IRS'. This lawsuit, combined with the IRS announcement of the 2009 Voluntary Disclosure Program, resulted in the collection of $3.4 billion from 15 000 disclosures. This programme had a window of opportunity that allowed tax evaders to come forward from 23 March 2009 to 15 October 2009. The desire of tax evaders to come clean following the closing of the 2009 OVD programme resulted in the IRS initiating a new OVD programme, in February 2011. The IRS reports that about 12 000 disclosures were made under the 2011 OVD. In 2012, the IRS announced a continuation of the OVD, with no defined endpoint, though the IRS reserved the right to change the programme at any time, including the possibility that specific groups of tax evaders could be disqualified from the programme. This programme was ended in September 2018, though there are still other programmes that are available to delinquent US taxpayers with offshore accounts.

Initiatives such as the IRS OVD programmes are unilateral in character and only effective if tax evaders have enough concern that the veil of secrecy will be lifted for offshore accounts at specific institutions. The limitations of this approach inspired a variety of incongruent initiatives of the EU, the OECD, the G20, Switzerland and the US to cobble together an international regime in which financial institutions and foreign tax authorities act to facilitate the ability of a given country to tax the offshore accounts of residents. Under the aegis of the OECD, these initiatives have coalesced as the GFTEITP. Restructured in 2009, the GFTEITP has made remarkable progress toward global implementation of the Automatic Exchange of Information on Request (AEIR) standard.[78] By joining, GFTEITP countries sign on to a standardized multilateral agreement, dramatically reducing the difficulties of negotiating bilateral agreements. Exploiting 'a growing consensus that financial institutions should act as cross-border tax intermediaries',[79] in much the same fashion as such inter-mediaries facilitate domestic tax collection, the GFTEITP further seeks to improve substantially the AEIR standard that the GFTEITP has managed to implement. The next stage is projected to introduce multilateral use of a Common Reporting Standard and Automatic Exchange of Information.

The success of the GFTEITP initiatives represent 'a remarkable shift in international norms'. In conjunction with increasing evidence of wide-spread use of globalization to evade taxes, a substantial initial impetus to change the older, largely unilateral approach to offshore accounts was the budgetary pressures brought on by the financial crisis of 2008–09. It was more than apparent that improved transparency was needed to combat offshore tax abuses. To achieve widespread agreement in the OECD, the participation from four member states with histories as offshore banking centers was needed – Austria, Belgium, Luxembourg, and Switzerland – countries firmly committed to bank secrecy as a bar to tax information exchange upon request. One of the countries, Switzerland, was estimated to be the location of more than 25 per cent of the global offshore wealth management industry, measured by assets under management. The situation in Switzerland was particularly complicated due to Swiss criminal law that makes the breaking of secrecy a serious crime. 'Recognizing its vulnerability to demands for transparency, Switzerland developed its own proposal: anonymous cross-border tax withholding in lieu of an information reporting scheme that would promote transparency.'[80] As of November 2019, all four countries were considered 'largely compli-ant' with the AEIR, with the same rating as Canada, the US, Japan and Germany.

Ability of the OECD to act collectively through the GFTEITP has seen important non-OECD financial centres, especially Hong Kong, Liechtenstein, Panama and Singapore, no longer 'follow the lead of Switzerland and the other OECD bank secrecy jurisdictions in rejecting exchange upon request of bank information'.[81] Singapore is considered fully compliant with the AEIR, with Hong Kong and Liechtenstein largely compliant. Panama is one of a few countries only partially compliant. Through GFTEITP information relevant for tax purposes is available from approximately 130 other jurisdictions, this includes all G20 and OECD countries, practically all international financial centres, together with an increasing number of developing countries. The 'global contest between automatic information reporting and anonymous withholding models for ensuring that states have the ability to tax offshore accounts'[82] is increasingly being decided in favour of automatic information reporting, which is preferred by non-tax haven countries that are losing revenue, while tax haven countries either want to keep the traditional secrecy model or, at best, convert to anonymous withholding.[83]

Though initiatives such as FATCA and the GFTEITP seek a multilateral solution, progress on bilateral agreements has also been made since 2008–09. Given the considerable progress getting Switzerland to loosen secrecy restrictions, the battle against wealthy tax evaders now shifts to the practical question: have these initiatives have been enough to offset 'the capacity to make, hold, and manage investments through offshore financial institutions . . . [making] it substantially easier to under-report or not to report investment [and business] earnings through the use of offshore accounts'.[84] In any event, automatic information reporting or an anonymous withholding model both involve global financial institutions cooperating with governments to act as cross-border tax intermediaries:

> the contest between information reporting and anonymous withholding models for how financial institutions will provide cross-border tax administrative assistance implicates broad questions about the future of tax sovereignty in a globalized economy and about the treatment of the wealthiest vis-à-vis other taxpayers. Whereas anonymous withholding delegates tax collection to a foreign entity, automatic information reporting shores up a government's capacity to tax its own citizens.[85]

NOTES

1. As quoted in Duclos (2006, p. 1078).
2. As MacMullen (1959, p. 207) observes: 'Of the many things that separate the Roman Empire from the Republic, the most obvious physically is the building activity of

Augustus and his successors in the provinces. The Republic had embellished its capital at the expense of the conquered; the Empire redressed the balance; and the political and psychological significance of this change, by which the wealth of Rome's subjects was in part, and sometimes very magnificently, restored to them, is sufficient to mark an era.'

3. Hale (1985) provides a useful discussion of property tax history starting from the medieval period. Recent changes in the property tax and the relationship with state and local relations are examined in Sokolow (1998). Shanske (2015) details why the current regime of fragmented property tax assessment and collection needs to be reformed.

4. The aid can be traced to the start of the 13th century. The aid was an assessment on 'personalty': movable property such as livestock, crops, tools and household goods, especially household luxuries such as silver plate (e.g., Hale, 1985, p. 388).

5. Hale (1985, p. 384).

6. Locke (1690, treatise 1, section 124).

7. See Myrdal (1965, pp. 164–5) and Groves (1974, 14–18, 30–32).

8. Seligman (1914 [1911], p. 640). For evidence of fervency, consider statements such as, 'wherever we find the spread of democracy, we find the growth of income taxation' (Seligman, 1914 [1911], p. 642).

9. Seligman (1914 [1911], p. 641).

10. Ibid.

11. Mehrotra (2005) is a useful source on conflict within the various elements of the Progressive movement and efforts to implement an income tax. Specifically, together with reform-minded Progressive economists at the leading American universities such as Richard Ely and Henry Carter Adams, Seligman faced 'formidable' opposition from the political left: 'There the populist attraction to the single-tax ideas of Henry George appeared to distract important constituencies away from the income tax movement. In defusing that opposition, the economists sought to debunk the amateur economic analysis conducted by George and his disciples. They also attempted to unmask the "ultraconservative" social theory that underpinned George's call for a single tax on land' (Mehrota, 2005, p. 943).

12. There is a voluminous literature on Henry George that continues to the present, O'Donnell (2015) being a recent example. The *American Journal of Economics and Sociology* has published numerous papers on George and the philosophy of 'Georgism', including an issue dedicated to the centenary of *Progress and Poverty* and an October 2014 issue providing a book featuring the ideas of George by T. Dwyer (2014). There are a number of institutes and foundations dedicated to Georgism and the work of George in the US, the UK and Australia. Of these, the Robert Schalkenbach Foundation, founded in 1925, features Ted Gwartney as President. An assessor by trade, Gwartney served as Assessment Commissioner and Chief Executive Officer of the British Columbia Assessment Authority from 1975 to 1986, and was responsible for implementing a property tax assessment system that is a model for property tax assessment based on market valuations. Together with the Francis Nelson Fund, the Schalkenbach Foundation provides grants to the *American Journal of Economics and Sociology*.

13. George (1882 [1879], p. 10).

14. Roberts (1971, p. 301).

15. *Progress and Poverty* (pp. 234, 316–17).

16. *Progress and Poverty* (p. 324).

17. See Goodwin (2008).

18. Harris (1994, p. 98).

19. Dietsch (2015, p. 14).

20. Hines and Summers (2009, p. 125).

21. Bowman and Rugg (2012, p. 3).

22. For example, was the ratio of income tax paid to property tax paid a significant contributor to an individual's survey responses?

23. Details on the structure of local property tax systems in the US and Canada are available in the surveys conducted by the International Association of Assessing Officers, the most recent in 2017 (Dornfest et al., 2019).

24. See Institute on Taxation and Economic Policy (2011). Krupa (2014) provides evidence that, confronted with a crisis in housing market values, market-based assessments will tend to exacerbate vertical inequity by undervaluing high-value properties and overvaluing lower-value properties.

25. See BC Assessment (2017). From 1860 to 1973, the property assessment process was not unlike that in many local US jurisdictions. In 1860, when the Real Estate Act for the colony of Vancouver Island was enacted, an annual tax of 1 per cent was assessed on the market value of real estate, with assessors appointed to perform the assessment function. Initially, assessment typically required 'minimal on-site or mass appraisal expertise. Instead, assessors established actual market values based on property owners' estimates to compile the assessment rolls.' Over time, as each city in BC created separate organizations using individual assessment criteria, much as in US localities, the lack of standard valuation methods meant 'assessments were frequently challenged and often difficult to defend. By 1973, with 140 independent assessment organizations in British Columbia, the situation had grown into a serious provincial crisis' (BC Assessment, 2017). Passed in 1974, the Assessment Authority Act granted the provincial government the power to create a province-wide assessment authority and, six months later, the British Columbia Assessment Authority produced the first impartial and independent assessment rolls and notices for the whole province, resolving issues of 'efficiency, professionalism, impartiality and uniformity' (ibid.).

26. Mieszkowski and Zodrow (1989, p. 1098).

27. Ibid.

28. Ibid.

29. Oates (1972, p. 143).

30. Wilson (1999, p. 269).

31. Ibid.

32. Cremer and Gahvari (1998).

33. Seligman (1914 [1911], p. 641).

34. Hines and Summers (2009, p. 126). The subtle difference between consumption and expenditure taxes is being ignored. More precisely, an expenditure tax involves tax on actual purchases (expenditures) of goods and services, while a consumption tax could be broader, possibly encompassing items that are 'consumed', such as imputed rent, without an identifiable expenditure associated with the tax. However, most sources treat the terms as synonyms.

35. The notion of introducing progressive consumption taxes is explored in McCaffery (2002) and Bank (2003). See also Zelanak (2010), McLure and Zodrow (2007), Shaviro (2007) and Bankman and Weisbach (2006).

36. Hines and Summers (2009, p. 126). See also Graetz (2002).

37. Hines and Summers (2009, p. 127).

38. Based on data from the Statistics Canada Survey of Financial Security, the advantages of having wealth at a early age are documented by Macdonald (2015): 'The major finding is that Canada's wealth gap is big and growing – the wealthiest 10 per cent of families enjoy a net worth that's millions more than families in the middle of the income spectrum – and that wealth advantage starts early in an affluent family's life. Young affluent families in their twenties have a major wealth advantage: their net worth is already higher than middle-class families in their fifties and sixties. If these millionaire babies stay at the top, they'll spend the rest of their lifetime accumulating even greater wealth, leaving their middle-class contemporaries behind in their gold dust.'

39. Modigliani (1988, p. 17).

40. Cagetti (2003) estimates that savings associated with the precautionary motive are approximately the same size as for the retirement motive.

41. Haugerud (2012, p. 148).

42. Bank (2003, pp. 2238–9).
43. Atkinson and Stiglitz (1976) is an influential early contribution to this argument. Such claims extend beyond the confines of economists. For example, Bankman and Weisbach (2006) develop the results of Atkinson and Stiglitz (1976) in a legal context.
44. More information can be found at: https://www.lta.gov.sg/content/ltaweb/en/roads-and-motoring/owning-a-vehicle/costs-of-owning-a-vehicle/tax-structure-for-cars.html.
45. An odd argument that is made against such mansion taxes is that there are asset-rich and cash-poor seniors that would be unable to make the additional tax payments. Presumably, there is some reason why a reverse mortgage could not be used. In some jurisdictions, such as British Columbia, such seniors can defer property taxes until the property is sold, and the tax bill can be settled out of the proceeds. Such seniors are not being taxed on the imputed rent and have either a deferred capital gain or, for a primary residence in most jurisdictions, have no capital gains tax to pay.
46. The study of death taxes, covering taxes on inheritance, estate, gifts, trusts and foundations, is vast. In the US, Stiglitz (1978) is often taken as a starting point for theoretical analysis. Stiglitz (1978, p. S317) finds the seemingly odd result that, 'because of capital accumulation effects, the estate tax may increase inequality of income and wealth. If the government takes actions to offset these accumulation effects, the tax will lead to an increase in equality of income and wealth.' Useful studies of death taxes include De Nardi and Yang (2016), Avery et al. (2015), Catetti and De Nardi (2009), Graetz and Shapiro (2011), Kopczuk and Slemrod (2003), Boadway et al. (2000) and Carroll (1989).
47. The eminent Roman historian P.A. Brunt (1984, pp. 435–7) refers to the tax as 'estate-duties' and provides details of the sources used to construct the narrative.
48. Circa 2019, there were six US states imposing an inheritance tax, with 12 states and DC having an estate tax. Since the 1960s many states have eliminated such taxes. The states that impose an inheritance tax are Iowa, Kentucky, Maryland, Nebraska, New Jersey and Pennsylvania. One impetus for such eliminations was the removal in 2005 of the credit against federal estate tax for non-federal estate taxes. This credit was phased out by passage of the Economic Growth and Tax Relief Reconciliation Act (2001). The federal Tax Cuts and Jobs Act (2017) raised the estate tax exclusion from $5.49 million to $11.2 million per person.
49. This simplifies some practical details. For example, if a capital asset is owned jointly by two individuals, then the death of one owner will not trigger the capital gain. However, if the remaining owner then adds another (arm's-length) owner to the title, then that would trigger the capital gain. Consequently, the wealthy in Canada often resort to the use of trusts where the triggering of the capital gain can either be avoided or transferred to a lower income beneficiary of the trust.
50. Cagetti and De Nardi (2009, p. 89).
51. Ibid.
52. Graetz and Shapiro (2011) provides a helpful discussion of such questions.
53. Gordon et al. (2016) discuss the empirical evidence on the choice between basis carry-over and estate tax.
54. Included in such studies are Gelber and Weinzierl (2016) for the US and Macdonald (2015) for Canada.
55. Included in the numerous studies of tax havens are the insightful efforts by the investigative journalist Nicholas Shaxson (2011) and the legal scholar James Hines (2010).
56. Studies on the connection between globalization and tax competition include Costa-Font et al. (2014), Hines and Summers (2009), Mittermaier (2009), Devereux et al. (2002) and Avi-Yonah (2000).
57. Studies on tax competition in the US predate the rise of globalization. Following on from the Tiebout model of local public goods and services provision introduced in 1956, theories of tax competition initially focused on competition between localities and states (e.g., Mieszkowski and Zodrow, 1989). Over time, these studies of local public goods were extended to a variety of areas of inter-governmental competition such as:

'competition for investment through weaker environmental standards or reductions in welfare payments by states trying to avoid attracting poor households' (Wilson, 1999, p. 270). It is not surprising that tax competition models have also been applied to competition between national governments for investment capital. Other recent studies of international tax competition include Dietsch (2015), Costa-Font et al. (2014), Haufler et al. (2009), Mittermaier (2009), Devereux et al. (2002), Scharf (2001), Haufler (2001), Feld (2000), Avi-Yonah (2000) and Janeba and Peters (1999).

58. Round-tripping is not restricted to FDI. Hanlon et al. (2015) consider round-tripping for portfolio investment, 'in which US individuals hide funds in entities located in offshore tax havens and then invest those funds in US securities markets'. More specifically, 'by making it appear that the investments are coming from true foreign investors, these individuals are able to evade most tax on the investment income because the United States taxes foreign investors in US securities much more favorably than domestic investors'. Jones and Temouri (2016) discuss the determinants of tax haven FDI.

59. Grubert and Altshuler (2016) and Graetz and Warren (2016) are studies that considered tax reforms needed to lower the US corporate tax rate to a level that would alleviate such tax competition.

60. The noted public finance economist John Diamond provided this insight in a preamble to a collection of papers from a *National Tax Journal* forum conducted in September 2016 (Diamond, 2016, p. 641).

61. A wealth of such data is available on the Tax Justice Network website, www.taxjustice. net.

62. Zucman (2014, p. 121). Estimates in GAO (2013) recognize that while initiative to limit offshore tax evasion has resulted in the IRS collecting 'billions of dollars' that would otherwise have escaped taxes, the GAO recognizes that the IRS 'may be missing continued evasion'. US Senate (2014) provides a useful overview of US government efforts to collect the unpaid taxes on the wealth hidden in offshore accounts. Slemrod (2007) discusses the economics of tax evasion.

63. See more at: http://www.timescolonist.com/news/local/victoria-family-cited-in-cra-crackdown-on-tax-evasion-1.2055917.

64. The British newspaper the *Daily Mail* (12 March 2014) reports that EU officials estimate tax fraud and aggressive cross-border tax avoidance schemes by companies to cost the EU governments an estimated €1 trillion (£830 billion) a year.

65. Dietsch (2015, p. 5).

66. Technically, it is Alphabet, the parent of Google, that is the entity avoiding tax. The Irish government recently closed the loophole that permitted the Dutch Sandwich.

67. Genschel and Schwarz (2011, pp. 346–7).

68. Knobel and Meinzer (2016).

69. Useful general studies on abuses of trusts include Knobel (2017), Harrington (2012) and Gaillard and Trautman (1987).

70. In Canada, there are two general types of trusts. A testamentary trust is a trust or estate that is generally created on the day a person dies. The terms of the trust are established by the will or by court order in relation to the deceased individual's estate under provincial or territorial law. An *inter vivos* trust is a trust that is not a testamentary trust. There are a sizeable number of variations on the *inter vivos* trust, such as the alter ego trust, real estate investment trust and unit trust.

71. Hansmann and Mattei (1998, p. 434).

72. See Knobel (2017) for a development of these reform measures.

73. Knobel (2017, p. 2).

74. There are a number of useful studies on the efforts such as FATCA to require financial institutions with global reach to proactively participate in the collection of income taxes on offshore wealth, in the same fashion as many such institutions participate in the collection of taxes on income generated from onshore wealth. In addition to Global Forum (2019), included in these studies are, especially, Grinberg (2012), Johannesen

and Zucman (2014), Song (2015) and Woldeab (2015). Other studies with useful content are Rahimi-Laridjani and Hauser (2016), Shaxson (2012), Sharman (2006) and Ahlawat and Telson (2015). GAO (2014) discusses participation in the offshore voluntary disclosure programme.

75. Grinberg (2012) is an essential source on the battle over taxing offshore accounts.
76. An overview of efforts in Canada to crack down on evasion and abusive avoidance is available at http://www.cra-arc.gc.ca/gncy/cmpgns/crckngdwn-eng.html.
77. The IRS reports on the results for three voluntary programmes that began in 2009: 'Overall, the three voluntary programs have resulted in more than 45000 voluntary disclosures from individuals who have paid about $6.5 billion in back taxes, interest and penalties' (https://www.irs.gov/newsroom/irs-offshore-voluntary-disclosure-efforts-produce-65-billion-45000-taxpayers-participate). The following discussion of the OVD is extracted from information on the IRS website.
78. Though the AEIR is a significant step forward, the standard is not a panacea for tax evasion and avoidance. Domestic tax authorities need to initially identify likely evaders and then contact specific countries for information about the suspect. If activities are spread across numerous tax jurisdictions using anonymous trusts or numbered corporations with nominees as trustees or directors, this could be a tedious task. Once the information has been obtained, then the domestic tax authorities would have to act in domestic tax courts. If the suspect had limited assets in the jurisdiction, then enforcing any judgment could be difficult.
79. Grinberg (2012, p.305).
80. The quotes in this paragraph are from Grinberg (2012).
81. Ibid.
82. Ibid.
83. An example of bilateral progress can be found in a *Financial Times* article of 29 December 2016 where it is reported that: 'Switzerland wants to update a tax deal with the US next year to allow the automatic, two-way exchange of information about bank accounts between the two countries, a senior official in Bern has said.'
84. Grinberg (2012, p.308).
85. Grinberg (2012).

6. Reforming taxes on equity capital

> The prime fact concerning us as a nation is the progressive diffusion of owner-
> ship on the one hand and the ever-increasing concentration of managerial
> power on the other.
>
> (William Ripley, *Main Street and Wall Street*, 1927)

CONCEIVING MODERN EQUITY CAPITAL[1]

The Separation of Ownership and Control

What are the proximate causes of increasing wealth and income inequality? Specifically, how have the wealthy and, especially, the wealthiest
managed to significantly increase the share of both wealth and income?
Examining the last 50 years of tax changes in the United States (US), a
recent study concluded that: 'Changes in taxes and transfers account for
nearly half of the rise in wealth concentration . . . Results highlight the
role of increasing wage dispersion during this period as the main driver
of trends in inequality.'[2] Recognizing the inherent limitations of the data
upon which such conclusions are based, it is not difficult to infer significant
contributors to the increasing wage dispersion that has benefited the
wealthy, the impact of technological change on the workplace, and the
increases in managerial compensation involving the substitution of equity
capital for cash compensation. In addition to changing the relationship
between capital and labour in many sectors, technological change has
generated unprecedented profits that have been increasingly captured by
corporations and other limited liability entities. In conjunction, increasing
separation of ownership from control has permitted the distribution of
these profits to be captured in managerial compensation that – combined
with realized and unrealized equity capital gains – has fuelled the increasing income and wealth of the wealthiest.

There are a small number of texts from the inter-war period with an
enduring influence that have survived to the present. A list of such texts
would include J.M. Keynes, *The General Theory* (1936),[3] and A. Berle
and G. Means, *The Modern Corporation and Private Property* (1932). The
persisting influence of such texts can be found in the diversity of issues

188

being addressed. While some issues still resonate, other aspects have long since been ignored. In the case of Berle and Means, the fundamental issues that still attract attention in corporation law, corporate finance and related subjects are shareholder primacy, and the separation of ownership and control. In modern corporate law, 'Berle and Means' is taken to represent 'shareholder primacy'; that is, that corporate managers have an over-riding responsibility to maximize shareholder value. Shareholder primacy is typically contrasted with two other viewpoints: one that allows for managerial discretion, and one that advocates corporate social responsibility. The debate between these different positions deals with 'the fundamental nature of corporate activity and the appropriate goals of corporate law'.[4]

Outside of corporate law, 'Berle and Means' is synonymous with the separation of ownership and control, a topic that continuously appears in numerous social, political, legal, economic and financial contexts. Specifically, the rise of fiduciary capitalism, where equity capital ownership is increasingly concentrated in passive investment entities, has facilitated the increasing separation of ownership from control initially identified by Berle and Means. In conjunction with the rise of managerial deferred equity compensation schemes that claim to address the agency problem associated with the separation of ownership from control, the door was opened to paying excessive managerial compensation that, in turn, exploits the 'realization principle' to defer paying personal income tax on the bulk of that compensation. In effect, not only is excessive managerial compensation a significant driver of increasing wealth and income inequality of the top 1 per cent, but also the method of paying the bulk of those gains effectively exploits deferred tax provisions associated with the payment of compensation as contingent equity capital, such as executive stock options or restricted stock.

Unfortunately, what has survived to modern times from Berle and Means has been sanitized, largely removed from the broader social and political context that is threaded through the text. To illustrate, consider the concluding paragraph on the reach and importance of the limited liability corporation:[5]

> The rise of the modern corporation has brought a concentration of economic power which can compete on equal terms with the modern state . . . Where its own interests are concerned, it even attempts to dominate the state. The future may see the economic organism now typified by the corporation, not only on an equal plane with the state, but possibly even superseding it as the dominant form of social organization.

Without the pressures of engaged stockholders, Berle and Means viewed managers 'as a self-perpetuating oligarchy, unaccountable to the owners whom they were expected to represent'.[6] In a broader context: 'Berle and Means warned that the ascendance of management control and unchecked corporate power had potentially serious consequences for the democratic character of the United States'.[7] It was a concern 'that economic power was becoming concentrated in the hands of a cluster of corporate managers' that initially brought together the research of Adolf Berle, a law professor, and economics graduate student Gardiner Means.[8]

Though *The Modern Corporation and Private Property* appeared in 1932 during the early part of the Great Depression, the text was more concerned with the period from 1890 until the 1920s, culminating in the stock market crash of 1929. The research was well formed before the stock market crash signalled the beginning of profound social and political concerns arising from the Great Depression. During the 1920s there was a pervasive view in law and economics that self-regulation was the appropriate approach to corporate governance. The conclusion of Berle and Means was that government control of publicly traded limited liability corporations was required to offset the power that the law and the political system had allowed to become overly concentrated, threatening democratic institutions. This reasoned and seemingly well-researched perspective fitted well with the New Deal reforms, such as the Securities Exchange Act (1934), that substantially altered the character of the relationship between the corporation and its owners, the common stockholders. For various reasons, such larger political and social concerns are largely absent from recent treatments. Instead, focus centres on concerns about 'the data', whether Berle and Means got it right back in the day, and whether similar data applies to more recent time periods.

Some studies have argued that the equity capital landscape has changed considerably since Berle and Means. More precisely: 'Equity ownership in the United States no longer reflects the dispersed share ownership of the canonical Berle–Means firm. Instead, we observe the re-concentration of ownership in the hands of institutional investment intermediaries.'[9] In addition to debates about the empirical evidence on ownership concentration after Berle and Means, questions have been raised about the validity of Berle and Means's interpretation of the degree of concentration, the separation of ownership and control, in earlier times. Similarly, 'Berle and Means'[s] omission of the role of investment funds led them to conclude that the separation of ownership from control problems was located between shareholders and company managers'.[10] This suggests a drawback in the agency theory approach based on corporate managers and diffusely distributed shareholders. Issues surrounding separation of equity capital fund ownership and shareholders in the funds are distinct from the traditional agency model, adding a layer of complexity involving insurance companies, pension funds, hedge funds, mutual funds, index funds and other exchange traded funds. To alleviate problems arising from the separation of owner-ship and control, the socially responsible corporate management will seek to maximize shareholder wealth, monitored by equity capital funds with a fiduciary responsibility to ensure that the interests of shareholders are looked after. Such is the basic theory of fiduciary capitalism.

What is Fiduciary Capitalism?

'Capitalism' is such an overused word that the underlying concept being referenced has become obscured by the variety of meanings that could be attached. Recently, many of those currently employing this term have preferred to explore 'varieties of capitalism'.[11] The economic and financial historian Larry Neal has synthesized this approach into:[12]

> Four elements . . . common in each variant of capitalism, whatever the specific emphasis:
>
> 1. private property rights
> 2. contracts enforceable by third parties
> 3. markets with responsive prices and
> 4. supportive governments.
>
> Each of these elements must deal specifically with *capital*, a factor of produc-tion that is somehow physically embodied, whether in buildings and equipment, or in improvements to land, or in people with special knowledge. Regardless of the form it takes, however, the capital has to be long lived and not ephemeral to have meaningful economic effects.

This approach identifies capital with the left-hand side of the balance sheet, that is, physical, financial and human capital. In contrast to those seeking common factors in varieties of capitalism, others do not find the term 'capitalism':[13]

> to be a useful one for the purposes of comparative economic or political analysis. By focusing on the ownership and accumulation of capital, this term distracts from the characteristics of societies which are more important in determining their economic development and the extent of inequality. For example, both Uzbekistan and modern Switzerland have private ownership of capital, but these societies have little in common in terms of prosperity and inequality because the nature of their economic and political institutions differs so sharply. In fact, Uzbekistan's capitalist economy has more in common with avowedly noncapitalist North Korea than Switzerland.

This could be interpreted as relating the capital in 'capitalism' to the right-hand side of the balance sheet, that is, the ownership claim of equity capital and the increase in value of equity with the accumulation of retained earnings over time.

Due to the scattered and disparate interpretations of 'capital', the capitalism associated with the equity capital of the right-hand side of the balance sheet often appears with an adjective: financial capitalism, money manager capitalism, fiduciary capitalism, agency capitalism, finance-dominated capitalism, investment bank capitalism, managerial capitalism. Though the broader concerns of these interpretations differ, a common theme is that the bulk of productive capacity in modern society is now owned by limited liability corporations with equity capital ownership that is increasingly concentrated in the hands of large financial institutions that are often passive investors: pension funds, life insurance companies, investment banks, mutual funds, exchange traded funds and, in some cases, hedge funds. The various adjectives reflect, to varying degrees, the positive or negative interpretations of the current state of capitalism. Those referring to fiduciary capitalism or agency capitalism see the increasing ownership of equity capital by fiduciaries as a positive development. Such fiduciaries work for fiduciary institutions with legally defined duties, such as prudent investor rules.

Some studies taking a positive view of fiduciary capitalism refer to such fiduciary institutions as 'universal investors':[14]

> whose investment portfolios are so large and so diverse, and whose time horizons are so long-term, that it no longer makes economic sense for them to focus on the goal traditionally thought to drive individual shareholders – the goal of maximizing the price of the company's shares ... the universal shareowner – unlike the typical individual investor – has both an interest in and an ability to promote corporate practices that advance not only the narrow interests of the firm's shareholders, but also those of the broader society.

In contrast to this positive view of fiduciary capitalism, others referring to money manager capitalism, finance-dominated capitalism, investment bank capitalism, and the like take a decidedly negative view.[15] For example, taking 'a systemic macroeconomic perspective on finance-dominated capitalism and its crisis', the financialization inherent in finance-dominated capitalism: 'has, since the early 1980's [*sic*], affected long-run economic developments in the developed capitalist economies in particular through the following three channels: re-distribution of income at the expense of low labour incomes, dampening of investment in real capital stock, and an increasing potential for wealth-based and debt-financed consumption'.[16] This concern with increasing redistribution and disparity of wealth is also a key theme in the widely discussed contributions by Piketty, but receives no attention from the renowned, if much more conservative, economist Robert Shiller.[17]

When viewed through the lens of equity capital, an alternative vision of capitalism appears. The negative view of capitalism claiming that increasing and inexorable wealth inequality leads to macroeconomic instability arguably finds no basis. The allocation of domestic production to various groups in society and the associated ability to carry wealth through time is largely a political and social matter unrelated to macroeconomic stability. Specifically, it is inherently inequality increasing through the increased use of personal income taxes, payroll taxes and consumption taxes, while reducing use of corporate taxes, taxes on wealth and death taxes to fund government activities that have traditionally supported inequality-alleviating support for those in lower-income groups. The macroeconomic implications of this political choice of tax structure are ambiguous, at best. Those with a positive view of capitalism also find no basis. By ignoring the fundamental social connection between the concentration of equity capital ownership in a narrow, privileged group and the use of that accumulated wealth to exercise political power, this approach fails to account for the perverse implications of a political process that is incapable of actions that could more fairly charge the wealthy for benefits received from access to 'the public space'.

Equity Capital in the 21st Century

The growth in the depth, extent and influence of equity capital during the 20th century was remarkable, and for some, profoundly disturbing. Circa 2009 the market capitalization of the 45 328 companies listed on the world's stock exchanges had reached $79 trillion dollars or 109 per cent of global gross domestic product (GDP) ($72.5 trillion).[18] These estimates can be compared to the 1913 values, using the estimates of Lyndon Moore. Recognizing the difficulties of determining equity capital market estimates prior to World War I, Moore calculated the value of corporate stocks quoted on the world's stock exchanges as $41.1 billion for 1913. Adjusting for 2009 prices produces a value of $918 billion, 'indicating an 86-fold increase in the absolute value of quoted corporate stocks in the course of, approximately, 100 years'. In relative terms, the market value of corporate common stocks was only 17 per cent of global GDP in 1913, using Angus Maddison's global GDP figure for that date. 'This implies a six-fold increase in the importance of corporate stocks, which was achieved against the background of an enormous destruction of stock market value during two world wars and successive bouts of government confiscation of privately held assets and the state ownership of many areas of business activity'. Such are the fundamental changes in the macroeconomic importance of equity capital.

Such dramatic change spanning several generations has not gone without considerable debate, discussion and criticism in different areas of the intellectual attention space. Perhaps the most influential recent contribution has been from Thomas Piketty: *Capital in the Twenty-first Century*. In the search for the inexorable laws of capitalism, Piketty observes:[19]

> Without real accounting and financial transparency and sharing of information, there can be no economic democracy. Conversely, without a real right to intervene in corporate decision-making (including seats for workers on the company's board of directors), transparency is of little use. Information must support democratic institutions; it is not an end in itself. If democracy is someday to regain control of capitalism, it must start by recognizing that the concrete institutions in which democracy and capitalism are embodied need to be reinvented again and again.

Being predicated on the notion that the limited liability corporation with autonomous shares needs, somehow, to be fixed by 'interven[ing] in corporate decision making' in order for democracy 'someday to regain control of capitalism', such popular impressions ignore the centuries of progress that have produced a legal form that is well adapted to commercial ventures requiring a large and permanent equity capital stock. Is the advancement of economic democracy and the goal of equality of opportunity aided by ad hoc intervention in commercial decisions? Is it possible that ensuring uniform rules are applied fairly is enough to have those benefiting the most from the 'public space' pay appropriately? The idealist's need to 'reinvent' democracy perceived by Piketty ignores the ability of the wealthiest to derail such reinventions and perpetuate the status quo.

A fundamental critique of Berle and Means in the modern context targets the assumption that 'social demands should be met by external regulation or wealth redistribution through taxation and transfer payments . . . Corporations take advantage of this open territory, using various means of regulatory arbitrage to escape domestic regulation and avoid paying income taxes.'[20] This illustrates the futility of taxing corporate and individual income instead of individual wealth and net corporate assets. The origins of this approach to taxation stretch back to the trust era:

> With the ratification of the Sixteenth Amendment to the Constitution, the income tax became a permanent fixture of American life. The passage of the income tax law in 1913 created another 'statistical community' as Americans became members of 'tax brackets', and income (rather than wealth) became the measure of the nation's well-being.[21]

The ability to almost instantaneously monetize an equity claim in a publicly traded limited liability corporation with global reach, and simultaneously transfer those funds to other locations on the globe, is a challenge which the national regulatory and tax authorities are unable and ill equipped to address. Are the wealthiest, once again, treating the rest with upper-class bigotry, or is there a systemic, inherent and irresistible social and political bias created by the economic pressures of global capitalism?

Though Berle and Means are perceived as seminal in observing that 'the rise of the modern corporation has brought a concentration of economic power which can compete on equal terms with the modern state', the 1893 statement of the American legal scholar William Cook in *The Corporation Problem*, made during the midst of the social and political reactions to the growth and abuses of the trusts in the US at the end of the 19th century, is revealing of issues identified by Berle and Means that still arise in current events:[22]

> [N]ot withstanding all the advantages, material, intellectual and moral, which have been derived from corporations, there is much to be said against them. And they have two peculiarities which have led to these abuses. These are, first, the ease with which all responsibility for bad acts is placed upon the corporation itself, while the real perpetrators are concealed; second, the separation of stockholders from corporate agents, of the investor from the investment, of the principal from the agent, with the expectation on the part of the investor, the principal, the stockholder, that profits will be made, honestly if possible, but that profits will be made.

While the infamous Bernie Madoff is vilified for defrauding hedge fund investors, the fraudulent violation of fiduciary duty produced a dramatic criminal sentence. Much larger losses created by corporations in the subprime mortgage crisis, seemingly based on the 'fraudulent' creation of toxic collateralized mortgage products and other collaterized debt obligations (CDOs), resulted in only monetary fines. Other recent examples where the perpetrators of bad acts are protected by the corporate veil abound (for example, SAC Capital). In the 21st century, it seems that the global search for corporate profits by agents acting separately from ownership is enough cover for egregious behaviour that, if committed by an individual or partnership, would attract significant legal sanction.

The severe stock market downtown at the start of the new millennium, colloquially referred to as the 'dot.com bubble', led to passage in the US of the Sarbanes–Oxley Act ensuring that corporate officers are legally responsible for the validity of financial statements. The dot.com bubble is a poor descriptor of the motivation for Sarbanes–Oxley, because the Act was inspired by the collapse of Worldcom and Enron, and the perpetration of accounting-related frauds at other firms, such as Tyco, that were not 'Internet' firms. The collapse of the major accounting firm Arthur

Anderson highlights the cosy managerial advisory services consulting relationship between accounting firms and the publicly traded and privately held companies that are being externally audited by those same accounting firms. This problem has plagued the accounting profession since early in the 20th century. Sarbanes–Oxley failed to adequately extend liability for inadequate supervision of corporate managers to all the directors, permitting the continuation of the practice of appointing ineffective boards populated by the well-connected, as opposed to the most competent, to represent the interests of shareholders. Ineffective legislators are joined by regulators that are, arguably, increasingly captured by the entities that are being regulated.[23]

EQUITY CAPITAL, SHARE BUYBACKS AND DIVIDENDS

Evolution of Stock Compensation

The 1990s witnessed the structure of pay for top corporate executives shifting markedly, as the use of managerial stock options and other forms of deferred equity compensation expanded substantially. A study from 2003 reports that for firms in the S&P 500, the value of stock options granted rose from $11 billion in 1992, averaging $22 million per firm, to $119 billion in 2000, averaging $238 million per firm.[24] The proportion in the 0.1 per cent of senior executives leading S&P 500 firms (lower pre-tax income threshold of $2 million and average of $6.15 million; see Table 1.3 in Chapter 1) is reflected in reported chief executive officer (CEO) compensation from annual Securities and Exchange Commission (SEC) proxy filings for 2015: median compensation of $10.4 million, with a lowest quartile average of $7.8 million and highest quartile average of $14.9 million.[25] This does not include other sources of income for CEOs and the substantial number of non-CEO senior executives who receive comparable compensation. Significantly, compensation mostly takes the form of salary, bonus, stock awards and stock options. For 2015 (2011), the median S&P 500 CEO compensation was divided as $1.13 million ($1.022 million) salary, $1.95 million ($2.018 million) bonus, $5.102 million ($3.26 million) stock awards, $1.111 million ($1.685 million) stock options with a remainder of $163 900 ($160 000).

The acceleration of stock awards and reduction in options between 2011 and 2016 reflects a change in sentiment away from time-based option grants to performance-based restricted stock awards. The rise of various types of stock awards parallelled the ascendency of academic theories to rationalize such schemes. Descending from the seminal work on agency theory by financial economists Jensen and Meckling, the conventional argument for equity-based compensation was to resolve the 'agency problem' by better alignment of the incentives for corporate management with those of shareholders. For a variety of reasons, such compensation initially was in form of executive stock options. Following the collapse of the dot-com bubble and plunge of the Nasdaq stock index, the risk encouragement associated with executive contingent equity compensation incentive schemes led to questioning of such schemes on a variety of grounds.[26] As a consequence, contingent equity compensation has gradually shifted away from stock option grants to time-vested stock, and restricted stock grants instead of options. Studies on the role of contingent equity compensation in the encouragement of excessive risk-taking and 'short-run-ism' – being costly and inefficient at providing managerial incentives – find that contingent equity compensation tempted managers at Enron, WorldCom and Tyco to commit fraud in order to ensure a high stock price at the time of option exercise.[27]

The evolution of managerial incentive schemes is detailed in a variety of studies.[28] The recent approach of granting contingent equity compensation to management, especially senior executives, stands in stark contrast to the early managerial incentive schemes introduced by General Motors (GM) and Du Pont in the 1920s. These plans involved lending to managers to purchase company stock at market prices. 'Managers paid market interest rates on such loans, and in the GM plan they were required to repay the principal gradually.'[29] The plans were seven to ten years in length, somewhat longer than the average term of modern contingent equity compensation plans. Compared to modern schemes, the GM and Du Pont schemes of the 1920s:

> were large relative to the salaries and wealth of the participating executives, and represented a nontrivial portion of the firm. In 1930, 58 managers purchased $93 million of stock (in 2004 dollars) at Du Pont, and at General Motors 246 managers purchased $578 million of stock (in 2004 dollars). The 1930 purchase by managers at GM represented 3.2 percent of the firm's stock, while the 1927 purchase by managers at Du Pont was 3.4 percent.[30]

Comparison of the 1930 purchases by executives at Du Pont with salaries is revealing. In 1930 dollars, the purchases averaged more than $152000 per participating executive, whereas the highest-paid officer at Dupont earned less than $100000/year. At GM, the average purchase was more than $223000 per participating executive. In 2004 dollars, this would be about $2.3 million per executive.

Equity compensation grants can take the form of time-vesting stock, time-vesting options or performance-based equity. Vesting of performance-based equity awards is ultimately dependent on prede-termined performance conditions, and most often takes the form of restricted stock or restricted stock units or – less commonly – options.[31] Consistent with the composition of equity compensation in S&P 500 firms, performance-based awards were the most common contingent equity compensation granted in each individual sector of the S&P 500. A mini-mum 73.3 per cent of companies offered performance awards regardless of sector. Conversely, the prevalence of time-vesting option awards varied substantially across sectors. Health care and utilities represented the high and low ends of the options grant spectrum at 83.3 per cent and 23.1 per cent prevalence, respectively. Against this backdrop:

> the rules regarding the taxation of stock options and restricted stock are . . . complex. With respect to ISOs [incentive stock options], the treatment of disqualifying dispositions and the impact of ISOs on the [alternative minimum tax] are especially challenging . . . The taxation of restricted stock is complex, especially regarding whether there is truly a substantial risk of forfeiture.[32]

The dominant use of contingent equity grants in managerial compensa-tion has received generally overwhelming support in academic studies. Few of these studies make any connection between the rise of such grants and the increasing use of share buyback programmes in lieu of dividend payout. In turn, no connection is made between contingent manage-rial equity compensation and increasing wealth and income inequality. Instead, academic explanations offered for share buybacks typically identify the motivations of information signalling or free cash flows.[33] The information signalling hypothesis claims that share buybacks are used to reveal favourable new information about prospects for the firm in the future. The free cash flow explanation posits that share buybacks reduce agency conflicts by returning excess cash to shareholders in a more tax-efficient form than dividend payout. Is it possible that managers of firms with high levels of contingent equity compensation for executives have an incentive to initiate buyback programmes? While it is possible 'that managers may be motivated to undertake on-market buyback programs in order to neutralize the dilution of earnings per share caused by their stock options, rather than for signaling purposes', there are other more self-serving explanations for the empirical observation that firms with a higher proportion of contingent equity compensation are more likely to undertake larger share buyback programmes.[34]

Dividends and Capital Gains Taxes

Recognition of the clean surplus, 'narrow dividend' relationship, where earnings are either retained or paid out in dividends, led to empirical studies on the properties of 'broad dividends', where both cash dividends and share buybacks are used to return cash to shareholders. To this end, there are numerous studies of narrow dividends that document an overall decline in aggregate dividend payout ratios since the 1950s, marked by periods of persistence where the dividend payout ratio is relatively constant. This declining importance of dividends has been parallelled by an increasing importance of share buybacks. For a sample of all industrial firms listed on the Compustat database from 1985 to 1996, the number of open-market share buyback programme announcements by US industrial firms increased 650 per cent from 115 to 755, with an announced value increase of 750 per cent from $15.4 billion to $113 billion.[35] Over the same period, dividends increased by a factor of just over two, with aggregate dividends rising from $67.6 billion to $141.7 billion. A similar study reports an increase in the value of share buybacks from $1.5 billion to $194.2 billion over a 1972 and 2000 sample, while dividends only rose from $17.6 billion to $171.7 billion.[36]

The study of share buybacks has progressed considerably as more firms have adopted this method of returning cash to shareholders.[37] Circa 1956, when the seminal work on corporate dividend policy by Lintner first appeared, it was acceptable for corporate income to be effectively distributed among dividends, retained earnings and taxes. Share buybacks were not a practical part of the mix. But times change, and from a significant number of recent academic studies some stylized facts have emerged. Specifically, it is claimed that share buybacks and dividends are used at different times and by different types of firms. While dividends are typically paid by firms with a higher level of 'permanent' operating cash flows, firms using share buybacks tend to have higher 'temporary', non-operating cash flows. Both cash flows and distributions from repurchasing firms tend to be substantially more volatile. Connection between the rise of contingent equity compensation and increased use of share buybacks goes largely unexplored.

In conjunction with increased usage of share buybacks in the US, a sample of 25 countries with more than 225 000 firm-year observations for firms paying dividends in the period from 1994 to 2007 also reflects a global decrease in the percentage of firms that are dividend payers.[38] Combined with the more detailed results from Fama and French[39] on US dividend payers for a 1926–99 sample, some key developments are apparent. Recognizing that there has been a significant increase in the total number of firms over the period, between 1994 and 2007 the percentage of firms paying dividends has fallen over 30 per cent in common law countries, from 74 per cent to 43 per cent, with a more modest reduction of 8 per cent from 70 per cent to 62 per cent for civil law countries.[40] The aggregate common law result brings these countries closer in line with the US, which saw dividend payers fall from 36 per cent to 25 per cent. Following a period in the 1970s when the payers exceeded non-payers, since 1980 the number of dividend non-payers in the US has increasingly exceeded payers. The civil law countries, which include European firms other than the UK and Ireland, and the important emerging markets of China and Brazil, even saw some increases in the percentage of dividend payers in smaller European countries such as Spain and Finland. The percentage of dividend paying firms in Germany fell from 71 per cent to 46 per cent, while the important sample of Japanese firms that have high corporate taxes fell only from 88 per cent to 86 per cent.

Share Buybacks and Managerial Compensation

Given the secular decline in the importance of cash dividend payout relative to share buyback programmes, details on such programmes assume increasing importance. For example, while various studies observe that the increases in stock buybacks have been procyclical, evidence on offshore cash holdings for the largest firms repatriated under the Trump tax plan indicate that such funds were primarily spent on share buybacks. Examining the ongoing process of corporations substituting share buybacks for dividends, there is evidence that firms are not simply cutting dividends and replacing them with buybacks. Rather, large dividend-paying firms are repurchasing stock rather than increasing dividends. Furthermore, much of the growth in popularity of share buybacks is due to large dividend-paying firms. Although the dividend payout ratio of US companies has been declining since the mid-1980s, the total payout ratio has remained more-or-less constant, which suggests that corporations have been substituting buybacks for dividends. While the average dividend payout ratio fell from 22.3 per cent in 1974 to 13.8 per cent in 1998, the average buyback payout ratio increased from 3.7 per cent to 13.6 per cent during the same period.[41]

The aversion of firms to cutting dividends is understandable given the significantly negative stock market reaction to dividend cuts. There are – admittedly crude – empirical estimates of an average stock price decline of about 6 per cent on the three days surrounding the announcement of a dividend cut.[42] This punitive market response to dividend decreases has been identified as an argument in favour of share buyback programmes where there is no commitment to initiate a new buyback programme when the old programme expires. As such, stock buybacks can be rationalized as a way for firms to pay out 'temporary' cash flows that have a high likelihood of not being sustainable. Even if the advantageous tax deferment of unrealized capital gains provided by the realization principle is ignored, the typically favourable investor tax treatment for realized capital gains over dividend income is yet another tax-related argument in favour of share buybacks. Such arguments in favour of share buybacks are so compelling that Fischer Black coined 'the dividend puzzle' in 1976: why do firms use dividends to distribute corporate income and investors prefer this form of distribution when dividends are subject to double taxation?[43]

In the US, the dividend puzzle has been largely resolved by the evolution of firm dividend policy: dividends are increasingly being replaced by share buybacks. In a widely cited contribution, Fama and French find that while almost all publicly traded firms paid dividends during the 1950s and into the 1960s when a significant number of non-dividend paying firms started to emerge, the percentage of firms paying cash dividends fell from 66.5 per cent in 1978 to 20.7 per cent in 1998.[44] What has emerged more than three decades after Black introduced the dividend puzzle is considerable heterogeneity in the dividend policy decision. This is particularly true if the scope of discussion includes international firms. Specifically, it is possible to demonstrate the importance across firms and countries of corporate ownership composition, particularly the presence of a large shareholder or shareholder group, to the determination of dividend policy. While not as significant an issue with US stocks, a sample of over 8000 firms from 37 countries had at least 50 per cent of the firms with one shareholder or a shareholder group owning at least 25 per cent of the equity in the firm, with the largest shareholder owning, on average, more than 30 per cent of total voting shares.[45]

Transformation of wage income, immediately taxed at personal income tax rates, into capital income, subject to the deferred taxation available under the realization principle and taxed at lower rates (if at all) when realized, is a long-standing method for the wealthy to avoid paying income taxes. A particularly relevant variant of this strategy appears in the awarding of managerial compensation. Casual examination of the extravagant compensation packages of senior managers at S&P 500 firms reveals a decided skew toward deferred equity capital compensation, in the form of executive stock options, restricted stock grants and the like. This is not to say that transforming wage income into capital income occurs only with managers of publicly traded corporations. Quite the contrary, such practices are systemic across publicly traded corporations and privately held companies. However, it is within a relatively small number of the largest corporations and companies where the ability of tax changes to significantly impact the top 0.1 per cent of the income distribution is located. Given the veil of privacy provided by privately held companies, and the flexibility of estimating private company valuation for tax purposes, is it possible that the transformation of wage income into capital income is more, not less, prevalent in privately held companies? What the publicly traded company provides is detailed information about pay packets that can only by inference be extended to practices at private companies.

RETHINKING TAXES ON THE WEALTHY AND THE WEALTHIEST

Net Wealth Taxes for the 21st Century?

The assessment of a tax based on individual or family wealth has ancient origins. Much of the art in the galleries of Florence and the opulent *palazzos* in the surrounding hillsides are witness to the desire of the wealthiest in Renaissance Florence to avoid a wealth tax. Swiss cantons have had a form of wealth tax since the 13th century. More recently, though not a major source of revenue, Sweden, Norway, Denmark and the Netherlands introduced a wealth tax early in the 20th century. Germany introduced a net wealth tax in 1922 modelled after the corresponding Prussian tax of 1819.[46] Following the introduction of the broad-based income tax, wealth taxes have received little attention as a mechanism for supplementing the income tax.[47] All Organisation for Economic Co-operation and Development (OECD) countries rely extensively on progressive personal income taxes to raise government revenue. No country derives significant revenue from net wealth taxes or taxes on the transfer of wealth at death or as gifts. Against a backdrop of increasing inequality in wealth and income, the failure for a net wealth tax to gain traction is both puzzling and revealing.

Not surprisingly, the wealth tax surfaced as part of Senator Elizabeth Warren's campaign for the Democratic Party nomination for the 2020 US presidential election. After recognizing that the property tax is a form of wealth tax, Warren proposed also taxing 'the diamonds, the yachts, and the Rembrandts'. This approach raises criticism reminiscent of the medieval English 'aid on movables' based on personalty that eventually proved to be unworkable and evolved into a land tax. Attempting to tax a wide category of 'wealth' items, including privately held businesses, artwork, gems, and the like, can pose significant valuation difficulties and administrative costs. Such taxes could also raise the inequity of double taxation if the wealth item was purchased using income that had already been taxed. These criticisms could be extended to include economic and financial distortions created by a tax avoidance bias against easy-to-value market-able and tangible wealth in favour of difficult-to-value non-marketable and intangible wealth that could be 'undervalued' for tax purposes; not to mention the complications raised by globalization and the ability to move capital offshore.

Instead of seeking to counter increasing wealth inequality with enhanced net wealth taxes, the trend has been in the opposite direction, with various European countries abandoning variants of the net wealth tax, though in 2018 Belgium did introduce a 0.15 per cent tax on certain financial instruments held in securities accounts valued over €500000. Circa 2012, the OECD reported that among countries still using a net wealth tax, the burden on net wealth differs considerably: 'In France, the tax-free threshold is relatively high with €1.3 million per taxpayer, and there are two tax bands at 0.25% and 0.5% (on fortunes above €3 million).'[48] In 2018, France replaced the wealth tax with a progressive tax on real estate. By contrast, in Switzerland, 'the tax burden differs between cantons and municipalities. Despite relatively low tax-free allowances, effective tax rates remain below 1% even for very high values of personal net wealth.' In Norway, 'the current overall (municipal and central government) tax rate is 1.1% for individuals with a net wealth above NOK 700k (about €90k), which implies a much higher burden for moderately wealthy indi-viduals compared to Switzerland and France'. As for tax revenue raised, 'the Swiss individual wealth tax generated tax revenue of 1% of GDP in 2010. The corresponding values for France and Norway are 0.2% and 0.5%, respectively'. In every case, 'the revenue from the net wealth tax is minuscule compared to the revenue from the personal income tax or from the VAT [value-added tax]'.

Despite the lack of contemporary usage, there are some potentially useful aspects of a wealth tax even if the revenue raised is not substantial. It has long been recognized that 'effective administration of an income tax requires that, even in the absence of a net wealth tax, the net wealth of taxpayers be calculated every year as a check on the investment income declared'.[49] In requiring residents to declare any foreign assets over C$100000, the Canadian government has taken a partial, if inadequate, step in this direction.[50] In this case, the government is implicitly acknowl-edging tax avoidance and evasion associated with the ownership of offshore assets. Significantly, requiring net wealth above some threshold to be declared on an annual basis, even if no tax is assessed, could be helpful for auditing income tax returns over a period of years. Such infor-mation is routinely required when financial institutions do credit scoring for loans, yet annual information on the net wealth of individuals is not demanded in many OECD countries, though countries with estate taxes do require such information for wealthy individuals with net assets above the filing threshold. There are no OECD countries administratively using net wealth declarations as a check on declared income. Half a century ago, it was observed: 'The absence of requirements for this information has been singled out as one of the weakest links in the enforcement chain for the administration of taxes on incomes – especially large incomes.'[51] Unfortunately, this sage advice has been largely ignored.

By construction, a net wealth tax is targeted at a broad list of items considered to be 'wealth'. For various reasons, such a tax would be difficult to implement at the local level. What features make the net wealth tax seemingly unworkable at the national level? If only administrative costs and valuation difficulties matter, then death taxes would be a workable alternative for managing costs and difficulties. Being proposed as a national supplement to the income tax, a net wealth tax would be assessed annually. In contrast, death taxes are typically aimed at the same, or a similar list of, wealth items. Being assessed only once, death taxes substantively mitigate administrative and valuation difficulties by reducing the number of times the tax is assessed. Death taxes are one of the oldest forms of tax, not new or practically unworkable as a net wealth tax. It is difficult to escape the conclusion that the failure to effectively utilize such taxes to alleviate increasing inequality speaks more to the ability of the wealthiest to influence the national agenda where such taxes would be imposed. Of course, controlling the threat to democratic institutions from concentrations of economic, social or political power is easier said than done.[52]

Taxes on Property and Capital Income

Could a progressive, *ad valorem* reformed property tax permit local jurisdictions, where the wealthy congregate, to capture much-needed tax revenue? Unfortunately, while property tax is substantively more difficult to avoid than income tax for those not willing to migrate, such enhanced property tax revenue would not be significant to many localities not favoured by the wealthy. The most that can be expected from the property tax is horizontal equity at the local level. As far as the use of property tax revenue to reduce reliance on the more-easily-avoided income tax is concerned, some potentially unachievable mechanism for redistribution of property tax revenue across localities is indicated if vertical equity across localities is desired. In turn, could localized revenue gains be enhanced by implementing progressive taxes on other forms of conspicuous consumption: luxury taxes, graduated vehicle licences and registration, user fees, and the like, that could be assessed at a higher level of government? While a national progressive consumption tax has been proposed at various times, difficulties of implementation deter such initiatives. Is the road to reform difficult and daunting, or unattainable?

Another problematic impediment to reforming taxes on the wealthy is the issue of tax-motivated migration. Though the US is able, at least for individuals, to partially mitigate this impediment by assessing income tax based on citizenship, other OECD countries assess income tax based on residence. Does the Tiebout hypothesis from local public finance apply to the wealthy in a globalized tax environment? Will the wealthy compulsively seek out jurisdictions of residence for tax purposes where the total tax burden is lower, while de facto living in and enjoying the benefits of a high-tax jurisdiction? Unlike the less-than-wealthy, there are a variety of public services that the wealthy can obtain from private resources. For example, living in a gated community with 24-hour manned security reduces significantly the need for police protection. Obviously, the top 1 per cent and 0.1 per cent have no need for publicly funded retirement plans, unemployment insurance and welfare programmes. Though it is possible for the wealthy to seek residence in low-income tax jurisdictions, there is also the compulsive need for many to seek status in owning high-value properties in premium locations with expensive automobiles, yachts, planes, and the like. As Thorsten Veblen observed, increasing the price of such items increases the status value, as fewer can afford the lifestyle. Could this be an Achilles heel for wealthy free riders?

Compared to limited potential revenue gains from taxing compulsive opulent consumption, there is a potentially much larger source of revenue if the income tax could be fixed by reform of the realization principle associated with deferring tax on capital income. Could this essential income tax reform be used to address increasing wealth and income inequality, both domestically and globally? Since the inception of the broad-based income tax, there have been a variety of efforts by the wealthy to enhance deferment of capital income associated with wealth increases, and to transform wage income into capital income, to access lower tax rates and tax deferment provisions for capital income. Specifically, the rise of fiduciary capitalism has facilitated an increasing separation of ownership from control in publicly traded corporations and large private limited liability companies, leading to the payment of substantial managerial compensation in the form of contingent equity grants (and other forms of compensation with deferred tax consequences). The theory that such grants better align the interests of managers and shareholders is increasingly being viewed as ill-conceived and implemented in a self-serving fashion. Recognizing that many of those in the top 1 per cent are senior executives at publicly traded corporations and privately held companies, tax fairness requires such managerial compensation to be treated as taxable income in the year it is received.

The increasing separation of ownership from control that has permitted the rise of managerial deferred tax compensation has, in turn, propelled an important, largely unanticipated, substitution of share buybacks, possibly accompanied by cash and investment asset accumulation, for traditional dividend payouts. Recognizing that contingent equity compensation typically depends on the expiration or vesting date share price, share buybacks and financial asset accumulation serve to drive up share prices, whereas dividend payments, taxable in the year earned, do not. Though rationalized using various arguments, such self-serving managerial actions have unintended implications both for income tax revenue and for wealth and income inequality. Instead of the traditional dividend payout to shareholders that is taxed in the year that profits are earned and paid out, the use of earnings for share buybacks and accumulation of cash and other liquid assets typically results in increased share prices, permitting tax deferment of the associated capital gain on the contingent equity compensation. Increased share price is essential for corporate management to achieve gains from such contingent compensation.

If using Haig–Simons income is problematic in practice, is it possible to use an alternative approach to counteract the implications of the realization principle for increasing wealth and income inequality? One possible method could be to integrate corporate and personal tax by providing a tax incentive for dividend payout relative to share buybacks. This could be achieved by eliminating the double taxation of dividends, allowing dividends to be tax deductible at the company level, with tax implications that 'flow through' to be taxed at full marginal income tax rates of the shareholder.[53] Alternatively, share buybacks could be coercively penalized by taxing profits retained within the firm that are used for share buybacks: a share buyback tax. Either approach would effectively encourage publicly traded corporations and privately held companies to operate as flow-through entities, with a possible additional proviso that profits retained within the firm for share buybacks would be subject to higher tax rates. Such changes would involve restricting the opaque types of flow-through structures that could be used, damping down the potential for tax avoidance and evasion using such entities that has recently appeared in the US.

Wealth and Power

It is misleading in the extreme to claim that tax authorities in different jurisdictions have not struggled to find appropriate responses to the use of globalization by wealthy tax evaders and free riders. With initiatives such as the Offshore Voluntary Disclosure programmes, the US Foreign Account Tax Compliance Act (2010) and payments to whistleblowers, the US initially led the way with continuing efforts to increase pressure on financial institutions to participate in multilateral initiatives to control offshore income tax evasion. However, while Automatic Exchange of Information on Request initiatives by the Global Forum on Transparency and Exchange of Information for Tax Purposes to deter the wealthy from avoiding and evading taxes by shifting assets and income offshore have been at least partly successful, efforts to simplify exceedingly and increasingly complex income tax codes have generally been failures in addressing wealth and income inequality. It is difficult to escape the fears of Thomas Paine and others about concentration and inter-generational transfer of wealth coming to fruition with an irreparably corrupted democratic process incapable of implementing tax reforms to address increasing income and wealth inequality in the US and elsewhere.

Even where tax reforms are well intentioned, when governments make substantial changes to the tax code then determining the ultimate impact is problematic. There are a multitude of inter-relationships, interactions and incentives amongst entities subject to a tax change. In addition, tax policy is a moving target. Incremental changes in the income tax code are regular events at the national level following an election. Extensive and pervasive tax reforms present a potentially intractable *ex ante* problem of determining direct and indirect impacts on the macroeconomy and the government revenue stream. These problems are typically skirted by only conducting a theoretical transactions analysis of tax change 'that proceeds by evaluating the tax treatment of various transactions according to ideal tax bases'.[54] Yet, there are profound philosophical, social and ethical questions associated with the threat to democracy and democratic ideals from the increasing concentration of wealth and income in the top 1 per cent and, especially, the wealthiest 0.1 per cent. Is it possible that, in the 21st century, the process of reform has become so complicated and compromised that those at the top of the wealth and income distributions have become largely bullet-proof to inequality mitigating tax reform?

What is clear at this stage? Though the precise amount cannot be known, available empirical evidence for increasing inequality of wealth and income is likely to involve substantive, possibly dramatic, under-estimation. Even if accurate empirical evidence were available, there is no 'one-size-fits-all' solution to reforming taxes on the wealthy and, especially, the wealthiest. How would flexibility and a variety of tax sources, across taxing jurisdictions, reduce the ability of the wealthiest to manipulate the reform agenda, especially for broad-based income taxes and death taxes levied mostly at the national level?[55] Unfortunately, a combination of globalization and favourable treatment of capital income has caused current progressive income tax structures to be too easily avoided and, in some cases, evaded by the wealthy. The highest levels of wealth and income generate the highest incentive to avoid and evade those taxes, especially income taxes, that are the largest source of total government revenue. It is evident that enhanced ability to locate wealth and income in different geographical locations requires creative rethinking of wealth and taxes in order to empathetically address increasing wealth and income inequality at a time of increasing poverty and homelessness within individual taxing jurisdictions.

If the relative government revenue burden is shifted from income tax, raised primarily at the national level where the wealthiest can exert decisive influence, what revenue sources are available to achieve vertical and horizontal equity? Achievement of horizontal equity at the local and, where applicable, state/provincial level could be achieved by a reinforced combination of alternative revenue sources that are hard for the wealthy to avoid: property tax, consumption tax, luxury vehicle levies and luxury tax. While such initiatives could address local inequities created by wealthy free riders, achieving vertical equity by reaching the 1 per cent and 0.1 per cent is decidedly more complicated. The political, social and economic influence exerted by the wealthiest feeds a public perception that accumulation of such wealth is a 'social good'. Even in the unlikely event that the public can be convinced to see the wealthiest as perpetuating a 'social bad', it is highly unlikely that adjustments to gift taxes and death taxes would be enough to address vertical equity concerns. Surcharges on high income would only exacerbate incentives for migration or tax avoidance and evasion. Some type of reform to the taxation of direct and indirect ownership of equity capital is required, but in the world of globalized capitalism the avenue to such reform is elusive. It is difficult to avoid the lack of potential for substantive reform of taxes on the wealthiest. To paraphrase John Donne again: 'As virtuous men pass mildly away And whisper to their souls, to goe, While some of their friends doe say, The breath goes now, and some say, no: So let us melt, and make no noise'.

NOTES

1. This section is based on Poitras (2016, Ch. 7).
2. Kaymak and Poschke (2016, p. 1). Such results are derived from available measurements of the wealth and income distributions and, as such, do not typically capture unrealized capital income, wealth and income that is domiciled offshore and not observ-

able, and various types of onshore wealth that are not captured by available estimation methods.
3. Keynes (2018 [1936]).
4. Bratton and Wachter (2008, p. 100). See also Millon (1990).
5. Berle and Means (1968 [1932], p. 313).
6. See Mizruchi (2004, p. 581).
7. Mizruchi (2004, p. 579).
8. Bratton (2001, p. 752).
9. Gilson and Gordon (2013, p. 863).
10. Bricker and Chandar (2000, p. 529).
11. Hall and Soskice (2001) are often credited with initiating this interpretation.
12. See Neal and Williamson (2014, p. 2).
13. Acemoglu and Robinson (2015, p. 4).
14. Stout (2001, p. 1248). See also Hawley and Williams (2000).
15. Rogers (2014) provides an example from an unlikely source.
16. Hein (2012, p. 179).
17. See Shiller (2013).
18. These estimates, and the following estimates and quotes, are from Michie (2012).
19. Piketty (2014, p. 570).
20. Bratton (2001, p. 770).
21. Previts and Merino (1998, p. 181).
22. Cook (1893, p. 7).
23. For example, despite repeated contacts indicating serious impropriety at the Bernie Madoff hedge fund, the SEC failed for years to uncover wrongdoing in the actions of this iconic Wall Street actor.
24. Hall and Murphy (2003, p. 49).
25. These and the following figures on CEO compensation are from Equilar (2016).
26. For example, see Bebchuk and Fried (2003), Hall and Murphy (2003), Ghosh et al. (2008) and Lamba and Miranda (2010).
27. Holden (2005, p. 135).
28. Two such studies of interest are O'Byrne and Young (2017), Bivens and Mishel (2010) and Holden (2005).
29. Holden (2005, p. 136).
30. Ibid.
31. A useful source on executive compensation practices can be found on the website for Meridian Compensation Partners, available at http://www.meridiancp.com/insights/thought-leadership/2016-ceo-pay-trends-report/.
32. Adkins (2016).
33. One exception is Lamba and Miranda (2010), which examines the evidence for Australia where share buybacks were prohibited until 1989 and, due to severe follow-on restrictions, there were few buybacks until 1995.
34. Lamba and Miranda (2010, p. 340).
35. Jagannathan et al. (2000).
36. Grullon and Michaely (2002).
37. For example, Stephens and Weisbach (1998), Jagannathan et al. (2000), Kahle (2002), Lee and Rui (2007).
38. Ferris et al. (2009).
39. Fama and French (2001).
40. Common law countries include the important equity markets of Australia, Canada, Hong Kong, Malaysia, Singapore, South Africa, the UK and the United States. The civil law countries include the important markets of France, Germany, Italy, Japan, Spain, Sweden and Switzerland.
41. These results appear in Grullon and Michaely (2002).
42. For example, see Ghosh and Woolridge (1988) and Denis et al. (1994).
43. See Black (1976), Crockett and Friend (1988), Christie (1990) and Frankfurter (1999).

Recognizing the dramatic reduction in the corporate tax burden since the 1960s, evidence provided in Burman et al. (2017) casts doubt on the empirical basis of the double taxation claim.

44. Fama and French (2001).
45. Truong and Heaney (2007, p. 684, Table 3).
46. Tanabe (1967, p. 126).
47. Studies of the net wealth tax in Canada are available in a 1991 issue of *Canadian Public Policy* that contains a variety of useful studies, including Banting (1991), Bird (1991), Brown (1991), Burbidge (1991), Davies (1991), Kessler and Pestieau (1991), Mintz (1991) and Mintz and Pesando (1991). Lehner (2000) discusses wealth taxes in Europe, in general, and Martinez-Vasquez and Sanz-Sanz (2007) discuss Spain, in detail. In the US, the *Tax Law Review* held a symposium in 2000 on the federal wealth tax featuring Rakowski (2000), Schenk (2000) and Lehner (2000), together with commentaries. Lindholm (1984) takes the debatable position that a federal net wealth tax in the US would be unconstitutional, while Michalos (1991) argues for a progressive annual wealth tax.
48. Figures given are from OECD (2012).
49. Tanabe (1967, p. 133).
50. This step is inadequate because, as Canadian income taxes are assessed on a residency basis, it is still possible for the primary income earned to be resident offshore and for funds to be transferred as gifts to lower-income individuals residing in Canada. Similarly, assets can be hidden in various ways to avoid the need to declare ownership of foreign assets. The greater the amount of family income generated offshore, the greater the incentive to disguise assets and income, leaving only 'small fish' in the pond. This suggests requiring that only gifts from income (or assets) previously subject to Canadian tax be permitted to be income tax exempt (allowing credit for foreign tax paid on the gift).
51. Tanabe (1967, p. 133).
52. Aaron and Munnell (1992) summarize these arguments in the context of death taxes, recognizing that these are one form of wealth tax.
53. Grubert and Altshuler (2016) discuss shifting the burden from the corporate to the personal level to permit the corporate tax rate to fall to a 15 per cent level that would alleviate international tax competition. Similarly, Graetz and Warren (2016) recommend integration of corporate and personal income taxes by providing shareholders a credit for corporate taxes paid with respect to corporate earnings distributed as dividends. This is administratively more complicated than allowing dividends to be tax deductible at the corporate level. Any such schemes need to account for taxation of dividend payments to non-resident entities.
54. Strnad (1985, p. 1023). The two leading tax bases are Haig–Simons and consumption tax bases.
55. As Dietsch (2015, p. 14) observes, 'a broad tax base, one which does not put all its eggs in one basket, tends to reduce incentives for evasion'.

Glossary of technical concepts and terminology

accrual basis accounting: Accrual basis accounting recognizes revenues and expenses in the period in which these occur and not, as in cash basis accounting, when the cash flow occurs. An example of accrual basis accounting occurs with estimated depreciation, where a charge is made to earnings based on a discretionary formula used to estimate depreciation, and not when cash is expended to purchase capital assets for replacement. Applied to capital income, accrual accounting would charge tax in the period in which the capital income was earned, and not when the cash flow was generated by sale of the asset. (See 'realization principle'.)

capitalization method: This is a method of determining the present value of a stream of cash flows used in accounting and business valuation. Conventionally, the value is determined by dividing the estimated cash flow by the 'capitalization rate', a variant of perpetuity estimation. In estimating the distribution of wealth, the capitalization method uses information for capital income from different tax brackets of individual and household income tax returns as the cash flow. This cash flow is divided by an assumed capitalization rate.

C corporation: This is a reference in the United States (US) federal tax code to the conventional limited liability corporation found in other jurisdictions that, as a result of having 'legal personality', is responsible for payment of corporate taxes on profits earned. To mitigate the impact of double taxation, the subsequent distribution of after-tax corporate profits to shareholders is subject to dividend tax rates that are lower than personal tax rates applied to regular income. In the US, both C corporations and S corporations have limited liability, with the main differences between a C corporation and an S corporation being that a C corporation is a separate legal entity with an unrestricted number of shareholders, able to issue more than one class of shares and subject to double taxation; whereas an S corporation is taxed once on a pass-through basis, with restrictions on the number and type of shareholders and only one class of stock permitted. (See 'S corporation'; 'limited liability company'.)

Chicago School: This term is associated with faculty in the Economics Department at the University of Chicago who maintain a strong, ideological adherence to free market principles. Two eras of the Chicago School can be identified: an earlier inter-war period led by Frank Knight and Jacob Viner; and a post-World War II period led by Milton Friedman, George Stigler, Harry Johnson and Gary Becker.

clean surplus (accounting): This refers to an assumption in accounting theory that the number of shares in an equity account has not been altered by share buybacks or secondary offerings of shares.

contingent equity compensation: This refers to the contingency (exposure to randomness) associated with deferred equity compensation. In certain cases, the introduction of a contingency makes it difficult to estimate the accrual value of the deferred compensation. Employee and executive stock options are the most common form of such compensation. (See 'deferred equity compensation'.)

death tax: This includes various types of tax that are assessed associated with the death of an individual, including estate tax, inheritance tax, and any capital gains tax that is a required realization of capital gains at death ending possible tax deferment available under the realization principle. (See also 'estate tax'; 'inheritance tax'; 'realization principle'.)

deferred equity compensation: Deferred equity compensation occurs when payment for a part of a wage or salary is delayed beyond the period when the compensation was earned, to be paid in some future period using some type of equity claim, usually common stock in the company. Typical types of equity compensation include employee and executive stock options, and managerial performance plans that make equity payments in the future if predetermined performance targets are achieved. Deferred equity compensation usually receives favourable tax treatment compared to wage or salary income. In the US, for example, the specific type of favourable tax treatment for a stock option grant will differ depending on whether the grant is qualified or non-qualified under Internal Revenue Service (IRS) rules. (See 'deferred tax on income'.)

deferred tax on income: It is conventional for assessment and payment of income tax on personal or business income to be made a few months following the year in which the income was earned. Deferred tax on income occurs when the assessment and payment occur at a later point in time, if ever. The most common type of deferred tax occurs with capital income, where the realization principle permits a capital gain to be taxed in the period in which the capital asset is sold instead of the period in which the gain occurred. A related variant of deferred tax occurs with deferred equity compensation paid as qualified stock option grants. In the US, such grants receive deferred tax treatment provided that the exercise price on the option is greater than or equal to the current stock price when the grant is awarded, and the exercise date is at least one year in the future. If the stock obtained at exercise is held for at least two years before sale, then sale of the stock will be taxed as a capital gain. If the stock is not sold, tax will be deferred. Deferred tax treatment of stock option grants in most other countries is similar. For example, in Canada when a stock option grant is exercised an employee is entitled to treat the (positive) difference between share price and fair market value as a capital gain. This differs slightly from the US treatment as the option grant exercise triggers a realization of capital gain. This ends the income tax deferment but allows the assessment of tax at the lower capital gains tax rate without having to hold the option for two years, as in the US. (See 'realization principle'.)

economic efficiency: There are various possible definitions of 'economic efficiency'. In this book, a loose definition is intended that alludes to the optimal production and distribution of scarce resources. Reference to more precise theoretical notions of economic efficiency, such as Pareto optimality, is not intended.

elasticity of demand: This refers to the relationship between the percentage change in quantity demanded for a percentage change in price. If demand is inelastic, then changes in price will have a limited impact on quantity demanded. Similarly, if demand is elastic, then quantity demanded will be sensitive to changes in price. A connection to tax follows from the impact that sales tax has on the price paid by the consumer. (See 'elasticity of supply'.)

elasticity of supply/inelastic supply: This refers to the relationship between the percentage change in quantity supplied for a percentage change in price. If supply is inelastic, then changes in price will have a limited impact on quantity supplied. In the case of labour supply, the relevant price is the wage rate. A connection to tax follows from the impact that income tax has on the after-tax wage paid for labour. (See 'elasticity of demand'.)

equity capital shares: Equity capital is defined by the balance sheet relationship (*Assets = Liabilities + Equity*) as the residual difference between asset and liabilities. Shares or ownership interests in equity capital are determined by the type of company organization. In a partnership, shares are determined by the partnership contract. For a publicly traded limited liability corporation, shares can be either common stock or preferred stock. In contrast to debt capital, there is no contractual obligation for a company to make dividend payments on equity capital shares, though preferred shares may have a cumulative provision. (See 'limited liability partnership'; 'limited liability company'.)

estate tax: According to the US Internal Revenue Service (IRS), an estate tax is a tax on the right of a deceased person to transfer property following death. Assessment of the tax requires an accounting of all property and certain interests in the person's possession at the date of death. Avoiding estate tax by gifting money, interests or property prior to death may be subject to gift tax. (See 'inheritance tax'; 'death tax'.)

estate tax multiplier method: This is a method of estimating the upper tail of the wealth distribution that uses information about wealth from estate tax filings, and applies a multiplier derived from the relationship between characteristics of the decedents – for example, age and income – with those still living to provide an aggregate estimate of wealth.

first past the post: This is an electoral system where the candidate with the largest number of votes is declared the winner, even if that candidate does not have a majority of votes. In a two-party system, first past the post is equal to a majority voting system. Where there are more than two parties, it is possible for first past the post to generate a majority government that does not have the ideological support of a majority of the voters.

Haig–Simons income: This is a definition of income motivated by concern about distributional equity. This definition defines income for a given period as equal to consumption plus the net change in wealth. (See also 'realization principle'.)

indenture contract: This is the legal contract that applies to a company bond issue. In addition to identifying the trustees, the indenture contract contains the priority of claim, amount of coupon and dates of payment, the maturity date, and other provisions such as a description of the call feature, if any.

inheritance tax: In contrast to an estate tax that is paid by a deceased person, an inheritance tax is paid by those receiving property or interest from an estate. Together, estate and inheritance tax can be referred to as 'death taxes'. (See also 'estate tax'; 'death tax'.)

life cycle savings model: This is a hypothesis about the consumption and savings behaviour of individuals over the life cycle from the early earnings years when consumption is high relative to savings; to the middle-income years when savings and asset accumulation increases to a 'hump' peak; to the retirement years when assets that have been accumulated by saving in previous years are used to support consumption in old age.

limited liability company: Use of this general terminology differs across jurisdictions, with the US interpretation having a special meaning. Subject to US federal income tax, a limited liability company (LLC) is a recently introduced hybrid structure, governed by state legislation, that combines the 'pass-through' feature of a partnership or S corporation with the limited liability of a corporation, though it is possible to adjust these default characteristics. For example, when an LLC elects to be treated as an S corporation, restrictions imposed on the number, status and citizenship of S corporation owners are avoided, though there are more restrictions on ownership transferability. In opposition to a limited liability C corporation, where both corporate tax on profits and personal tax on dividends are assessed, the LLC confers considerable flexibility to choose an organizational structure that achieves the lowest tax liability. Upon formation, a LLC is 'organized', not chartered or incorporated; with founding documentation referred to as 'the articles of organization', with equity capital ownership interests of members, not shareholders, referred to as 'membership units', not shares. (See 'C corporation'; 'S corporation'.)

limited liability partnership: In a traditional general partnership, the partners have unlimited liability for debts incurred by the business. The precise legal implications of a general partnership differ by jurisdiction; for example, whether partners are severally liable or whether liability is limited by the partnership share. In a limited liability partnership (LLP), there are two classes of partners specified in a partnership contract: limited partners that have shares with limited liability and do not typically participate in the operation of the business; and general partners that have unlimited liability and typically run the business, receiving a management fee for services provided. For tax purposes, in both general and limited liability partnerships the tax implications of firm profit flow through to the partners, where it is taxed at personal tax rates. (See also 'limited liability company'.)

Lindahl taxes: This is a theoretical concept employed in economics where the tax assessed equals the marginal benefit (somehow defined) of the public goods provided by government services. In effect, the objective of Lindahl taxes is to have individuals pay tax based on the individual benefit received from the public good provided by the government. In public finance economics, the Lindahl tax is an achievable equilibrium concept that identifies the optimum level for the supply of public goods or services.

marginal tax rates: This refers to the highest percentage of income an individual is required to pay in tax. In a progressive tax system, the percentage of tax to be paid increases according to tax brackets. Individuals with incomes falling into higher tax brackets are required to pay a higher percentage of income in tax; that is, such individuals have a higher marginal tax rate. In a flat tax system, the marginal tax rate will be the same across taxpayers, after allowance for personal and other deductions. In this case, individuals with higher incomes would still pay more tax, but the marginal rate of tax would not be higher.

mark-to-market accounting: A variation of accrual accounting that uses market prices, if available, to determine the accrual value.

neoliberal: This is a term that has evolved over time. 'Neoliberal' was a term initially employed by economists to identify policies and theories that stressed the benefits of free market competition, removing barriers to domestic and international trade, and privatizing government services. 'Neoliberal' is now used largely by non-economists to stress the negative implications of free market competition, especially the increasing wealth and income inequality associated with globalization and privatization.

nonlinear function: This refers to a mathematical representation of the relationship between two or more variables. In contrast to a linear function that expresses the relationship between a dependent and a set of independent variables in terms of intercept and slope, a non-linear function uses more complicated representations, such as logarithms, powers or roots of the variables, to describe the relationship.

optimal tax theory: This refers to a vast literature, mostly in academic economics, that attempts to obtain the best method of raising taxes.

realization principle: A fundamental feature of broad-based income taxes, the realization principle allows capital income to be taxed in the period a capital asset is sold (realization basis), rather than in the period the capital income is earned (accrual principle). Put differently, the realization principle allows the taxing of capital gains when realized rather than when earned.

S corporation: The S corporation is an entity specified in the US tax code that has many similarities to a limited liability company. The Internal Revenue Service (IRS) states that S corporations are limited liability corporations that elect to pass corporate income, losses, deductions and credits through to their shareholders for federal tax purposes. Shareholders of S corporations report the flow-through of income and losses on their personal tax returns, and are assessed tax at their individual income tax rates. To qualify for S corporation status, the corporation must be a domestic corporation, and only have shareholders that are individuals, or certain trusts and estates; that is, shareholders may not be partnerships, corporations or non-resident alien shareholders. S corporations cannot have more than 100 shareholders; must have only one class of stock; and must not be ineligible, that is, certain financial institutions, insurance companies and domestic international sales corporations are ineligible. Small businesses are typically set up as a partnership, S corporation or LLC, depending on the specific objectives of the owners. While LLCs provide more organizational flexibility than S corporations, LLCs have more restrictive rules on transferring membership units. (See 'limited liability company'; 'C corporation'.)

separable utility function: This is a theoretical relation that imposes a specific structure on the utility function of an individual. Different types of separability are available. In practical terms, separability requires the individual to divide goods into separate categories and make decisions on how much to spend on each category. This leads to a second 'separated' stage of budgeting where the individual then decides on how much to spend on each good within a category. The assumption of additive separability is often invoked for preferences of consumption over time, to allow decisions in one period to be unaffected by decisions in other time periods.

social welfare function: A theoretical construct in economics that seeks to generalize the utility function for an individual to a preference function for society, usually by making some assumptions needed to aggregate individual preferences into a social preference function. Under reasonable theoretical conditions it can be shown that aggregation of individual preferences into a social preference function is not possible.

stationary equilibrium: This refers to a concept adapted from physics, especially thermodynamics and the kinetic theory of gases, to describe a theoretical economic system at rest. Stationary equilibria can be either static or dynamic, depending on the structure of the economic model.

tax evasion versus tax avoidance: Recognizing difficulties associated with determining the legal boundary between these notions, tax evasion refers to illegal actions consciously taken to reduce tax paid, while tax avoidance involves legal actions that result in tax paid that is inconsistent with horizontal and vertical equity. The tax courts are left to determine where the boundary in the grey area between these two notions lies. A wealthy individual who consciously engages an accounting or legal firm to engineer a tax avoidance scheme later deemed to be tax evasion is a tax evader, not a tax avoider, even though criminal penalties are not likely to be imposed.

Most tax evaders are wealthy individuals, not corporations, though the corporate veil of secrecy could be used as part of an evasion scheme.

unrealized capital gains: This refers to the capital income that is accumulating prior to being taxed at realization. (See 'realization principle'.)

References

Aaron, H. and A. Munnell (1992), 'Reassessing the Role for Wealth Transfer Taxes', *National Tax Journal* **45**: 119–43.

Acemoglu, D. and J. Robinson (2015), 'The Rise and Decline of General Laws of Capitalism', *Journal of Economic Perspectives* **29**: 3–28.

Adkins, E. (2016), 'Taxation of Stock Options and Restricted Stock: The Basics and Beyond', Grant Thornton LLP.

Ahlawat, S. and H. Telson (2015), 'The Foreign Account Tax Compliance Act's Unintended Consequences', *Banking and Finance Review* **7**: 137–54.

Alm, J. (2018), 'Is the Haig–Simons Standard Dead? The Uneasy Case for a Comprehensive Income Tax', *National Tax Journal* **71**: 379–98.

Alm, J., J. Martinez-Vazquez and S. Wallace (eds) (2004), *Taxing the Hard-to-Tax: Lessons from Theory and Practice*, Amsterdam: Elsevier.

Almås, I. and M. Mogstad (2012), 'Older or Wealthier? The Impact of Age Adjustment on Wealth Inequality', *Scandinavian Journal of Economics* **114**: 24–54.

Alstadsæter, A. and W. Kopczuk (2014), 'Are Closely Held Firms Tax Shelters?', *NBER Tax Policy and the Economy* **28**: 1–32, http://www.nber.org/chapters/c13052.

Alstadsæter, A., N. Johannesen and G. Zucman (2019), 'Tax Evasion and Inequality', *American Economic Review* **109**: 2073–103.

Alvaredo, F. (2018), 'The Distribution of Wealth: Evidence from Five Data Sources', paper presented to the OECD Conference on Wealth Inequalities: Measurement and Policies, 26 April, http://www.oecd.org/statistics/oecd-conference-on-wealth-inequalities-measurement-and-policies-april-2018.htm.

Alvaredo, F., A. Atkinson and S. Morelli (2016), 'The Challenge of Measuring UK Wealth Inequality in the 2000s', *Fiscal Studies* **37**: 13–33.

Alvaredo, F., L. Chancel, T. Piketty, E. Saez and G. Zucman (2017), 'Global Inequality Dynamics: New Findings from WID.world', *American Economic Review: Papers and Proceedings* **107** (5): 404–9.

Alvaredo, F., L. Chancel, T. Piketty, E. Saez and G. Zucman (2018), 'The Elephant Curve of Global Inequality and Growth', *American Economic Association Papers and Proceedings* **108**: 103–8.

Alvaredo, F., L. Chancel, T. Piketty, E. Saez and G. Zucman (2019), 'World Inequality Report 2018', World Inequality Lab/Wid.World, available at: https://wir2018.wid.world/files/download/wir2018-full-report-english.pdf.

American Bar Association (AAA) (2011), 'Revised Prototype Limited Liability Company Act', Revised Prototype Limited Liability Company Act Editorial Board, LLCs, Partnerships and Unincorporated Entities Committee, ABA Section of Business Law, *Business Lawyer* **67** (November): 117–225.

Armour, P., R.V. Burkhauser and J. Larrimore (2013), 'Deconstructing Income and Income Inequality Measures: A Crosswalk from Market Income to Comprehensive Income', *American Economic Review: Papers and Proceedings* **103**: 173–7.

Armour, P., R.V. Burkhauser and J. Larrimore (2014), 'Levels and Trends in US Income and its Distribution: A Crosswalk from Market Income towards a Comprehensive Haig–Simons Income Approach', *Southern Economic Journal* **81**: 271–93.

Ashton, R. (1956), 'Revenue Farming under the Early Stuarts', *Economic History Review* **3**: 310–22.

Atkinson, A. (1970), 'On the Measurement of Inequality', *Journal of Economic Theory*, **2**: 244–63.

Atkinson, A. (1971), 'Capital Taxes, the Redistribution of Wealth and Individual Savings', *Review of Economic Studies* **38**: 209–27.

Atkinson, A. (1977), 'Optimal Taxation and the Direct versus Indirect Tax Controversy', *Canadian Journal of Economics* **10**: 590–606.

Atkinson, A. (2005), 'Top Incomes in the UK over the Twentieth Century', *Journal of the Royal Statistical Society*, Series A **168**: 325–43.

Atkinson, A. and J. Stiglitz (1976), 'The Design of Tax Structure: Direct Versus Indirect Taxation', *Journal of Public Economics* **6**: 55–75.

Atkinson, A., T. Piketty and E. Saez (2011), 'Top Incomes in the Long Run of History', *Journal of Economic Literature* **49**: 3–71.

Auerbach, A. (1991), 'Retrospective Capital Gains Taxation', *American Economic Review* **81**: 167–78.

Auerbach, A. and K. Hassett (2015), 'Capital Taxation in the Twenty-First Century', *American Economic Review: Papers and Proceedings* **105**: 38–42.

Avery, R., D. Grodzicki and K. Moore (2015), 'Death and Taxes: An Evaluation of the Impact of Prospective Policies for Taxing Wealth at the Time of Death', *National Tax Journal* **68**: 601–32.

Avi-Yonah, R. (2000), 'Globalization, Tax Competition, and the Fiscal Crisis of the Welfare State', *Harvard Law Review* **113**: 1573–676.

Baack, B. and E. Ray (1985), 'Special Interests and the Adoption of the Income Tax in the United States', *Journal of Economic History* **45**: 607–25.

Bach, S., R. Beznoska and V. Steiner (2014), 'A Wealth Tax on the Rich to Bring Down Public Debt? Revenue and Distributional Effects of a Capital Levy in Germany', *Fiscal Studies* **35**: 67–89.

Bahl, R. (2004), 'Reaching the Hardest to Tax: Consequences and Possibilities', in J. Alm, J. Martinez-Vazquez and S. Wallace (eds), *Taxing the Hard-to-Tax: Lessons from Theory and Practice*, Amsterdam: Elsevier, pp. 337–54.

Balafoutas, L., A. Beck, R. Kerschbamer and M. Sutter (2015), 'The Hidden Costs of Tax Evasion: Collaborative Tax Evasion in Markets for Expert Services', *Journal of Public Economics* **129**: 14–25.

Balestra, C. and R. Tonkin (2018), 'Inequalities in Household Wealth across OECD Countries: Evidence from the OECD Wealth Distribution Database', Statistics Working Papers No. 88, OECD.

Bang, P. (2008), *The Roman Bazaar: A Comparative Study of Trade and Markets in a Tributary Empire*, Cambridge, UK: Cambridge University Press.

Bank, S. (2003), '"The Progressive Consumption Tax Revisited", review of "Fair Not Flat: How to Make the Tax System Better and Simpler" by Edward J. McCaffery', Survey of Books Relating to the Law, *Michigan Law Review* **101**: 2238–60.

Bankman, J. and D. Weisbach (2006), 'The Superiority of an Ideal Consumption Tax over an Ideal Income Tax', *Stanford Law Review* **58**: 1413–56.

Banting, K. (1991), 'The Politics of Wealth Taxes', The Role of Wealth Taxes in Canada, *Canadian Public Policy* **17**: 351–67.

Bastani, S., S. Blomquist and L. Micheletto (2013), 'The Welfare Gains of Age-Related Optimal Income Taxation', *International Economic Review* **54**: 1219–49.

BC Assessment (2017), 'BC Assessment Corporate History 1974 Onwards', Victoria, BC, https://www.bcassessment.ca/About-Us/about-BC-Assessment/history.

Bebchuk, L. and J.M. Fried (2003), 'Executive Compensation as an Agency Problem', *Journal of Economic Perspectives* **17** (Summer): 71–92.

Benson, G. (1965), *The American Property Tax: Its History, Administration, and Economic Impact*, Claremont, CA: Institute for Studies in Federalism.

Berle, A. and G. Means (1968 [1932]), *The Modern Corporation and Private Property*, New York: Harcourt, Brace & World; 1968 revised reprint.

Birch, T. (1988), 'Justice in Taxation: An Appraisal of Normative Tax Theory', *Social Science Quarterly* **69**: 1005–13.

Bird, R. (1976), 'The Incidence of the Property Tax: Old Wine in New Bottles?', Supplement: Property Tax Reform, *Canadian Public Policy* **2**: 323–34.

Bird, R. (1991), 'The Taxation of Personal Wealth in International Perspective', The Role of Wealth Taxes in Canada, *Canadian Public Policy* **17**: 322–34.

Bird, R. and Wallace (2004), 'Is it Really so Hard to Tax the Hard-to-Tax? The Context and Role of Presumptive Taxes', in J. Alm, J. Martinez-Vazquez and S. Wallace (eds), *Taxing the Hard-to-Tax: Lessons from Theory and Practice*, Amsterdam: Elsevier, pp. 121–55.

Bivens, J. and L. Mishel (2013), 'The Pay of Corporate Executives and Financial Professionals as Evidence of Rents in Top 1 Percent Incomes', *Journal of Economic Perspectives* **19** (Fall): 135–44.

Black, F. (1976), 'The Dividend Puzzle', *Journal of Portfolio Management* **2**: 5–8.

Block, F. (2009), 'Read Their Lips: Taxes and the Right Wing Agenda', in I. Martin, A. Mehrotra and M. Prasad (eds), *The New Fiscal Sociology: Taxation in Comparative and Historical Perspective*, Cambridge, UK: Cambridge University Press, pp. 68–85.

Blough, R. (1948), 'Review: "Agenda for Progressive Taxation" by William Vickrey', *American Economic Review* **38**: 670–73.

Boadway, R., M. Marchand and P. Pestieau (2000), 'Redistribution with Unobservable Bequests: A Case for Taxing Capital Income', *Scandinavian Journal of Economics* **102**: 253–67.

Böhm-Bawerk, E. (1970 [1891]), *Capital and Interest: A Critical History of Economical Theory*, trans. W. Smart, New York: A.M. Kelley.

Bonus, H. (1982), 'On Social Justice', Social Policy in a Free Market Economy: A Symposium, *Journal of Institutional and Theoretical Economics*, **138** (3): 599–617.

Boran, I. (2008), 'Do Cosmopolitans Have Reasons to Object to Global Distributive Justice?', *American Philosophical Quarterly* **45**: 1–17.

Bowman, K. and A. Rugg (2012), 'Public Opinion on Taxes: 1937 to Today', American Enterprise Institute for Public Policy Research, AIE Public Opinion Studies.

Brackney, M. (2015), 'Reporting Foreign Partnerships', *Journal of Passthrough Entities* (May/June): 35–8.

Bradford, D. (1995), 'Fixing Realization Accounting: Symmetry, Consistency and Correctness in the Taxation of Financial Instruments', *Tax Law Review* **50**: 731–85.

Bratton, W. (2001), 'Berle and Means Reconsidered at the Century's Turn', *Journal of Corporation Law* **26**: 733–70.

Bratton, W. and M. Wachter (2008), 'Shareholder Primacy's Corporatist Origins: Adolf Berle and the Modern Corporation', *Journal of Corporation Law* **33**: 118–52.

Bricker, R. and N. Chandar (2000), 'Where Berle and Means Went Wrong: A Reassessment of Capital Market Agency and Financial Reporting', *Accounting, Organizations and Society* **25**: 529–54.

Bricker, J., A. Henriques, J. Krimmel and J. Sabelhaus (2016), 'Measuring Income and Wealth at the Top Using Administrative and Survey Data', *Brookings Papers on Economic Activity* (Spring): 261–312.

Brock, G. (2008), 'Taxation and Global Justice: Closing the Gap between Theory and Practice', *Journal of Social Philosophy* **39**: 161–84.

Brown, H.G. (1924), *The Economics of Taxation*, New York: Henry Holt & Co.

Brown, R. (1991), 'A Primer on the Implementation of Wealth Taxes', The Role of Wealth Taxes in Canada, *Canadian Public Policy* **17**: 335–50.

Brucker, G. (1993), 'Florentine Voices from the "Catasto", 1427–1480', *I Tatti Studies in the Italian Renaissance* **5**: 11–32.

Brunner, J., P. Eckerstorfer and S. Pech (2013), 'Optimal Taxes on Wealth and Consumption in the Presence of Tax Evasion', *Journal of Economics* **110**: 107–24.

Brunt, P. (1984), 'The Role of the Senate in the Augustan Regime', *Classical Quarterly* **34**: 423–44.

Buchanan, J. and G. Brennan (1980), *The Power to Tax: Analytical Foundations of a Fiscal Constitution*, Cambridge, UK: Cambridge University Press.

Burbidge, J. (1991), 'The Allocative and Efficiency Effects of Wealth Taxes', The Role of Wealth Taxes in Canada, *Canadian Public Policy* **17**: 264–78.

Burkhauser, R., S. Feng, S. Jenkins and J. Larrimore (2009), 'Recent Trends in Top Income Shares in the USA: Reconciling Estimates from March CPS and IRS Tax Return Data', *Review of Economics and Statistics* **94**: 371–88.

Burman, L., K. Clausing and L. Austin (2017), 'Is US Corporate Income Double-Taxed?', *National Tax Journal* **70**: 675–706.

Burton, G. (2004), 'The Roman Imperial State, Provincial Governors and the Public Finances of Provincial Cities, 27 BC–AD 235', *Historia: Zeitschrift für Alte Geschichte* **53**: 311–42.

Butcher, J. and H. Dick (eds) (1993), *The Rise and Fall of Revenue Farming: Business Elites and the Emergence of the Modern State*, New York: St Martin's Press.

Cagetti, M. (2003), 'Wealth Accumulation over the Life Cycle and Precautionary Savings', *Journal of Business and Economic Statistics* **21**: 339–53.

Cagetti, M. and M. De Nardi (2009), 'Estate Taxation, Entrepreneurship, and Wealth', *American Economic Review* **99**: 85–111.

Calkins, H. (1991), 'Can Florence in the *Quatrocento* Help Shape Tax Policy Today?', *Tax Lawyer* **44**: 685–95.

Campbell, A. (2009), 'What Americans Think of Taxes', in I. Martin, A. Mehrotra and M. Prasad (eds), *The New Fiscal Sociology: Taxation in Comparative and Historical Perspective*, Cambridge, UK: Cambridge University Press, pp. 48–67.

Canadian Department of Finance (2008), 'Tax and Other Issues Related to Publicly Listed Flow-Through Entities (Income Trusts and Limited Partnerships)', http://www.fin.gc.ca/activty/pubs/toirplf1-eng.asp.

Canadian Public Policy (1991), Special Issue, 'The Role of Wealth Taxes in Canada'.

Carroll, S. (1989), 'Taxing Wealth: An Accessions Tax Proposal for the US', *Journal of Post Keynesian Economics* **12**: 49–69.

Carter, K. (1968), 'Canadian Tax Reform and Henry Simons', *Journal of Law and Economics* **11**: 231–42.

Cave, R. and H. Coulson (1965), *A Source Book for Medieval Economic History*, New York: Biblo & Tannen.

Cirillo, R. (1984), 'Léon Walras and Social Justice', *American Journal of Economics and Sociology* **43**: 53–60.

Clausing, K. (2009), 'Multinational Firm Tax Avoidance and Tax Policy', *National Tax Journal* **62**: 703–25.

Cobham, A. and P. Janský (2017), 'Global Distribution of Revenue Loss from Tax Avoidance: Re-estimation and Country Results', WIDER Working Paper #55, March.

Conesa, J., S. Kitao and D. Krueger (2009), 'Taxing Capital? Not a Bad Idea after All!', *American Economic Review* **99**: 25–48.

Cook, W. (1893), *The Corporation Problem: The Public Phases of Corporations, Their Uses, Abuses, Benefits, Dangers, Wealth, and Power, with a Discussion of the Social, Industrial, Economic, and Political Questions to Which They Have Given Rise*, New York: G. Putnam.

Cooper, M., J. McClelland, J. Pearce, R. Prisinzano, J. Sullivan, et al. (2015), 'Business in the United States: Who Owns It, and How Much Tax Do They Pay?', NBER and Office of Tax Analysis, Working Paper 104, October.

Costa-Font, J., F. De-Albuquerque and H. Doucouliagos (2014), 'Do Jurisdictions Compete on Taxes? A Meta-regression Analysis', *Public Choice* **161**: 451–70.

Cowell, F. and M. Victoria-Feser (1996), 'Robustness Properties of Inequality Measures', *Econometrica* **64**: 77–101.

Cox, H.B. (1919), 'Origin and Growth of Income Tax', *Journal of Comparative Legislation and International Law*, Third Series, **1**: 42–57.

Crawford, R., D. Innes and C. O'Dea (2016), 'Household Wealth in Great Britain: Distribution, Composition and Changes, 2006–12', *Fiscal Studies* **37**: 35–54.

Cremer, H. and F. Gahvari (1998), 'On Optimal Taxation of Housing', *Journal of Urban Economics* **43**: 315–35.

Crockett, J. and I. Friend (1988), 'Dividend Policy in Perspective: Can Theory Explain Behavior?', *Review of Economics and Statistics* **70**: 603–13.

Christie, W. (1990), 'Dividend Yield and Expected Returns: The Zero-Dividend Puzzle', *Journal of Financial Economics* **28**: 95–126.

Davies, J. (1991), 'The Distributive Effects of Wealth Taxes', The Role of Wealth Taxes in Canada, *Canadian Public Policy* **17**: 279–308.

Davies, J. and A.F. Shorrocks (2000), 'The Distribution of Wealth', in A. Atkinson and F. Bourguignon (eds), *Handbook of Income Distribution*, Amsterdam: North-Holland, pp. 605–75.

Davies, J., R. Lluberas and A. Shorrocks (2017), 'Estimating the Level and Distribution of Global Wealth 2000–2014', *Review of Income and Wealth* **63**: 731–59.

Davies, J., S. Sandstrom, A. Shorrocks, A. Wolff and E. Wolff (2008), 'The World Distribution of Household Wealth', Working Paper Series DP2008/03, World Institute for Development Economic Research (UNU-WIDER).

Davis, P. and A. Ko (n.d.), 'Investing in Canada Through a US Limited Liability Company: The Impact of New Paragraph 6 to Article IV of the Canada–US Tax Treaty', Lane Powell PC, Seattle, Washington.

De Nardi, M. and F. Yang (2016), 'Wealth Inequality, Family Background, and Estate Taxation', *Journal of Monetary Economics* **77**: 130–45.

Denis, D.J., D.K. Denis and A. Sarin (1994), 'The Information Content of Dividend Changes: Cash Flow, Signaling, Overinvestment and Dividend Clienteles', *Journal of Financial and Quantitative Analysis* **29**: 567–87.

Devereux, M., R. Griffith, A. Klemm, M. Thum and M. Ottaviani (2002), 'Corporate Income Tax Reforms and International Tax Competition', *Economic Policy* **17**: 449–95.

Diamond, J. (2016), 'Forum: Corporate Tax Reform', *National Tax Journal* **69**: 641–2.

Diamond, P. and J. Mirrlees (1971), 'Optimal Taxation and Public Production I: Production Efficiency', *American Economic Review* **61**: 8–27.

Diamond, P. and E. Saez (2011), 'The Case for a Progressive Tax: From Basic Research to Policy Recommendations', *Journal of Economic Perspectives* **25** (Fall): 165–90.

Diamond, P. and J. Spinnewijn (2011), 'Capital Income Taxes with Heterogeneous Discount Rates', *American Economic Journal: Economic Policy* **3** (November): 52–76.

Dietsch, P. (2015), *Catching Capital: The Ethics of Tax Competition*, New York: Oxford University Press.

Domeij, D. and J. Heathcote (2004), 'On the Distributional Effects of Reducing Capital Taxes', *International Economic Review* **45**: 523–54.

Donohoe, M., P. Lisowsky and M. Mayberry (2015), 'Who Benefits from the Tax Advantages of Organizational Form Choice?', *National Tax Journal* **68**: 975–98.

Dornfest, A., J. Rearich, T. Brydon and R. Almy (2019), 'State and Provincial Property Tax Policies and Administrative Practices (PTAPP): 2017 Findings and Report', *Journal of Property Tax Assessment and Administration* **16**: 43–130.

Dowd, T., R. McClelland and A. Muthitacharoen (2015), 'New Evidence on the Tax Elasticity of Capital Gains', *National Tax Journal* **68**: 511–44.

Duclos, J. (2006), 'Innis Lecture: Equity and Equality', *Canadian Journal of Economics* **39**: 1073–104.

Dugger, W. (1990), 'The Wealth Tax: A Policy Proposal', *Journal of Economic Issues* **24**: 133–44.

Dwyer, T. (2014), 'Taxation the Lost History', *American Journal of Economics and Sociology* **73**: 627–988.

Dyson, T. (2012), 'On Demographic and Democratic Transitions', Population and Public Policy: Essays in Honor of Paul Demeny, *Population and Development Review* **38**: 83–102.

Eckerstorfer, P., J. Halak, J. Kapeller, B. Schütz, F. Springholz and R. Wildauer (2016), 'Correcting for the Missing Rich: An Application to Wealth Survey Data', *Review of Income and Wealth* **62**: 605–27.

Economic Journal (1999), Special Issue, June, 'Controversy: On the Hidden Economy'.

Edwards, C. and D. Mitchell (2008), *Global Tax Revolution: The Rise of Tax Competition and the Battle to Defend It*, Washington, DC: Cato Institute.

Emory, M. (1965), 'The Early English Income Tax: A Heritage for the Contemporary', *American Journal of Legal History* **9**: 286–319.

Equilar (2016), *2016 CEO Pay Trends*, Lake Forest, IL: Meridian Compensation Partners.

Erickson, M. and Shiing-wu Wang (2007), 'Tax Benefits as a Source of Merger Premiums in Acquisitions of Private Corporations', *Accounting Review* **82**: 359–87.

Escobar, L. (2007), 'Personal Wealth Taxes: The Inheritance and Gift Taxes and the Net Wealth Tax', in J. Martinez-Vazquez and J. Sanz-Sanz (eds), *Fiscal Reform in Spain: Accomplishments and Challenges*, Cheltenham, UK and Northampton, MA, USA: Edward Elgar Publishing, pp. 241–90.

Evans, C. (2011), 'Reflections on the Mirrlees Review: An Australasian Perspective', *Fiscal Studies* 32: 375–93.

Fagereng, A., L. Guiso, D. Malacrino and L. Pistaferri (2016), 'Heterogeneity in Returns to Wealth and the Measurement of Wealth Inequality', *American Economic Review: Papers and Proceedings* 106: 651–5.

Fama, E. and K. French (2001), 'Disappearing Dividends: Changing Firm Characteristics or Lower Propensity to Pay?', *Journal of Financial Economics* 60: 3–43.

Feige, E. (1990), 'Defining and Estimating Underground and Informal Economies: The New Institutional Economics Approach', *World Development* 18: 989–1002.

Feige, E., M. Boldrin and H. Huizinga (2000), 'Taxation for the 21st Century: The Automated Payment Transaction (APT) Tax', *Economic Policy* 15: 473–511.

Feld, L. (2000), 'Tax Competition and Income Redistribution: An Empirical Analysis for Switzerland', *Public Choice* 105: 125–64.

Feldstein, M. (1978), 'The Welfare Cost of Capital Income Taxation', Research in Taxation, *Journal of Political Economy* 86 (April): S29–S51.

Ferris, S., N. Sen and E. Unlu (2009), 'An International Analysis of Dividend Payment Behavior', *Journal of Business Finance and Accounting* 36: 496–522.

Fetter, F. (1900), 'Recent Discussion of the Capital Concept', *Quarterly Journal of Economics* 15: 1–45.

Fetter, F. (1907), 'The Nature of Capital and Income', *Journal of Political Economy* 15: 129–48.

Finnerty, J. (2002), 'Adjusting the Comparable-Company Method for Tax Differences when Valuing Privately Held "S" Corporations and LLCs', *Journal of Applied Finance* (Fall/Winter): 15–30.

Fisher, I. (1896), 'What is Capital?', *Economic Journal* 6: 509–34.

Fisher, I. (1904), 'Precedents for Defining Capital', *Quarterly Journal of Economics* 18: 386–408.

Foreign Policy (2004), 'Measuring Globalization', *Foreign Policy* 141 (March–April): 54–69.

Frankfurter, G. (1999), 'What is the Puzzle in the "Dividend Puzzle"?', *Journal of Portfolio Management* 26 (Summer): 76–85.

Gaillard, E. and D. Trautman (1987), 'Trusts in Non-Trust Countries: Conflict of Laws and the Hague Convention on Trusts', *American Journal of Comparative Law* 35: 307–40.

Galbraith, J.K. (2012), *Inequality and Instability: A Study of the World Economy Just Before the Great Crisis*, New York: Oxford University Press.

Galbraith, J.K. (2016), *Inequality: What Everyone Needs to Know*, New York: Oxford University Press.

Galbraith, J.K. (2019), 'Sparse, Inconsistent and Unreliable: Tax Records and the *World Inequality Report 2018*', *Development and Change* **50** (2): 329–46.

Gelber, A. and M. Weinzierl (2016), 'Optimal Taxation when Children's Abilities Depend on Parents' Resources', *National Tax Journal* **69**: 11–40.

Genschel, P. and P. Schwarz (2011), 'Tax Competition: A Literature Review', *Socio-Economic Review* **9**: 339–70.

George, H. (1882 [1879]), *Progress and Poverty: An Inquiry into the Cause of Industrial Depressions, and of Increase in Want with Increase in Wealth. A Remedy*, London: Kegan Paul, Trench & Company.

Ghosh, C. and J. Woolridge (1988), 'An Analysis of Shareholder Reaction to Dividend Cuts and Omissions', *Journal of Financial Research* **11**: 281–94.

Ghosh, C., J. Harding, O. Sezer and C. Sirmans (2008), 'The Role of Executive Stock Options in REIT Repurchases', *Journal of Real Estate Research* **30**: 27–44.

Gibrat, R. (1931), *Les Inegalites Economiques*, Paris: Sirey.

Gilson, R. and J. Gordon (2013), 'The Agency Costs of Agency Capitalism: Activist Investors and the Revaluation of Governance Rights', *Columbia Law Review* **113**: 863–927.

Glennerster, H. (2012), 'Why Was a Wealth Tax for the UK Abandoned? Lessons for the Policy Process and Tackling Wealth Inequality', *Journal of Social Policy* **41**: 233–49.

Goldberg, P. and N. Pavcnik (2007), 'Distributional Effects of Globalization in Developing Countries', *Journal of Economic Literature* **45**: 39–82.

Golosov, M., A. Tsyvinski, I. Werning, P. Diamond and K. Judd (2006), 'New Dynamic Public Finance: A User's Guide (with Comments and Discussion)', *NBER Macroeconomics Annual* **21**: 317–63, 365–79, 381–7.

Goodwin, B. (2008), 'Taxation in Utopia', *Utopian Studies* **19**: 313–31.

Gordon, H. (1980), *Welfare, Justice and Freedom*, New York: Columbia University Press.

Gordon, R., D. Joulfaian and J. Poterba (2016), 'Choosing Between an Estate Tax and a Basis Carryover Regime: Evidence from 2010', *National Tax Journal* **69**: 981–1002.

Government Accountability Office (GAO) (2013), 'Offshore Tax Evasion: IRS Has Collected Billions of Dollars, But May Be Missing Continued Evasion', GAO-13-318.

Government Accountability Office (GAO) (2014), 'IRS's Offshore Voluntary Disclosure Program: 2009 Participation by State and Location of Foreign Bank Accounts', GAO-14-265R.

Government Accountability Office (GAO) (2016), 'Corporate Income Tax: Most Large Profitable US Corporations Paid Tax but Effective Tax Rates Differed Significantly from the Statutory Rate', GAO-16-363, 17 March.

Graetz, M. (2002), '100 Million Unnecessary Returns: A Fresh Start for the US Tax System', *Yale Law Journal* **112** (November): 261–310.

Graetz, M. and I. Shapiro (2011), *Death by a Thousand Cuts: The Fight over Taxing Inherited Wealth*, Princeton, NJ: Princeton University Press.

Graetz, M. and A. Warren (2016), 'Integration of Corporate and Shareholder Taxes', *National Tax Journal* **69**: 677–700.

Green, R. (1984), 'Ethics and Taxation: A Theoretical Framework', *Journal of Religious Ethics* **12**: 146–61.

Greenhouse, C. (1994), 'Democracy and Demography', Symposium: Global Migration and the Future of the Nation-State, *Indiana Journal of Global Legal Studies* **2**: 21–29.

Grinberg, I. (2012), 'The Battle Over Taxing Offshore Accounts', *UCLA Law Review* **60**: 305–83.

Gross, J. (1993), 'Progressive Taxation and Social Justice in Eighteenth-Century France', *Past and Present* **140**: 79–126.

Groves, H. (1974), *Tax Philosophers*, Madison, WI: University of Wisconsin Press.

Grubert, H. and R. Altshuler (2016), 'Shifting the Burden of Taxation from the Corporate to the Personal Level and Getting the Corporate Tax Rate down to 15 Percent', *National Tax Journal* **69**: 643–76.

Grullon, G. and R. Michaely (2002), 'Dividends, Share Repurchases and the Substitution Hypothesis', *Journal of Finance* **57**: 1649–84.

Haig, R. (ed.) (1921), *The Federal Income Tax: A Series of Lectures Delivered at Columbia University in December, 1920*, New York: Columbia University Press.

Hale, D. (1985), 'The Evolution of the Property Tax: A Study of the Relation between Public Finance and Political Theory', *Journal of Politics* **47**: 382–404.

Hall, B. and K. Murphy (2003), 'The Trouble with Stock Options', *Journal of Economic Perspectives* **17** (Summer): 49–70.

Hall, P. and D. Soskice (eds) (2001), *Varieties of Capitalism: The Institutional Foundations of Comparative Advantage*, Oxford: Oxford University Press.

Hanlon, M., E. Maydew and J. Thornock (2015), 'The Long Way Home: US Tax Evasion and Offshore Investments in US Equity and Debt Markets', *Journal of Finance* **70**: 257–87.

Hanna, C. (2000), 'Some Observations on a Pure Income Tax System', *International Lawyer* **34**: 125–35.

Hansen, M. (2014), 'Self-Made Wealth or Family Wealth? Changes in Intergenerational Wealth Mobility', *Social Forces* **93**: 457–81.

Hansmann, H. and U. Mattei (1998), 'The Functions of Trust Law: A Comparative Legal and Economic Analysis', *New York University Law Review* **73**: 434–79.

Harrington, B. (2012), 'Trust and Estate Planning: The Emergence of a Profession and Its Contribution to Socioeconomic Inequality', *Sociological Forum* **27**: 825–46.

Harris, C.L. (1994), 'An Address on Land Taxation as an Evasion-Proof Revenue Source', *American Journal of Economics and Sociology* **53**: 97–8.

Harrod, R. (1930), 'Progressive Taxation and Equal Sacrifice', *Economic Journal* **40** (December): 704–7.

Harvard Law Review (1909), 'The Proposed Income Tax Amendment', *Harvard Law Review* **23** (November): 49–51.

Haufler, A. (2001), *Taxation in a Global Economy*, Cambridge, UK: Cambridge University Press.

Haufler, A., A. Klemm and G. Schjelderup (2009), 'Economic Integration and the Relationship between Profit and Wage Taxes', *Public Choice* **138**: 423–46.

Haugerud, A. (2012), 'Satire and Dissent in the Age of Billionaires', Politics and Comedy, *Social Research* **79**, (Spring): 145–68.

Hawley, J. and A. Williams (2000), *The Rise of Fiduciary Capitalism: How Institutional Investors Can Make Corporate America More Democratic*, Philadelphia, PA: University of Pennsylvania Press.

Hayek, F. (1976), *The Mirage of Social Justice*, Chicago, IL: University of Chicago Press.

Hays, J. (2003), 'Globalization and Capital Taxation in Consensus and Majoritarian Democracies', *World Politics* **56**: 79–113.

Head, J. (1970) 'Henry Simons Regained. Report of the Canadian Royal Commission on Taxation', *FinanzArchiv* New Series, **29**: 197–237.

Head, J. (1972), 'Canadian Tax Reform and Participatory Democracy', *FinanzArchiv*, New Series, **31**: 48–68.

Hein, E. (2012), *The Macroeconomics of Finance Dominated Capitalism and Its Crisis*, Cheltenham, UK and Northampton, MA, USA: Edward Elgar Publishing.

Henry, J. (2012), 'The Price of Offshore Revisited: New Estimates for Missing Global Private Wealth, Income, Inequality and Lost Taxes', Tax Justice Network, July, https://taxjustice.net/cms/upload/pdf/Priceof OffshoreRevisited120722.pdf.

Hines, J. (2010), 'Treasure Islands', *Journal of Economic Perspectives* **24** (4): 103–26.

Hines, J. and L. Summers (2009), 'How Globalization Affects Tax Design', *Tax Policy and the Economy* **23**: 123–58.

Hirschman, A. (1945), *National Power and the Structure of Foreign Trade*, Berkeley, CA: University of California Press.

Hobbes, T. (1676), *Leviathan*, London: J. Thomson.

Hodder, L., M. McAnally and C. Weaver (2003), 'The Influence of Tax and Nontax Factors on Banks' Choice of Organizational Form', *Accounting Review* **78**: 297–325.

Holden, R. (2005), 'The Original Management Incentive Schemes', *Journal of Economic Perspectives* **19** (Fall): 135–44.

Hont, I. (2015), *Politics in Commercial Society: Jean-Jacques Rousseau and Adam Smith*, Béla Kapossy and Michael Sonenscher (eds), Cambridge, MA: Harvard University Press.

Hubbard, G. (2015), 'Taking Capital's Gains: Capital's Ideas and Tax Policy in the Twenty-first Century', *National Tax Journal* **68**: 409–24.

Hufbauer, G. (1966), 'Progressivity and Horizontal Equity in Personal Income Taxation', *Southwestern Social Science Quarterly* **47**: 181–90.

Institute on Taxation and Economic Policy (2011), *The ITEP Guide to Fair State and Local Taxes*, Washington, DC: ITEP.

Jacobson, K. (2001), 'Fiduciary Duty Considerations in Choosing between Limited Partnerships and Limited Liability Companies', *Real Property, Probate and Trust Journal* **36**: 1–36.

Jagannathan, M., C. Stephens and M. Weisbach (2000), 'Financial Flexibility and the Choice between Dividends and Stock Repurchases', *Journal of Financial Economics* **57**: 355–84.

Janeba, E. and W. Peters (1999), 'Tax Evasion, Tax Competition and the Gains from Nondiscrimination: The Case of Interest Taxation in Europe', *Economic Journal* **109**: 93–101.

Jäntti, M. and E. Sierminska (2007), 'Survey Estimates of Wealth Holdings in OECD Countries Evidence on the Level and Distribution across Selected Countries', UNU-WIDER Research Paper No. 2007/17.

Jewell, H. (1972), *English Local Administration in the Middle Ages*, New York: Barnes & Noble.

Johannesen, N. and G. Zucman (2014), 'The End of Bank Secrecy? An Evaluation of the G20 Tax Haven Crackdown', *American Economic Journal: Economic Policy* **6**: 65–91.

Johnson, N. (2006), 'Banking on the King: The Evolution of the Royal Revenue Farms in Old Regime France', *Journal of Economic History* **66**: 963–991.

Jones, C. (2015), 'Pareto and Piketty: The Macroeconomics of Top Income and Wealth Inequality', *Journal of Economic Perspectives* **29** (Winter): 29–46.

Jones, C. and Y. Temouri (2016), 'The Determinants of Tax Haven FDI', *Journal of World Business* **51**: 237–50.

Kahle, K.M. (2002), 'When a Buyback Isn't a Buyback; Open Market Repurchases and Employee Options', *Journal of Financial Economics* **63**: 235–61.

Kaldor, N. (1955), *An Expenditure Tax*, London: G. Allen & Unwin.

Katic, P. and A. Leigh (2016), 'Top Wealth Shares in Australia 1915–2012', *Review of Income and Wealth* **62** (June): 209–22.

Kaymak, B. and M. Poschke (2016), 'The Evolution of Wealth Inequality over Half a Century: The Role of Taxes, Transfers and Technology', *Journal of Monetary Economics* **77**: 1–25.

Kellner, D. (2002), 'Theorizing Globalization', *Sociological Theory* **20**: 285–305.

Kennedy, W. (1913), 'English Taxation: 1640–1799; An Essay on Policy and Opinion', Series of the London School of Economics and Political Science, No. 33, London: G. Bell & Sons.

Kennickell, A. (2006), 'Currents and Undercurrents: Changes in the Distribution of Wealth, 1989–2004', Finance and Economics Discussion Series Working Paper No. 2006-13.

Kennickell, A. (2009), 'Ponds and Streams: Wealth and Income in the U.S., 1989 to 2007', Finance and Economics Discussion Series Working Paper No. 2009-13, Divisions of Research & Statistics and Monetary Affairs, Federal Reserve Board, Washington, DC.

Kennickell, A. (2017), 'Lining Up: Survey and Administrative Data Estimates of Wealth Concentration', Finance and Economics Discussion Series Working Paper No. 2017-17, Divisions of Research and Statistics and Monetary Affairs, Federal Reserve Board, Washington, DC.

Kennickell, A. (2019), 'The Tail that Wags: Differences in Effective Right Tail Coverage and Estimates of Wealth Inequality', *Journal of Economic Inequality* **17**: 443–59.

Kessler, D. and P. Pestieau (1991), 'The Taxation of Wealth in the EEC: Facts and Trends', The Role of Wealth Taxes in Canada, *Canadian Public Policy* **17**: 309–21.

Keynes, J.M. (2018 [1936]), *The General Theory of Employment, Interest and Money*, Cham: Springer International Publishing.

Knobel, A. (2017), 'Trusts: Weapons of Mass Injustice?', Tax Justice Network, 13 February. https://papers.ssrn.com/sol3/papers.cfm?abstract id=2943493.

Knobel, A. (2018), 'Reporting Taxation: Analysing Loopholes in the EU's Automatic Exchange of Information and how to Close Them', Report Commissioned by the Greens/EFA Group in the European Parliament, 15 October.

Knobel, A. and M. Meinzer (2016), 'Drilling Down to the Real Owners – Part 2', Tax Justice Network, 28 June. https://www.taxjustice.net/2016/06/28/europe-trust-trusts/.

Kolm, S. (1976), 'Unequal Inequalities', *Journal of Economic Theory*, **12**: 416–42.

Kopczuk, W. (2015), 'What Do We Know about the Evolution of Top Wealth Shares in the United States?', *Journal of Economic Perspectives* **29**: 47–66.

Kopczuk, W. and E. Saez (2004), 'Top Wealth Shares in the United States, 1916–2000: Evidence from Estate Tax Returns', *National Tax Journal* **57**: 445–87.

Kopczuk, W. and J. Slemrod (2003), 'Dying to Save Taxes: Evidence from Estate-Tax Returns on the Death Elasticity', *Review of Economics and Statistics* **85**: 256–65.

Kotz, D. (2015), *The Rise and Fall of Neoliberal Capitalism*, Cambridge, MA: Harvard University Press.

Krupa, O. (2014), 'Housing Crisis and Vertical Equity of the Property Tax in a Market Value–based Assessment System', *Public Finance Review* **42**: 555–81.

Kuznets, S. (1953), *Shares of Upper Income Groups in Income and Savings*, New York: National Bureau of Economic Research.

Lamba, A. and K. Miranda (2010), 'The Role of Executive Stock Options in On-Market Share Buybacks', *International Review of Finance* **10**: 339–63.

Land, S.B. (1996), 'Defeating Deferral: A Proposal for Retrospective Taxation', *Tax Law Review* **52**: 45–117.

Landier, A. and G. Plantin (2017), 'Taxing the Rich', *Review of Economic Studies* **84**: 1186–209.

Lee, B. and O. Rui (2007), 'Time-Series Behavior of Share Repurchases and Dividends', *Journal of Financial and Quantitative Analysis* **42**: 119–42.

Lehner, M. (2000), 'The European Experience with a Wealth Tax: A Comparative Discussion', *Tax Law Review* **53**: 615–91.

Levmore, S. (2015), 'Inequality in the Twenty-First Century', *Michigan Law Review* **113**: 833–54.

Lindholm, R. (1984), 'The Constitutionality of a Federal Net Wealth Tax: A Socioeconomic Analysis of a Strategy Aimed at Ending the Under-Taxation of Land', *American Journal of Economics and Sociology* **43**: 451–4.

Locke, J. (1690), *Two Treatises of Government*, London: Awnsham Churchill.

Locke, J. (1728), *Two Treatises of Government (Essay Two)*, 2nd edn with corrections, London: Awnsham & Churchill.

Lofft, K., P. Maniar and T. Rosenberg (2012), 'Are Hybrids Really More Efficient? A "Drive-By" Analysis of Alternative Company Structures', *Business Law Today* (September): 1–6.

Looney, A. and K. Moore (2016), 'Changes in the Distribution of After-Tax Wealth in the US: Has Income Tax Policy Increased Wealth Inequality?', *Fiscal Studies* **37**: 77–104.

Macdonald, D. (2015), *The Wealth Advantage, The Growing Wealth Gap Between Canada's Affluent and the Middle Class*, Canadian Centre for Policy Alternatives, June.

MacMullen, R. (1959), 'Roman Imperial Building in the Provinces', *Harvard Studies in Classical Philology* **64**: 207–35.

Mankiw, G., M. Weinzierl and D. Yagan (2009), 'Optimal Taxation in Theory and Practice', *Journal of Economic Perspectives* **23** (Fall): 147–74.

Maris, B. (1999), *Lettre ouverte aux gourous de l'économie qui nous prennent pour des imbeciles* (Open Letter to the Gurus of Economics Who Take Us for Idiots), Paris: Albin Michel.

Martin, I. (2013), *Rich People's Movements: Grassroots Campaigns to Untax the One Percent*, New York: Oxford University Press.

Martin, I., A. Mehrotra and M. Prasad (eds) (2009), *The New Fiscal Sociology: Taxation in Comparative and Historical Perspective*, Cambridge, UK: Cambridge University Press.

Martines, L. (1988), 'Forced Loans: Political and Social Strain in "Quattrocento" Florence', *Journal of Modern History* **60**: 300–311.

Martinez-Vazquez, J. and J. Sanz-Sanz (eds) (2007), *Fiscal Reform in Spain: Accomplishments and Challenges*, Cheltenham, UK and Northampton, MA, USA: Edward Elgar Publishing.

McCaffery, E. (2002), *Fair not Flat: How to Make the Tax System Better and Simpler*, Chicago, IL: University of Chicago Press.

McCollim, G. (2012), *Louis XIV's Assault on Privilege: Nicolas Desmaretz and the Tax on Wealth*, Rochester, NY: Rochester University Press.

McLean, P. (2005), 'Patronage, Citizenship, and the Stalled Emergence of the Modern State in Renaissance Florence', *Comparative Studies in Society and History* **47**: 638–64.

McLure, C. and G. Zodrow (2007), 'Consumption-based Direct Taxes: A Guided Tour of the Amusement Park', *FinanzArchiv* **63**: 285–307.

Meade, J. (1978), *Report of a Committee Chaired by J. Meade: The Structure and Reform of Direct Taxation*, London: Allen & Unwin.

Mehrotra, A. (2005), 'Edwin R.A. Seligman and the Beginnings of the US Income Tax', Legal Studies Research Paper #56, Tax Notes, Indiana University, Maurer School of Law, 14 November.

Meyer, B., W. Mok and J. Sullivan (2015), 'Household Surveys in Crisis', *Journal of Economic Perspectives* **29**: 199–226.

Michalos, A. (1991), 'A Case for a Progressive Annual Net Wealth Tax', *Public Affairs Quarterly* **2**: 105–40.

Michie, R. (2012), 'The Stock Market and the Corporate Economy: A Historical Overview', in G. Poitras (ed.), *Handbook of Research on Stock Market Globalization*, Cheltenham, UK and Northampton, MA, USA: Edward Elgar Publishing, pp. 28–67.

Micklethwait, J. and A. Wooldridge (2001), 'The Globalization Backlash', *Foreign Policy* **126**: 16–26.

Mieszkowski, P. and George R. Zodrow (1989), 'Taxation and The Tiebout Model: The Differential Effects of Head Taxes, Taxes on Land Rents, and Property Taxes', *Journal of Economic Literature* **27**: 1098–146.

Mill, J.S. (1849), *Principles of Political Economy*, 2nd edn, Vol. I and II, London: John Parker.

Millon, D. (1990), 'Theories of the Corporation', *Duke Law Journal* **201**: 220–29.

Mintz, J. (1991), 'The Role of Wealth Taxation in the Overall Tax System', The Role of Wealth Taxes in Canada, *Canadian Public Policy* **17**: 248–63.

Mintz, J. and J. Pesando (1991), 'Wealth Taxation in Canada: An Introduction', The Role of Wealth Taxes in Canada, *Canadian Public Policy* **17**: 227–36.

Mirrlees, J. (1971), 'An Exploration in the Theory of Optimum Income Taxation', *Review of Economic Studies* **38**: 175–208.

Mirrlees, J., S. Adam, T. Besley, R. Blundell, S. Bond, et al. (2010), *Dimensions of Tax Design, Mirrlees Review*, Institute of Fiscal Studies (ed.), Oxford: Oxford University Press.

Mirrlees, J., S. Adam, T. Besley, R. Blundell, S. Bond, et al. (2011), 'The Mirrlees Review: Conclusions and Recommendations for Reform', *Fiscal Studies* **32**: 331–59.

Mitchell, S. (1951), *Taxation in Medieval England*, S. Painter (ed.), New Haven, CT: Yale University Press.

Mittermaier, F. (2009), 'The Role of Firm Ownership in Tax Competition', *FinanzArchiv* **65**: 297–312.

Mizruchi, M. (2004), 'Berle and Means Revisited: The Governance and Power of Large US Corporations', *Theory and Society* **33**: 579–617.

Modigliani, F. (1988), 'The Role of Intergenerational Transfers and Life Cycle Saving in the Accumulation of Wealth', *Journal of Economic Perspectives* **2** (Spring): 15–40.

Morissette, R. and Z. Xuelin (2006), 'Revisiting wealth inequality', *Perspectives on Labour and Income* **7** (December). Statistics Canada Catalogue no. 75-001-X.

Murdock, C. (2001), 'Limited Liability Companies in the Decade of the 1990s: Legislative and Case Law Developments and Their Implications for the Future', *Business Lawyer* **56**: 499–590.

Musgrave, R. (1968), 'The Carter Commission Report', *Canadian Journal of Economics* **1** (Suppl., February): 159–82.

Myrdal, G. (1965), *The Political Element in the Development of Economic Theory*, Paul Streeten (transl.), Cambridge, MA: Harvard University Press.

Nayar, P. (2008), 'Social Justice in a Globalised World: Encounters with State and Civil Society', *Sociological Bulletin* **57**: 3–29.

Naylor, R. (2005), 'A Ruse by Any Other Name: The Underground Economy', *Challenge* **48** (November–December): 32–49.

Neal, L. and J. Williamson (eds) (2014), *The Cambridge History of Capitalism*, Cambridge, UK: Cambridge University Press.

Novokmet, F., T. Piketty and G. Zucman (2018), 'From Soviets to Oligarchs: Inequality and Property in Russia 1905–2016', *Journal of Economic Inequality* **16**: 189–223.

Nozick, R. (1973), 'Distributive Justice', *Philosophy and Public Affairs* **3**: 45–126.

Oates, W. (2001), 'Fiscal Competition or Harmonization? Some Reflections', *National Tax Journal* **54** (September): 507–12.

Oates, W. (1972), *Fiscal Federalism*, New York: Harcourt Brace Jovanovich.

O'Brien, P. (1959), 'British Incomes and Property in the Early Nineteenth Century', *Economic History Review*, New Series, **12**: 255–67.

O'Brien, P. (1988), 'The Political Economy of British Taxation, 1660–1815', *Economic History Review* **41**: 1–32.

O'Byrne, S. and S. Young (2017), 'The Evolution of Executive Pay Policy at General Motors, 1918–2008', *Journal of Applied Corporate Finance* **29** (Winter): 36–49.

O'Donnell, E. (2015), *Henry George and the Crisis of Inequality: Progress and Poverty in the Gilded Age*, New York: Columbia University Press.

OECD (2012), *Revenue Statistics 1965–2011*, OECD Publishing. http://dx.doi.org/10.1787/10.1787/revstats-2012-en-fr.

OECD (2016), *Tax Policy Reforms 2016: OECD and Selected Partner Economies*, Paris: OECD Publishing.

OECD (2019a), 'Wealth Distribution', *OECD Social and Welfare Statistics* (database). https://doi.org/10.1787/7d7b803c-en.

OECD (2019b), *Tax Policy Reforms 2019: OECD and Selected Partner Economies*, Paris: OECD Publishing. http://dx.doi.org/10.1787/97892642 60399-en.

Oppenheimer, M. (2008), 'The End of Liberal Globalization', *World Policy Journal* **24** (Winter, 2007/2008): 1–9.

Paine, T. (1791), *The Rights of Man: Being an Answer to Mr Burke's Attack on the French Revolution*, London: J.S. Jordan.

Palan, R., R. Murphy and C. Chavagneux (2010), *Tax Havens: How Globalization Really Works*, Ithaca, NY: Cornell University Press.

Phelps, E. (1979), 'Justice in the Theory of Public Finance', Seventy-Sixth Annual Meeting of the American Philosophical Association, Eastern Division, *Journal of Philosophy* **76**: 677–92.

Piketty, T. (2014), *Capital in the Twenty-First Century*, Cambridge, MA: Harvard University Press.

Piketty, T. (2015a), 'About *Capital in the Twenty-First Century*', *American Economic Review: Papers and Proceedings* **105**: 48–53.

Piketty, T. (2015b), 'Putting Distribution Back at the Center of Economics: Reflections on "Capital in the Twenty-First Century"', *Journal of Economic Perspectives* **29** (Winter): 67–88.

Piketty, T. (2020), *Capital and Ideology*, Cambridge, MA: Harvard University Press.

Piketty, T. and E. Saez (2003), 'Income Inequality in the United States, 1913–1998', *Quarterly Journal of Economics* **118**: 1–39.

Piketty, T. and E. Saez (2013), 'Top Incomes and the Great Recession: Recent Evolutions and Policy Implications', *IMF Economic Review* **61**: 456–78.

Piketty, T., E. Saez and G. Zucman (2018), 'Distributional National Accounts: Methods and Estimates for the United States', *Quarterly Journal of Economics* **133**: 553–609.

Piketty, T., L. Yang and G. Zucman (2019), 'Capital Accumulation, Private Property, and Rising Inequality in China, 1978–2015', *American Economic Review* **109**: 2469–96.

Poitras, G. (2011), *Valuation of Equity Securities: History, Theory and Application*, Singapore: World Scientific.

Poitras, G. (2016), *Equity Capital: From Ancient Partnerships to Modern Exchange Traded Funds*, New York: Routledge.

Poitras, G. and M. Geranio (2016), 'Trading in Shares of the *Societates Publicanorum*?', *Explorations in Economic History* **61**: 95–118.

Porter, E. (2016), 'The Haves and their Havens', *Democracy: A Journal of Ideas* **40** (Spring): 116–22.

Previts, G. and B. Merino (1998), *A History of Accountancy in the United States: The Cultural Significance of Accounting*, Columbus, OH: Ohio State University Press.

Priest, G. (1994), 'The Ambiguous Moral Foundations of the Underground Economy', Symposium: The Informal Economy, *Yale Law Journal* **103**: 2259–88.

Rahimi-Laridjani, E. and E. Hauser (2016), 'The New Global FATCA: An Overview of the OECD's Common Reporting Standard in Relation to FATCA', *Journal of Taxation of Financial Products* **13**: 9–15.

Rakowski, E. (2000), 'Can Wealth Taxes Be Justified?', *Tax Law Review* **53**: 263–374.

Ramsey, F. (1927), 'A Contribution to the Theory of Taxation', *Economic Journal* **37**: 47–61.

Raub, B. and J. Newcomb (2012), 'Personal Wealth 2007', *Internal Revenue Service Statistics of Income Bulletin* (Winter): 156–79.

Rawls, J. (1971), *A Theory of Justice*, Cambridge, MA: Harvard University Press.

Rawls, J. (1999), *The Law of Peoples: With the Idea of Public Reason Revisited*, Cambridge, MA: Harvard University Press.

Ripley, W. (1927), *Main Street and Wall Street*, Boston, MA: Little, Brown, & Company.

Roberts, J. (1971), 'Progress and Poverty's Continuing Challenge', *American Journal of Economics and Sociology*, **30**: 301–16.

Rogers, J. (2014), 'A New Era of Fiduciary Capitalism? Let's Hope So: Guest Editorial', *Financial Analysts Journal* **70** (May–June): 6–12.

Rousseau, J.-J. (1762), *The Social Contract*, J. Bennet (transl.). http://www.earlymoderntexts.com/assets/pdfs/rousseau1762.pdf.

Saez, E. and M. Veall (2005), 'The Evolution of High Incomes in Northern America: Lessons from Canadian Evidence', *American Economic Review* **95**: 831–49.

Saez, E. and G. Zucman (2016), 'Wealth Inequality in the United States since 1913: Evidence from Capitalized Income Tax Data', *Quarterly Journal of Economics* **131**: 519–78.

Sahm, M. (2008), 'Methods of Capital Gains Taxation and the Impact on Asset Prices and Welfare', *National Tax Journal* **61**: 743–68.

Sahm, M. (2009), 'Imitating Accrual Taxation on a Realization Basis', *Journal of Economic Surveys* **23**: 734–61.

Sandford, C. (1971), *Taxing Personal Wealth: An Analysis of Capital Taxation in the United Kingdom – History, Present Structure and Future Possibilities*, London: Allen & Unwin.

Sandford, C., J. Willis and D. Ironside (1975), *An Annual Wealth Tax*, London: Heinemann Educational Books.

Savage, T. (1958), 'The Proposed Virginia Estate Tax', *Virginia Law Review* **44**: 1009–27.

Scharf, K. (2001), 'International Capital Tax Evasion and the Foreign Tax Credit Puzzle', *Canadian Journal of Economics* **34**: 465–80.

Scheffler, S. (2008), 'Cosmopolitanism, Justice and Institutions', On Cosmopolitanism, *Daedalus* **137** (Summer): 68–77.

Schenk, D. (2000), 'Saving the Income Tax with a Wealth Tax', *Tax Law Review* **53**: 423–76.

Schluter, C. (2012), 'On the Problem of Inference for Inequality Measures for Heavy-Tailed Distributions', *Econometrics Journal* **15**: 125–53.

Schneider, F. (2009), 'Size and Development of the Shadow Economy in Germany, Austria and Other OECD Countries: Some Preliminary Findings', *Revue économique* **60**: 1079–116.

Schneider, F. and D. Enste (2000), 'Shadow Economies: Size, Causes, and Consequences', *Journal of Economic Literature* **38**: 77–114.

Schnellenbach, J. (2012), 'The Economics of Taxing Net Wealth: A Survey of the Issues', *Public Finance and Management* **12**: 368–400.

Selg, P. (2012), 'Justice and Liberal Strategy: Towards a Radical Democratic Reading of Rawls', *Social Theory and Practice* **38**: 83–114.

Seligman, E. (1895), *Essays in Taxation*, New York: Macmillan.

Seligman, E. (1908), *Progressive Taxation in Theory and Practice*, 2nd edn, Princeton, NJ: American Economic Association.

Seligman, E. (1914 [1911]), *The Income Tax: A Study of the History, Theory and Practice of Income Taxation at Home and Abroad*, 2nd edn, New York: Macmillan.

Sewalk, S. and R. Leaman (2014), 'A Comprehensive Net Wealth Tax: The Solution to Tax Simplification, Fairness, Equity and Saving Social Security', *Franklin Business and Law Journal* **1**: 2–43.

Shakow, D. (1986), 'Taxation without Realization: A Proposal for Accrual Taxation', *University of Pennsylvania Law Review* **134** (June): 1111–205.

Shanske, D. (2015), 'Revitalizing Local Political Economy Through Modernizing the Property Tax', *Tax Law Review* **68**: 143–206.

Sharman, J. (2006), *Havens in a Storm: The Struggle for Global Tax Regulation*, Ithaca, NY: Cornell University Press.

Shaviro, D. (2007), 'Beyond the Pro-Consumption Tax Consensus', *Stanford Law Review* **60**: 745–88.

Shaxson, N. (2012), *Treasure Islands: Tax Havens and the Men Who Stole the World*, London: Vintage Books.

Shiller, R. (2013), 'Capitalism and Financial Innovation', *Financial Analysts Journal* **69** (January–February): 21–5.

Sikka, P. (2015), 'The Hand of Accounting and Accountancy Firms in Deepening Income and Wealth Inequalities and the Economic Crisis: Some Evidence', *Critical Perspectives on Accounting* **30**: 46–62.

Simons, H. (1938), *Personal Income Taxation: The Definition of Income as a Problem of Fiscal Policy*, Chicago, IL: University of Chicago Press.

Slemrod, J. (1990), 'Optimal Taxation and Optimal Tax Systems', *Journal of Economic Perspectives* **4** (Winter): 157–78.

Slemrod, J. (2016), 'Caveats to the Research Use of Tax-Return Administrative Data', *National Tax Journal* **69**: 1003–20.

Slemrod, J. and J. Bakija (2000), *Taxing Ourselves: A Citizen's Guide to the Great Debate over Tax Reform*, Cambridge, MA: MIT Press.

Smith, A. (1776), *An Inquiry into the Nature and Causes of the Wealth of Nations*, London: Strahan & Cadell.

Smith, J. (2001), 'Why is Wealth Inequality Rising?', in F. Welch (ed.), *The Causes and Consequences of Increasing Inequality*, Chicago, IL: University of Chicago Press, pp. 83–115.

Smith, R. (1993), *Personal Wealth Taxation: Canadian Tax Policy in a Historical and an International Setting*, Toronto: Canadian Tax Foundation.

Smith, W., W. Wayte and G. Marindin (eds) (1890), *A Dictionary of Greek and Roman Antiquities*, London: John Murray.

Sokolow, A. (1998), 'The Changing Property Tax and State–Local Relations', The State of American Federalism, *Publius* **28**: 165–87.

Song, J. (2015), 'The End of Secret Swiss Accounts? The Impact of the US Foreign Account Tax Compliance Act (FATCA) on Switzerland's Status as a Haven for Offshore Accounts', *Northwestern Journal of International Law and Business* **35**: 686–718.

Spragens, T. (1993), 'The Antinomies of Social Justice', *Review of Politics* **55**: 193–216.

Steinmo, S. (1993), *Taxation and Democracy: Swedish, British, and American Approaches to Financing the Modern State*, New Haven, CT: Yale University Press.

Stephens, C. and M. Weisbach (1998), 'Actual Share Reacquisitions in Open-Market Repurchase Programs', *Journal of Finance* **53**: 313–33.

Stewart, K., M. Webb, L. Bovenberg and C. Favero (2006), 'International Competition in Corporate Taxation: Evidence from the OECD Time Series', *Economic Policy* **21**: 153, 155–201.

Stiglitz, J. (1978), 'Notes on Estate Taxes, Redistribution, and the Concept of Balanced Growth Path Incidence', Research in Taxation, *Journal of Political Economy* **86**: S137–S150.

Stout, L. (2001), 'Review: *The Rise of Fiduciary Capitalism: How Institutional Investors Can Make Corporate America More Democratic* by James P. Hawley and Andrew T. Williams', *Journal of Economic Literature* **39**: 1248–9.

Strnad, J. (1985), 'Taxation of Income from Capital: A Theoretical Reappraisal', *Stanford Law Review* **37**: 1023–107.

Swank, D. (2002), *Global Capital, Political Institutions, and Policy Change in Developed Welfare States*, Cambridge, UK: Cambridge University Press.

Tait, A. (1967), *The Taxation of Personal Wealth*, Urbana, IL: University of Illinois Press.

Tanabe, N. (1967), 'The Taxation of Net Wealth', *IMF Staff Papers* **14** (March): 124–68.

Tax Foundation (2016), 'State–Local Tax Burden Rankings FY 2012', 20 January.

Tax Law Review (2000), Special Issue, 'Symposium on Wealth Taxes'.

Thiel, H. (1967), *Economics and Information Theory*, Amsterdam: North-Holland.

Thomas, J. (1999), 'Quantifying the Black Economy: "Measurement without Theory" Yet Again?', *Economic Journal* **109**: F381–89.

Thorndike, J. (2009), '"The Unfair Advantage of the Few": The New Deal Origins of "Soak the Rich Taxation"', in I. Martin, A. Mehrotra and M. Prasad (eds), *The New Fiscal Sociology: Taxation in Comparative and Historical Perspective*, Cambridge, UK: Cambridge University Press, pp. 29–47.

Tilly, C. (1992), *Coercion, Capital, and European states, AD 990–1992*, Cambridge, MA: Blackwell.

Timmons, J. (2010), 'Does Democracy Reduce Economic Inequality?', *British Journal of Political Science* **40**: 741–57.

Toder, E. and A. Viard (2016), 'Replacing Corporate Tax Revenues with a Mark-to-Market Tax on Shareholder Income', *National Tax Journal* **69**: 701–32.

Truong, T. and R. Heaney (2007), 'Largest Shareholder and Dividend Policy around the World', *Quarterly Review of Economics and Finance* **47**: 667–87.

United Nations Development Programme (UNDP) (2019), *Human Development Report 2019: Beyond Income, Beyond Averages, Beyond Today; Inequalities in Human Development in the 21st Century*, New York: UNDP.

Uppal, S. and S. LaRochelle-Côté (2015), 'Changes in wealth across the income distribution, 1999 to 2012', Insights on Canadian Society, Statistics Canada, 3 June, Catalogue no. 75-006-X.

Veblen, Thorstein (1899), *The Theory of the Leisure Class: An Economic Study of Institutions*, New York: Macmillan.

Veblen, Thorstein (1919), *The Vested Interests and the Common Man*, New York: B.W. Huebsch.

Venugopal, R. (2015), 'Neoliberalism as Concept', *Economy and Society* **44**: 165–87.

Vermeulen, P. (2018), 'How Fat is the Top Tail of the Wealth Distribution?', *Review of Income and Wealth* **64**: 357–86.

Vickrey, W. (1947), *Agenda for Progressive Taxation*, New York: Ronald.

Vickrey, W. (1992), 'An Updated Agenda for Progressive Taxation', *American Economic Review: Papers and Proceedings* **82**: 257–62.

Vogelgesang, U. (2000), 'Optimal Capital Income Taxation and Redistribution', *FinanzArchiv* **57**: 412–34.

Ward, P (2014), 'Measuring the Level and Inequality of Wealth: An Application to China', *Review of Income and Wealth* **60** (December): 613–35.

Warren, A. (1980), 'Would a Consumption Tax Be Fairer Than an Income Tax?', *Yale Law Journal* **89**: 1081–124.

Webber, C. and A. Wildavsky (1986), *A History of Taxation and Expenditure in the Western World*, New York: Simon & Schuster.

Welch, F. (ed.) (2001), *The Causes and Consequences of Increasing Inequality*, Chicago, IL: University of Chicago Press.

Weller, C. and M. Rao (2010), 'Progressive Tax Policy and Economic Stability', *Journal of Economic Issues* **44**: 629–59.

White, E. (2004), 'From Privatized to Government-Administered Tax Collection: Tax Farming in Eighteenth-Century France', *Economic History Review* **57**: 636–63.

Wildasin, D. (1990), 'R.M. Haig: Pioneer Advocate of Expenditure Taxation?', *Journal of Economic Literature* **28**: 649–54.

Wilson, J. (1999), 'Theories of Tax Competition', *National Tax Journal* **52** (June): 269–304.

Winnick, A. (1989), *Toward Two Societies: The Changing Distributions of Income and Wealth in the United States since 1960*, New York: Praeger.

Woldeab, Y. (2015), '"Americans: We Love You, But We Can't Afford You": How the Costly US–Canada FATCA Agreement Permits Discrimination of Americans in Violation of International Law', *American University International Law Review* **30**: 611–47.

Wolff, E. (1990), 'Methodological Issues in the Estimation of the Size Distribution of Household Wealth', *Journal of Econometrics* **43**: 179–95.

Wolff, E. (1992), 'Changing Inequality of Wealth', *American Economic Review* **82**: 552–8.

Wolff, E. (1994), 'Trends in Household Wealth in the United States, 1962–83 and 1983–89', *Review of Income and Wealth* **40**: 143–74.

Wolff, E. (1995), *Top Heavy: A Study of the Increasing Inequality of Wealth in America*, New York: Twentieth Century Fund Press.

Wolff, E. (1996), 'International Comparisons of Wealth Inequality', *Review of Income and Wealth* **42**: 433–51.

Wolff, E. (1998), 'Recent Trends in the Size Distribution of Household Wealth', *Journal of Economic Perspectives* **12** (Summer): 131–50.

Yunker, J. (1994), 'Evaluating Changes in the Distribution of Capital Wealth', *Economic Inquiry* **32**: 597–615.

Yunker, J. (2014), 'Capital Wealth Taxation: Theory and Application', *Review of Political Economy* **26**: 85–110.

Zelenak, L. (2010), 'Foreword: The Fabulous Invalid nears 100', Turning Points in the History of the Federal Income Tax, *Law and Contemporary Problems* **73**: i–xvii.

Zucman, G. (2014), 'Taxing across Borders: Tracking Personal Wealth and Corporate Profits', *Journal of Economic Perspectives* **28** (Fall): 121–48.

Zucman, G. (2015), *The Hidden Wealth of Nations: The Scourge of Tax Havens*, transl. T. Fagan, Chicago, IL: University of Chicago Press.

Index